D1596223

The Romance of Engines

by Takashi Suzuki, Ph.D.

Published by:
Society of Automotive Engineers, Inc.
400 Commonwealth Drive
Warrendale, PA 15096-0001
Phone: (412) 776-4841
Fax: (412) 776-5670
http://www.sae.org

Translation from Japanese to English was sponsored by Southwest Research Institute, San Antonio, Texas. The team effort was led by Mr. Charles D. Wood while he was Vice President of the Institute's Division of Engine and Vehicle Research.

Library of Congress Cataloging-in-Publication Data

Suzuki, Takashi, 1928-
   [Enjin no roman. English]
   The romance of engines / by Takashi Suzuki.
     p. cm.
   Includes bibliographical references and index.
   ISBN 1-56091-911-6 (hc)
   1. Heat-engines--History. I. Title.
TJ255.S9813   1997
621.43'09--dc21   96-52945
                                         CIP

SAE Order No. R-188

Foreword to the Revised Edition

The magnificent and splendid Versailles Palace built by King Louis XIV served as the source of inspiration for Christiaan Huygen's idea of an engine. To provide water for a mile-long canal, numerous water fountains, and diverse kinds of trees, shrubs, and bushes that were within the palace garden, a tremendous volume of water had to be drawn from the Seine River every day and transported to the palace grounds. Seeing this effort, Huygen sought a way to ease the arduous task of transporting water, a task placed on both humans and animals. He had the idea of an engine. Since then, the blood, sweat, and tears of many people have been shed to invent and then develop the engine.

While circumstances differ from one generation to the next, the human yearning for new knowledge and new discoveries is a constant, and the complicated challenges that technology presents serve only to stimulate the human imagination.

Today, technology is in a highly advanced stage, and the engine is used in virtually all branches of technological development. The engine has provided innumerable conveniences for the entire human race. Unfortunately, solutions to problems such as environmental pollution and safety hazards that have resulted from the extensive use of the engine can come only from a sacrifice of some of that convenience. The engine has become a fixture in human society in the form of the automobile and numerous other conveniences. Society as we know it cannot continue to exist without the engine. Just as Huygen's concern for humanism was the basis for his solution to a problem, so must the solutions to today's problems be rooted in humanism. The search for new technology is still driven by curiosity and the desire to fulfill dreams. By re-examining the thorny paths blazed by our predecessors as they struggled to improve their existing technology, we hope to learn from their challenges and failures and use this knowledge to solve the problems that are facing us now. Our ultimate goal is to create an engine that functions in harmony with nature while still meeting the demands of an ever-advancing civilization. With this purpose in mind, we put together this manuscript and published it as *The Romance of Engines*.

I have included material I have written and compiled since the publication of an earlier edition, *The Heart of the Engine*. I have also made a number of changes to update the information in the book originally published eight years ago. Technical descriptions and additional information pertaining to the main issues discussed in each chapter are included in the appendices at the end of the individual chapters. If you are interested in the subject matter, please read them. If not, the appendices may be skipped without losing the flow of thought.

I want to thank Messrs. Shohei Kakizoe and Makoto Iwamoto for their diligence in promoting the publication of this book. I also thank Messrs. Tomio Futami and Kyohei Kuse, who provided the opportunity to publish the first edition, and all the companies that sponsored the project and their personnel who organized the information. Finally, I express my deepest gratitude to Mr. Tamotsu Kawashima of the publishing house President Publishing Company for his efforts.

Takashi Suzuki
Summer 1988

Preface to the English Edition

My sincere thanks to U.S. friends for the publication of the English edition.

One day, I gave a copy of my book *The Romance of Engines,* published in 1983, to my honorable friend, Mr. Martin E. Goland of Southwest Research Institute. I told him that I hoped he could understand my meaning and my affection for the subject of my book through the cartoons and photographs, even though the captions and the text were written in Japanese. Later, when I saw him again, he told me that he wanted to be able to read the book because the drawings and photographs were so interesting. He asked me how many copies of the book had been sold in Japan. I replied that some 20,000 copies had been sold. He said that number seemed to be a reasonable number and that he wanted to have my book translated and published in the United States. Even after this conversation I did not work on the book, but Mr. Goland proceeded with the translation of my book in collaboration with another friend of mine, Mr. Charles D. Wood, Jr., also of Southwest Research Institute, who even negotiated with the Society of Automotive Engineers for publication.

In Japan, an enlarged and revised edition was published. The translation was based on this later edition. In working with the translation from Japanese to English, I took great care with the meaning because the book contained many technical terms and delicate concepts. I finished the translation thanks to the dedicated assistance of numerous people. I particularly want to thank Mr. Wood for his technical editing and Mr. James Pryor, also of Southwest Research Institute, for his help with phrasing and grammar. I took the opportunity of the translation to incorporate changes in response to Mr. Wood's valuable advice, added events that occurred since the issuance of the first revised edition, adjusted some comments for a foreign edition, and corrected some typographical errors that had appeared in earlier editions.

Through my long years of association with my companion, the "engine," I have made numerous friends in foreign countries. The United States of America was the destination of my first overseas trip in 1966. In the United States, as well as worldwide, I have had the good fortune to meet and become friends with many people who shared my interest in automotive history. This English edition could only have been completed as a result of the crystallization of our friendships. I am grateful for my friends' help and for my luck in having them as friends.

In addition to technical nomenclature and terminology, every book contains unusual phrasing and methods of wording as a result of the author's writing style and his literary and technical background. In translating these phrases and names, however, they must often be changed because priority must always be given to accuracy rather than to style. Particularly in *The Romance of Engines*, I used rather philosophical words because I wanted to relate many historical facts in such a way as to provide lessons to today's people. I think the translation does indeed carry out my goal of teaching. Unfortunately, many of the puns and plays on words that make a book so enjoyable to the reader could not survive in the new language.

As an aside to the reader, please realize that this book describes many historical events, and the lessons and impressions that I received from those happenings. I am confident of the historical accuracy of those events that happened inside Japan and Hino Motors; however, those events that took place in foreign countries may have some errors because of restricted or unrecoverable documents and records. The lessons to be learned on manufacture, though, remain the same. As far as possible, the cited documents are listed at the end of this book. I welcome any comments or suggestions on the contents of this book.

I hope that you can glimpse the engineers' spirits through this book.

Takashi Suzuki
Autumn 1995

Preface to the Revised Edition

More than five years have passed since the publication of the original edition of *The Romance of Engines*. During this time, I have received comments and impressions from a number of readers, some of whom were quite unexpected. I am very pleased to have had people read and understand from my book some aspect of the engine, its technology and production, and the spirit of management. I offer my heartfelt thanks to my readers for the time and effort in reading and responding to my book.

Recently, Mr. Tamotsu Kawashima of the President Publishing Company asked me to consider revising my book. I considered this request because substantial improvements to the engine have been made during the last five years . Many of these changes have occurred on the diesel engine as a result of recent environmental measures. In addition, I have gathered a great deal of new information—both historical accounts and more recent data—to which I added some of my own impressions and personal experiences. In addition, I have revised some of the older data in the light of new information and new experiences.

Today, due to the rapid development of technology, we are enjoying conveniences that as recently as half a century ago would have been unimaginable. This convenience has as its price an explosive increase in the consumption of raw materials and energy. The increase in the rate of consumption is threatening our global environment. Environmental problems are becoming more serious day by day. Moreover, international problems, such as the overemphasis on economic development and the disparity in the standard of living between the developed nations and the Third World countries, are becoming increasingly complicated. Against this background, newly considered methods of production are being demanded. There are two roads to this "new production": One is in the pursuit of a more sophisticated and high-quality product; the other is the search for harmony with nature. The search for technical improvement has as its origins the system of reasoning developed by Descartes; the longing for harmony with nature is the principle that has guided the Japanese people through their long cultural history. I feel that the true path to our future lies in the merging of these two different roads so that these "new dreams" can be pursued on a foundation of humanism laid down by our ancient wise men. If this book can serve as a roadmap to reach this "new dream," I will be overjoyed.

I express my heartfelt gratitude to Mr. Tamotsu Kawashima for his assistance in the publication of the revised edition, to the staffs of the new ACE and Hino Motors for their data arrangement and presentation, and to those many other people who provided me with valuable information and suggestions.

Takashi Suzuki
October 1993

From the Preface of "The Heart of the Engine"

In the winter of 1969, I traveled to Europe for the first time. Everything I saw and heard was fresh and marvelous to me. This awe was because at that time the direct-injection diesel engine was still in its infancy in Japan, and I was shocked by our significant lag in technological development as compared to Europe. I took the opportunity one day to visit the German museum, and I was astonished to see the aircraft engine made by Benz in 1910. This amazement was because of the way that Benz had mounted the oil pump to the aircraft engine. During the summer of 1966, I had been working to resolve an unexplained power loss in Hino's racing car HINO-PROTO each time it was tested on the Fuji Speedway. After much effort and hard work, I determined that the oil pump was causing the power losses. Again, after much effort, I found a solution to the problem. Fortunately, the HINOPROTO won the next race. What had amazed me was that my innovative solution had already been used on that old engine originally made in 1910. I was again surprised in the museum of the Mahle Piston Company, my next destination. I found that my invention for reducing oil consumption, which I believed was applicable to any engine, had been rather casually exhibited as an example of a particular solution that had been arrived at half a century ago.

This is how my interest in museum visiting began. From my experience with museums, I began to understand that it is occasionally necessary to look down and observe the river of technology instead of always struggling in its currents.

When one stands on a bridge, he can see upstream and predict the direction of the stream flow. Similarly, each significant accomplishment in the past offers, to those who can see, clues and suggestions as to how we may overcome the technological challenges we face today. In this book, I have gathered those suggestions and clues offered by history that impressed me, in the hope that they will guide and inspire those who labor everyday to improve technology.

Some people believe that our civilization based on mobility is close to its end because it has become too immense to function properly. They may also believe that, because of excessive automation, modern technology has reached a critical juncture. Many people do not realize that technologies as advanced and seemingly remote as rockets and nuclear power are actually close to them. Having traveled the journey of the internal-combustion engine, I have learned that technology stems from the simple wish to improve human life. Because of this basic desire, one cannot help but find an unlimited sense of humanity within each advance in history of technology.

More than 100 years have passed since the invention of the internal-combustion engine. But even today this engine is at the leading edge of technological advancement, along with the automobile. The reason for this is simply that the engine has become more and more closely tied to human life.

With the worldwide concern over the depletion of energy sources and environmental pollution, the technological improvements that can be made on the engine and the automobile are limitless. Thus, automotive engineers who can merge modern technologies with humanism are indeed fortunate. I am one of those people who envisage the future continuously improving, thanks to the efforts of the innovator and the engineer.

Takashi Suzuki
August 1980

Table of Contents

Chapter 1

Why Was the Engine Needed?

The needs for human happiness and water for Versailles result in the need for an invention.

❊

Water Keeper Christiaan Huygens' Idea

According to the historical records[1-1], the first long-distance automobile trip, that is, the grand touring, was made by Madam Bertha Benz, wife of German engineer and inventor Karl Benz, and her two children. The second long-distance driving trip was made by Armand Peugeot, who founded the Peugeot Motor Company. Peugeot traveled the Paris-Brest-Paris route.

If a traveler were riding on an express train from Brest to Paris, he would see on the left side of the track, approximately 20 minutes to the Montparnasse train station in Paris, the famous Palace of Versailles. The Palace of Versailles was converted by King Louis XIV from a royal hunting lodge to the premier palace of the Western world. The palace and its auxiliary buildings took 21 years to complete, from 1667 to 1688. The 425-meter-long main building was large enough to entertain 10,000 guests and was noted for its lavish furniture and innovative architecture (see Photo 1-1).

The palace grounds were extensive. A mile-long canal was dug at the front of the building, permitting boaters to leisurely sip a glass of aperitif before a glorious dinner. The formal gardens of Versailles were the pride of Louis XIV and complemented the splendor of the palace with a beauty that was admired by all the royalty of Europe. Broad avenues were lined with symmetrical plantings of trees. Hedges were planted in elaborate embroidered patterns, and fountains spewed jets of water into pools (see Photo 1-2). Flowers and bushes were arranged in patterns of vibrant colors.

Photo 1-1 Versailles Palace (1667 to 1688): From the center of the main building to the south wing.

Photo 1-2 Versailles Palace: Viewing mile-long canal for honored guests from Latone Fountain (the garden alone has more than ten luxurious fountains).

Although the gardens were designed by Andre LeNortre, providing water for the plants and fountains in the garden as well as for the palace itself was the responsibility of Christiaan Huygens, who was a member of King Louis XIV's court, serving as a water keeper at this time. Water to keep the gardens luxuriant was drawn from the nearby Seine River. More than 3000 cubic meters of water were needed to provide the palace and its grounds with its daily supply of water. Both the effort, man or animal power, and time necessary to transport the water from the river to the palace were enormous. Huygens, who was in charge of the palace waterworks, was constantly thinking of how to simplify obtaining the water necessary for the gardens and the palace. Finally, in 1673, he devised a prototype of an internal-combustion engine.[1-2]

The concept of this primitive engine is illustrated in Fig. 1-1. The line A-B represents the cylinder. Gunpowder is placed at point C and then ignited. The explosive gases force piston D to the top of the cylinder, and one-way leather release valves (E-F) allow the waste gases to exhaust to the atmosphere. A near vacuum then exists in the cylinder. Atmospheric pressure forces the piston back toward the bottom of the cylinder, raising substance G, which could be water.

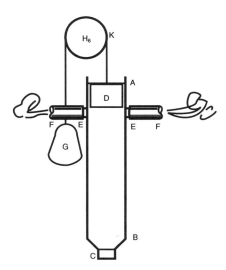

Fig. 1-1 Conceptual drawing of internal-combustion engine originated by Huygens (1673).

Huygens documented this first internal-combustion engine in a letter to his brother. Several versions of the engine were built and tried.[1-3] Obviously, the man who originated this innovative concept was not an ordinary courtier.

In fact, Christiaan Huygens was one of the foremost natural philosophers of his era (Fig. 1-2). In 1673, the year the engine was built, Huygens was the first foreign member to be accepted into the Paris Academy. He was a Dutch physicist who originated the principle of light known as Huygens' Principle. He discovered that Saturn was surrounded by a flattened ring. He patented the first pendulum clock, which keeps accurate time.

In 1685, 12 years after its design, the water pump was built by using 14 water wheels, each with a 12-meter diameter, to transport 3000 cubic meters of water daily from the Seine River to the gardens of Versailles, barely enough to meet its needs.[1-4] The enormous quantity of water required daily by the palace can be realized if the reader knows that the entire Hino plant of Hino Motors, Ltd. uses only 4000 cubic meters of water daily in its total manufacturing process.

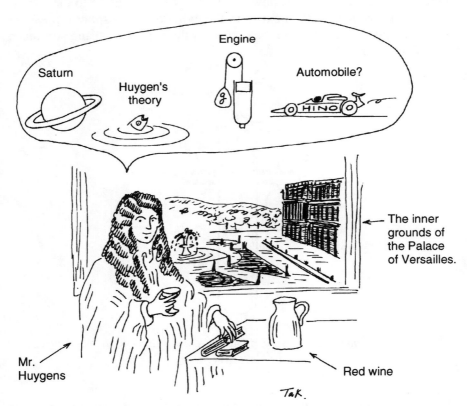

Fig. 1-2 Water keeper and his elegant idea (1629 to 1695).[1-5]

If early internal-combustion engines are to be reviewed, then one more genius must be mentioned here. This genius was the Italian Leonardo da Vinci, who sketched a gunpowder engine in 1509. The sketch is very similar to Huygens' concept. However, the da Vinci engine was never built. The gunpowder engine was one of da Vinci's many inventions and ideas that were noted only in drawings. Since Huygens had never seen da Vinci's sketch, Huygens' idea was his own.[1-3]

Beginning of the Steam Engine

Denis Papin was a French inventor, medical student, and industrial artist. He served as an assistant in developing the Huygens engine, and he developed ideas concerning a steam engine instead of a gunpowder engine around 1670. However, it is believed that he never fully developed his ideas into practical machines. This development was left for future generations.

Englishman Thomas Savery devised the first practical apparatus for harnessing steam power. His machine and Papin's idea also led to the invention by Thomas Newcomen in 1712 of the first successful steam engine. James Watt modified and improved the Newcomen steam engine, which resulted in Watt's new steam engine being recognized as a practical engine powerplant.

Joseph Cugnots was the first inventor to use the steam engine in a vehicle for transportation, around 1763-1771. Later, in 1890, Clement Ader attempted to install the steam engine into an airplane. Both the vehicle (Photo 1-3) and the airplane (Photo 1-4) are on display at the Conservatoir National de Arts et Matiers in Paris. However, neither vehicle was practical for transportation. The invention of the really useful engine for transportation was left for future generations of dreamers. The internal-combustion engine suitable for vehicle use was not available until the invention of an engine by Nicolaus August Otto. As noted in this chapter, the reason for developing an engine is to meet the needs of the people and to have these machines relieve them of the tremendous burdens previously borne by the human back. This need to improve the condition of humanity, of course, is the primary reason for all inventions and progress. Even though an idea may be conceived by the single person responsible, for example, for providing water to trees, plants, and fountains, the dedication of many skilled and imaginative people are required to nurture and grow that idea. New technology is the realization of critical thinking and originality through the application of skill and knowledge. This principle is illustrated on the first pages of the history of the engine.

Photo 1-3 Cugnots' steam engine car (1770) (Conservatoir National de Arts et Matiers in Paris).

Photo 1-4 Clement Ader's steam airplane (1890) (Conservatoir National de Arts et Matiers in Paris).

Chapter 2

A Great Work of the Early Period: Newcomen's Steam Engine

*Success comes from the careful compilation of information. The
key to success is one young man's tenacity.*

❄

Fundamental Reformation of the Heat Engine

When a visitor walks into the Science Museum in London, one of the first
exhibits that he sees is the Newcomen engine (Photo 2-1). The engine
appears to rise from the floor like a diving board stand at poolside. The significance of this engine is that it was the first practical use of the piston-
cylinder assembly in a work-producing configuration. Thomas Newcomen,
a blacksmith and inventor, was born in Dartmouth, England.[2-1] His work
was based on the earlier discoveries of Christiaan Huygens and Denis
Papin, both discussed in Chapter 1. He combined their concepts by using
the spray jet developed by Dr. Desaguliers, and he, with help from glass
and lead pipe worker John Calley, modified and redesigned the engine built
earlier by Thomas Savery in 1698.[2-2]

Fig. 2-1 illustrates the Newcomen engine. A piston (Photo 2-2) and a cylinder are placed above an old distillation boiler. The steam from the boiler
expands, is directed into the cylinder, and pushes the piston to the top of the
cylinder. When the piston reaches its peak, the interior jet spray sprays
water into the cylinder, condensing the steam into water. Concurrently with
the water spray, the valve separating the cylinder from the boiler is closed.
At this point, a near-vacuum is created in the cylinder. The atmospheric
pressure pushes the piston down, causing the drawing pump to operate
through the beam. This engine, in effect, demonstrates the concept that had

Photo 2-1 Huge Newcomen engine: Exhibited engine was manufactured in 1791 by Francis Thompson. 1454-mm bore, 2100-mm stroke, 25 PS, 18 strokes/minute (London Science Museum. Bore, stroke, and PS indicate cylinder diameter, piston stroke, and horsepower, respectively).

been postulated by Huygens with his earlier engine. In this version, however, gunpowder had been replaced by steam as the powering force.

Young Man Potta's Tenacious Spirit

In Newcomen's engine, actuating the valve, shutting off the steam, and spraying the water had to be done for each pumping stroke. Since these parts of the cycle had to be performed manually, an attendant was hired to carry out this function. One of the first men hired to monitor the condensation cycle was Humphrey Potta. This young man is credited with having automated some of these laborious procedures to simplify operation of the engine. After extensive trial and error, he had the water flowing into the cylinder on the top of the piston. This water flow also cooled the leather seal on the piston. Potta also attached a clasp and a strap to a lever, which opened and closed the valve.

The Newcomen engine was the first steam engine that could successfully pump the ground water from flooded mine shafts. The removal of this obstacle allowed the sinking of deeper shafts to mine coal seams that previously would have been unworkable. The Newcomen engine spread rapidly among

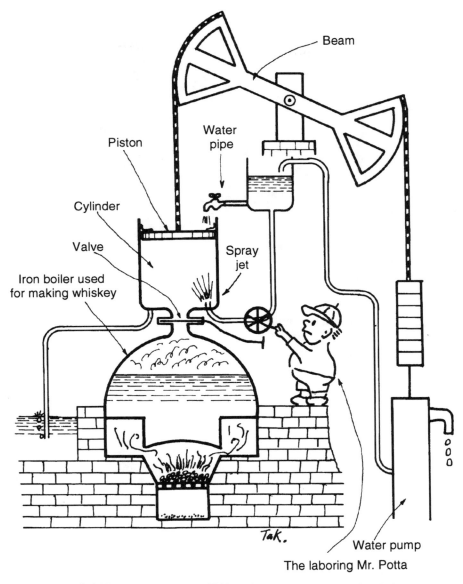

Beam

Water pipe

Piston

Cylinder

Valve

Iron boiler used for making whiskey

Spray jet

Tak.

Water pump

The laboring Mr. Potta

Fig. 2-1 Newcomen engine (1712): The engine was completed thanks to the Potta proposal.

the British mining districts, greatly expanding the production of coal. This engine removed one of the great bottlenecks restraining the economic growth

Photo 2-2 Piston area of the Newcomen engine (Munich, German museum).

of England. As a result, the industrial revolution exploded in England. Thus, Potta's tenacious spirit served as the trigger for the industrial change in England and subsequently the world.

Chapter 3

The Watt Steam Engine Grew from a Model Steam Engine

A new engine is created as a result of failure analysis.

❧

An Indispensable Problem-Solving Technique

In 1763, a model of the Newcomen steam engine that had been used as a teaching tool at the University of Glasgow stopped working. Since James Watt was the instrument maker at the University, he was asked to repair the engine. Watt's work with this engine is the reason that his engine appears to be so similar to the Newcomen engine. Watt, rather than Newcomen, is recognized as the inventor of the modern steam engine because his steam engine was the forerunner of the engines that utilize the pressure of steam itself, unlike an atmospheric engine, as detailed later.

Watt began a systematic examination to determine why the Newcomen engine model failed to operate satisfactorily, even though it was made on almost the same scale as that of a full-size engine. In modern terminology, his approach to locate the problem can be called a failure analysis. In effect, failure analysis means that if the machine has broken down or has been damaged, then the investigator must systematically determine the cause of the problem. Then he must study the problem in a logical manner to provide a solution. Even though these problem-solving techniques may not have been called failure analysis over the years, it has been one of the most important aspects of improving and developing the engine.

The *White Pigeon*

Since failure analysis is so important in modern development, I will digress from my story somewhat to give two examples of successful failure analyses. These examples include the midair disintegrations of the Japanese Airline Dornier Wal *White Pigeon* in 1932 and the De Havilland *Comet 4* aircraft in 1954. No one witnessed either accident or was able to determine the cause of the crashes. The only way to determine the cause of these accidents was detective work. The parts, which had been strewn about the accident sites, were recovered, and records of the flying conditions were examined for adverse weather conditions. The maintenance records of all the parts were reviewed to determine the condition of the structures at the time of the accident. Then reconstructions were performed, a hypothesis was established, and the structures were re-examined in light of the hypothesis. These steps were repeated until a hypothesis was found that fit all the circumstances of the accident. Needless to say, repeating these steps time after time required considerable patience and great faith that the cause of the accident would be discovered.

In the investigation of the airplane *Comet* accident, I was deeply impressed by the attitude of P.B. Walker, a staffmember of the British Air Force Research Laboratory, an organization of the Royal Aircraft Establishment (RAE). At first, everyone thought that the accident was caused by a faulty layout of the main wings. Walker, however, insisted on subjecting the entire fuselage to a stress test. In this stress test, the huge fuselage was immersed in water, and the cyclic pressure amplitude between ground level and high altitude was repeated until failure was reached.[3-1] By its very nature, a hypothesis is never a certainty at the beginning, so mistakes may be made. Walker resolutely worked to determine the cause of the air catastrophe. He ordered the fatigue tests in a specially fabricated gigantic water bath. Then he may have felt that he could only do his best, and he would leave the rest to Providence. However, every decision should be based on logical thinking, rather than aimless hunches. To Walker's relief, the *Comet* was found to have crashed because of fatigue failure of the fuselage due to repetitive loads or pressurizations, as he had predicted (Photos 3-1 and 3-2).

The second example involved the destruction of the *White Pigeon*. Torahiko Terada, who was a great scientist and also a pupil of the Japanese novelist Sohseki Natsume, published the details of the *White Pigeon* investigation[3-2] in the journal *Chuo Kohron* in July 1935. The research team was headed by Professor Syuhei Iwamoto of the Aeronautical Research Institute of Tokyo University. Its failure analysis began with the

Photo 3-1 World's first jet passenger plane De Havilland Comet: It now lies in a corner of the Ducksford Airfield, cherishing its dramatic history.

Photo 3-2 Hydraulic pressure test of passenger plane: It has become standard practice in developmental experiments to immerse the entire fuselage of an airplane in a water bath and to carry out a repetitive pressure test according to Walker's proposal. (This photo, courtesy of Nippon Kokuki Seizo Company, Ltd., shows the YS11 under test.)

study of the failed parts. Duplicates of these structurally failed parts were prepared, and they were subjected to different modes of fatigue stress such as folding, pushing, and twisting. The different modes of stressing were continued until the resulting fatigue cracks on the test specimens appeared the same as those on the crashed airplane.

As a result of the patient trial-and-error methodology, the midair disintegration was determined to have been caused by a weak wire. The proposed scenario has the wing being repeatedly subjected to a fluctuating load, eventually breaking a lock-wire. This lock-wire had prevented the rotation of the turnbuckle that secured the wing-bracing wires. With the loss of the lock-wire, the turnbuckle came loose, the screw loosened, and the bracing wire slipped off. The wing and the aileron began to vibrate heavily (fluttering). At last, the wing disintegrated, and the flying boat crashed. It was reported that the final hypothesis was verified with a wind tunnel test. As I read Terada's report of their work, I was deeply impressed, and I felt that I had heard the analysis group shout with joy when the wind tunnel tests confirmed their hypothesis. Success in solving any technological problem can be reached only through patient trial-and-error, experiments, and bravely and persistently continuing the work. This historical event suggests that both the designer and the manufacturer of even small parts such as the turnbuckle and lock-wire should recognize the importance of their products (Fig. 3-1).

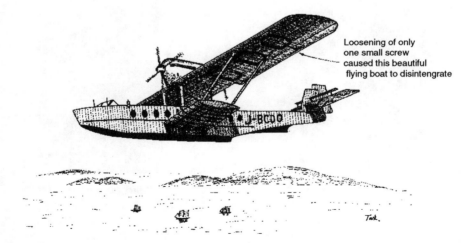

Loosening of only
one small screw
caused this beautiful
flying boat to disintengrate

Fig. 3-1 Dornier Wal Flying Boat (1930): The loosening of one small screw caused this beautiful flying boat to disintegrate in midair.

Watt's Idea for His New Engine Came from the Newcomen Engine

When Watt began repairing the Newcomen model engine at the University of Glasgow, he felt that the engine produced an insufficient volume of steam in view of the amount of heat put into the engine. Today, we know that the cylinder wall of the Newcomen engine model may have been too thick, requiring excessive steam to raise the temperature of the cylinder and then an excessive amount of water to cool the cylinder. Watt heated and cooled the engine for several cycles, finally determining the exact volume of steam required to operate the machine. During this process, Watt uncovered a contradictory point in the Newcomen engine in that a large amount of water was required to cool the heated cylinder, and in the next cycle, the cylinder had to be heated again by a large amount of steam. To reduce his need for so much water and steam, Watt added to the engine a separate chamber for condensing steam, that is, a condenser. Further, he thought that even better results might be obtained by supplementing atmospheric pressure with the pressure of the steam itself after the steam was returned to the condenser. As a result, he applied the steam's pressure to the cylinder. However, the pressure was reportedly only one atmosphere above ambient pressure.

In this manner, Watt installed the condenser and completed a steam engine in which the piston is being driven directly by steam pressure.[2-1] The steam engine was said to have been completed in 1776, 13 years after Watt's failure analysis began. Photo 3-3 shows Watt's early steam engine. Note that almost all the teeth in the gear used to transfer the power from the engine were broken.

The gear teeth used in today's engines are based on a curved line called the involute, and their strength has been sufficiently calculated. However, in Watt's era around the 1770s, the industrial gear was still in its formative stages. Since the involute curve-based gear had not appeared yet, gears were based on the curved line known as an epicycloid. The first person who calculated the strength of gear teeth was Watt. His assistant, Matthew Boulton, wrote Watt a letter advising that gear profiles must be machined more precisely to protect gear teeth from damage.[3-3] Machining processes and their accuracy are inseparable problems that are not limited to engines, but are the basis of all mechanical products (see Chapter 38). Machining or manufacturing process and the accuracy for the desired product are the most basic and important parts of all mechanical products. This concept originated with Watt's engine.

Photo 3-3 The use of Watt's steam engine spread like wildfire throughout modern European nations. This engine is the one made by Watt in 1788 with 476-mm bore, 1200-mm stroke, and 13.75 PS. The fact that the power-transmitting gear teeth are all broken convinces me that Watt was the first person to perform the strength calculation of gear teeth (London Science Museum).

Although Watt did add one atmospheric pressure of steam into the cylinder, it served only to transport the steam to the cylinder. Therefore, Watt's engine can still be classified as an atmospheric engine. He never attempted to convert his atmospheric pressure machine into something more efficient through the use of a higher pressure. When Watt separated the condenser from the cylinder, the efficiency of his engine was increased four times, that is, coal consumption was reduced to one fourth. Watt continued to feel that high pressures in the engine would be dangerous and avoided its use: Still, the basic structure of his engine pointed to the need for higher pressures and served to transition from the atmospheric pressure machine. It was obvious

that a higher steam pressure would be required to achieve a higher efficiency. In spite of Watt's opposition, Richard Trevithick completed his
high-pressure steam engine in 1804.

Chapter 4

How Was an Internal-Combustion Engine Established?

The discovery of the century was the result of a faulty idea. The earliest theory was buried due to an unpaid tax bill.

Barrier Against the Birth of the Internal-Combustion Engine

Progress in any technology, particularly in natural science, is made when a hypothesis is established that has been based on experiments that reproduce a phenomenon and confirm the consistency of some rule (design standard).[4-1] In this case, the hypothesis can be a mere conjecture and does not have to be a valid theory from its very beginning. Because a hypothesis serves as merely a single step on the road toward solving a problem, it can be revised freely if a contradiction arises, just as a hiker can change directions if a fallen tree blocks his path.

The German experimenter Nicolaus August Otto invented the first successful four-stroke internal-combustion engine. This first engine was the forerunner for the multipurpose engines used today. He was working on the engine with the goal of improving the low efficiency of the new Lenoir two-stroke, noncompression engine. However, the conjecture that was the basis for his inquiry, that is, his basis for improving the low efficiency of the Lenoir engine, was far removed from the factors that eventually produced the high efficiency of the Otto engine.

After Watt had commercialized the steam engine, attempts to design a high-performance internal-combustion engine were never made because no one had thought to compress the air/gasoline mixture prior to its ignition. Jean Joseph Etienne Lenoir, a French inventor, is generally credited with designing the world's first internal-combustion engine in 1860, 155 years after the Newcomen steam engine had been assembled. His engine was still not a compression machine because it ignited its fuel at atmospheric pressure. In those cases with minimal heat transfer, when the air/fuel mixture is compressed in the cylinder before ignition, then the temperature in the cylinder will rise in proportion to the power of the volume ratio (compression ratio). As a result, the thermal efficiency increases rapidly with the increase in the compression ratio (Appendix A4). This increase in thermal efficiency is the reason engine manufacturers attempt to maximize the compression ratio of gasoline and diesel engines even today.

The idea of compressing the air/fuel mixture before ignition had been presented by some people shortly after the invention of the Lenoir engine. Otto's idea was very different in that he felt the poor thermal efficiency was attributable to an abrupt explosion. Otto felt that if the combustion process could be slowed, then the efficiency would rise. His idea to slow down the rate of combustion was to stratify the air/fuel area (a region of several different mixture ratios) and to initiate the combustion more slowly at ignition. Next, he promoted combustion in a rich mixture (a mixture with a higher proportion of fuel) and then followed with a lean mixture (a mixture with a lower proportion of fuel).

Although not directly related to the four-stroke cycle engine, it is interesting to note that Otto separated the intake stroke (in an attempt at stratification) through his invention of the slide valve system for intake and exhaust and also of his improvement of the flamed ignition, which he had inherited from the Lenoir engine. This improvement eventually led to the four-stroke cycle compression engine. Historical records indicate that his design had a compression ratio of about 2.5. For comparison, today's gasoline engine has a compression ratio of approximately 8 while a diesel engine has a ratio of approximately 18.

Who Conceived the Principle of the Four-Stroke Cycle Engine?

If Otto merely improved the two-stroke cycle Lenoir engine, then who originally conceived the idea of the four-stroke cycle engine? In my opinion, that would be a French citizen named Alphonse Beau de Rochas. In 1862, right after Lenoir completed his two-stroke cycle engine, Rochas developed his idea sufficiently to build his four-stroke cycle engine 14 years before the Otto engine. Thus, because of this chronological record, the credit for the four-stroke engine should go to Rochas. If this is the case, then why is Rochas generally not acknowledged for his engine? After Otto had built his engine in 1876 and attempted to patent his idea, a patent attorney named C. Wigand researched possible patent infringement for Otto. Wigand came across unpublished documents and papers that showed Rochas had invented the four-stroke cycle engine.[4-2] However, Rochas' French patent had been invalidated because he had failed to pay taxes on the patent. During this time in French history, the penalty for delinquent taxes was to invalidate the patent that had been granted to the inventor. I am deeply impressed that Rochas did not protest when Otto was awarded a gold prize for his engine at the Paris Exposition the year after Otto's invention. However, Rochas was officially commended as the inventor of the four-stroke cycle engine two years before his death and was awarded a £3000 prize. This attitude of the French government also made a deep impression on me.

Because some French people were humiliated by this turn of history, a French textbook later wrote that the Otto engine had a Beau de Rochas cycle instead of a four-stroke cycle. However, this statement still seems a little odd to me.

Appendix A4 Compression Ratio and Thermal Efficiency

An Otto cycle is a process in which air is compressed adiabatically (without the transfer of heat to or from the air) by the piston in the cylinder, heat is added to the air during the constant-volume heating process (in a real engine heat is obtained by burning fuel), and the air is subjected to adiabatic expansion from the maximum pressure point. This Otto cycle is currently regarded as the ideal cycle for the spark-ignition engine.

When pressure, temperature, and volume are represented with $P_1...P_4$, $T_1...T_3$, and $V_1...V_4$, the following equations can be established because of the relationship between the heat added, Q_h, and the heat rejected, Q_L (see Fig. A4-1).

$$Q_h = mC_v(T_3 - T_2) = mC_v T_1 \varepsilon^{K-1}(\xi - 1)$$
$$Q_L = mC_v(T_4 - T_1) = mC_v T_1(1 - \xi)$$

where

m = Weight of gas
C_v = Specific heat at constant volume

ε = Ratio of compression and expansion (compression ratio) = V_1/V_2

K = Specific heat at constant pressure/specific heat at constant volume
  = C_p/C_v

ξ = P_3/P_2

Then, theoretical thermal efficiency is given by the equation below.

$$\eta_{th} = 1 - \frac{Q_L}{Q_h} = 1 - \frac{1}{\varepsilon^{K-1}} = 1 - \frac{T_1}{T_2} = 1 - \frac{T_4}{T_3}$$

That is, the theoretical thermal efficiency is related only to the compression ratio and K, and it corresponds to the efficiency of the Carnot cycle active between temperatures T_1 and T_2 or T_3 and T_4. (Refer to Chapter 9.)

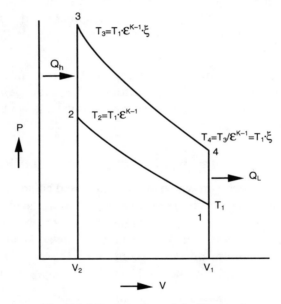

Fig. A4-1 Explanation of the Otto cycle.

Chapter 5

The Mind of Nicolaus August Otto

A vision toward stratified charge combustion.

The Source of Inspiration in Solving a Problem Is Consciousness

Otto, who as an employee of Deutz Gas Motoren Fablic GmBH, now the KHD Corporation, had devoted much of his time to improving the efficiency of the engine. One day he noticed that smoke rising from a factory smokestack continued to rise straight up without mixing with the air. As he began to wonder why the smoke was responding in this way, he was struck by an inspiration; that is, what would happen if this smoke were fuel gas? He thought that if the gas were ignited just at the exit of the smokestack (i.e., in the region that had more fuel [rich mixture] in the air), then combustion would propagate slowly to the other areas in which concentration gradually falls (i.e., in the region that has a higher amount of air [lean mixture] and less fuel). As a result, a quiet and efficient combustion would occur due to the slower propagation of combustion instead of abrupt explosions (this process corresponds to stratified charge combustion) (Fig. 5-1).

Otto knew he had hit upon an idea of great potential. To realize that potential, however, he would have to find a way to put smoke like that which came from the smokestack directly into an engine cylinder. Without wasting any time, he built a model engine equipped with a transparent cylinder, a hand-operated piston, and an intake and exhaust valve using a side valve system. He then put cigarette smoke into the intake valve and observed the reaction. He repeated the process while changing some conditions and observed the smoke again. For six years, he searched for the best way to inject the air and fuel into the cylinder. Otto felt that the fuel mixture in the

Fig. 5-1 Otto's idea was the result of seeing smoke rise from a smokestack (1870).

combustion chamber would explode prematurely if any of the gas from the previous explosion cycle were to remain in the chamber. He also believed that any uncombusted gas would be ejected from the cylinder as a result of the explosion. Through utilization of these principles, he finally completed a four-stroke-cycle gas engine.

Otto's Dream Surviving in Present Measures on Exhaust Gas

In the 1970s, rapidly increasing social concern about exhaust emissions resulted in the stratified charge engine receiving renewed attention. The engine was put on the market as the Honda CVCC, the Ford PROCO, and the Volkswagen PCI, among others. Fig. 5-2 illustrates the principle of the Honda CVCC. A fuel-rich mixture is brought close to the ignition plug and ignited. Then, the flame propagates to a fuel-lean mixture progressively farther from the ignition source. NO$_x$ (nitrogen oxides) are the most difficult of the exhaust gases to eliminate. NO$_x$ can be reduced in the emission by decreasing the concentration of fuel in the mixture; however, the combustion temperature also falls, reducing the output power. The Honda CVCC is an attempt to spread combustion sequentially into the fuel-lean mixture, which normally will not burn, by igniting locally the mixture with a high fuel content. Although the objective was different, this method is a realization of Otto's dream after a time lapse of 100 years. Also Otto's method of observing the engine mechanics through a transparent cylinder has been recognized as a significant research tool in the quest to reduce exhaust emissions. The use of the transparent cylinder is called a visualization method and is popular among research institutions. If Otto, who did not know the meaning of NO$_x$, were alive and saw the use of this "visualization method," he might say, "These guys are doing the same thing as I did even though 100 years have passed."

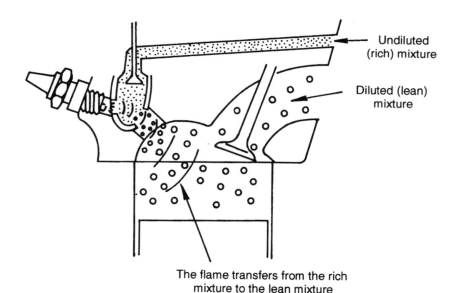

The flame transfers from the rich
mixture to the lean mixture

Fig. 5-2 The Honda CVCC realized Otto's idea.

Photo 5-1 shows photographs of the airflow taken through a transparent cylinder in a modern diesel engine. It can be seen that a strong eddy was formed in the cylinder. This eddy is called a swirl by engine manufacturers and is considered to be an important component in combustion performance.

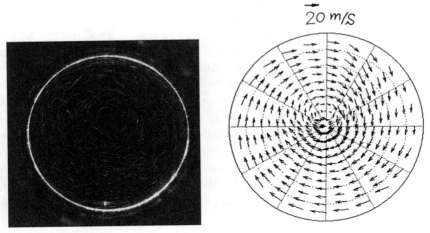

Photo 5-1 Air is vigorously whirling in cylinder: (1) In-cylinder air motion observed by the laser light sheet method. (2) Flow velocity and direction of air in left picture as measured with laser Doppler velocimetry.

To remove the NO_x exhaust emission from gasoline engines, a three-way catalyst has been put into general use, and the elimination of NO_x has been achieved due to the fuel-lean combustion resulting from research on in-cylinder airflow. As a result of this innovation, the engine that depended on stratified charge combustion has faded from the industrial scene. However, some organizations still do some research on this engine.

Chapter 6

Truth About the Completion of the Otto Engine

Invented by Otto, but completed by Maybach. The never-ending problem of lubrication still remains to be solved.

�֎

Have a Support Person

Every major achievement has a history. Many people contribute their thoughts, their talents, and their dedication to accomplish this achievement. In fact, it can be said that no one person can accomplish any great achievement; instead, it takes the combined efforts of a team to complete the job. This statement is especially true in mechanical engineering.

For example, the Huygens engine had Denis Papin, and the Lenoir engine needed the ideas of many people and other earlier techniques. Alphonse Beau de Rochas, who invented the four-stroke-cycle engine, did not have a good assistant to help with the invention of his new device.

Otto was fortunate in having many people help him design and improve the Otto engine. One of Otto's assistants was Wilhelm Maybach, who later became the chief engineer of the Daimler company. He designed the Mercedes engine, which can be said to be the origin of the Daimler and even the Rolls-Royce aeroengines used in World War II war planes (refer to Chapter 22).

Maybach's Two Distinguished Services

When Otto was first building an experimental engine, Maybach was traveling in America. When Maybach returned home, he made many changes to the still experimental engine for the actual production. Lyle C. Cummins,

author of *Internal Fire: The Internal Combustion Engine, 1673-1900*, wrote
that there were two major distinguishing points in the modified Otto
engine.[(4-2)] First, a device was invented to make starting easier by releasing
the compressed gas in the cylinder. This device is the same as the decom-
pression system that was used in the heavy-duty precombustion engines for
a long time even after World War II. In this method, the engine is rotated
with either the suction or exhaust valve open so as to release the compression pressure. After the engine gets a rotating inertia, the engine can be
rotated at high speed with less effort. Then the open valve is closed, the air/
fuel mixture is ignited, and the engine is operated in the normal way.

According to Cummins, the other major improvement was in lubrication.
An unmistakable difference between the experimental and production
engines was that the production engines had a crosshead. The crosshead is a
sliding piece between the piston and the connecting rod that prevents lateral
motion due to the forces (side thrust) transmitted from the connecting rod, as
shown in Fig. 6-1. Traditionally used in steam engines, the crosshead is used
today only in large ships with low-speed, two-stroke-cycle engines having a
cylinder diameter of 500 to 600 mm and more. However, the sliding portion

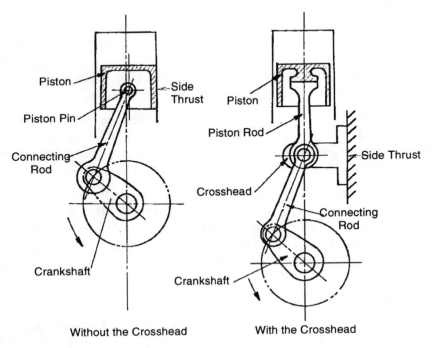

Fig. 6-1 Explanation of crosshead.

and piston pin, which receive the side thrust, are separated from the hot piston and are much cooler. Therefore, providing adequate lubrication in this area is easier, serving to minimize problems that are likely to occur in that area such as seizure and abnormal wear. Maybach examined the problems that had resulted on Otto's first experimental engine. Otto had simplified the design of this later model by omitting the crosshead. Maybach immediately returned the crosshead and added an oil reservoir above the cylinder. This story exemplifies Maybach's superb insight. However, we would like to point out that his returning to the original design is one of the basic techniques in troubleshooting.

Otto's first experimental engine is preserved (top of Photo 6-1) at the KHD Museum in Koln (Germany) or Cologne city (the word "cologne" gets its etymology from the French *eau de Cologne*, drawing from the waters at the city of Cologne). Its production model, on the other hand, is exhibited at the Smithsonian Museum in the United States. This engine is one of the products that KHD put on the U.S. market circa 1880. The area showing the crosshead is shown at the bottom of Photo 6-1. The bevel gear shown in this photo is a part of the slide valve opening/closing mechanism for intake and exhaust through the cylinder head and for the ignition flame (the electric spark plug was not in practical use at that time). Bevel gears to control the valve mechanisms were used in World War II fighter aircraft. The crosshead was seldom used in the smaller engines, but the lubrication of pistons and cylinders was a recurring problem that still requires extensive engineering attention. As a result, I want to discuss this problem next.

Photo 6-1 [Top] Experimental engine (in KHD Museum) with 160-mm bore, 300-mm stroke, and 3 PS/180 rpm (1876). [Bottom] Production engine (in Smithsonian Museum) (circa 1880): With the addition of the crosshead, which the experimental Otto engine did not have.

Chapter 7

The Problems of Piston and Cylinder

Engine life ensured by lubrication. New technology attributable to a serviceman.

✂

We Still Have Seizure Problems

If a vehicle were to be driven with insufficient cooling, then the friction of the piston against the cylinder walls would generate enough heat to cause the piston to seize in the cylinder. In a car race, for instance, engines sometimes overheat, causing the water in the radiator to boil over and be lost. Sometimes, smoke may even roil out from the engine as a result of the lubricant burning in the engine, after the piston (or other components such as bearings) has seized.

Seizure is not limited to an instance in which the radiator has no water. It also occurs when the material, surface finish, and lubrication of the piston and cylinder are not satisfactory. However, we rarely experience these other failures now because, under normal conditions, today's cars are designed to resist the seizure problem.

Although specific details are not available, I suppose that the first Otto engine mentioned in the previous chapter was troubled by piston seizure. This problem of piston seizure may have been waiting for Maybach to solve when he returned from the United States. It can be imagined that Maybach solved the problem by returning the engine design to the old crosshead type.

The problems of materials, surface finish, oil consumption, and lubrication are still some of the major subjects in seizure research. This combination of topics is called "tribology." Even though modern engines almost never experience piston seizure, piston rings and cylinders do wear, resulting in a shortened engine life. Oil consumption must be controlled, particularly in view of environmental concerns.

Lubricating Oil Consumption and Engine Life

The Japanese artist Yuzo Saeki, renowned as a master artist, visited Paris in the 1920s. The year after he was in Paris, Saeki painted a beautiful picture entitled *The Gas Station.* In his painting, the entrance of the service station had a sign that read "HUILE (oil) - ESSENCE (gasoline)." Today, we do not even think about oil when pumping gasoline at a service station because oil consumption is so much lower than gasoline. However, in the 1920s when Yuzo Saeki strolled through Paris with his canvas over his shoulder, it was probable that several liters of oil must have been required every time one added 30 liters of gasoline. Therefore, "HUILE" and "ESSENCE" were painted side by side on the shop's signboard (Fig. 7-1, Photo 7-1). Fig. 7-2 illustrates the decline in engine oil consumption from 1910 to now. As shown in the figure, the oil consumption of today's engine has decreased to about 1/700 of the 1910 level. The consumption values in this figure cover the early aircraft engine[7-1] (the engine was often used in common for both automobiles and airplanes in the early days) and the more recent commercial engine. The commercial engine, because of its requirement for a long life, is sensitive to lubrication and oil consumption. Reducing the engine's access to oil may lead to a reduction in engine life. Fig. 7-3 shows an increase in the average life of a truck engine after the end of World War II. Owners of commercial vehicles have especially been concerned about extending the life of the truck engine. This figure shows a steady increase in truck engine life.

Fig. 7-4 traces the oil consumption in a typical truck since it was first put into service. As plotted in this graph, the oil consumption is relatively low in the beginning, but then increases significantly. After reaching the first peak, oil consumption begins falling. In the final curve, oil consumption increases slowly and steadily. The lubrication oil in the oil sump lubricates only the frictional faces. What, then, causes this trend in oil consumption? For what other function could the oil be used?

For instance, the transmission also contains lubricating oil, but this oil is not consumed as fast as the engine lubricating oil. After lubricating the piston and cylinder, most of the engine oil is returned to the sump by the wiping action of the piston rings. However, that portion that is not returned is either burned in the cylinder or discharged through the exhaust port in its unburned state. Another cause of engine oil consumption is that some of the

The lemon-colored body of the 1923 Citroën dominated a generation.

Fig. 7-1 Oil consumed by 10% of fuel. (Reference is made to Yuzo Saeki's painting.
"HUILE [oil]" and "ESSENCE [gasoline]" are written side by side
on the signboard.)

combustion gas in the cylinder leaks between the piston and the cylinder.
This leakage gas is known as blowby gas. As this gas passes the piston, it
entrains a small amount of lubricating oil. This gas is either discharged to
the atmosphere or mixed with the intake air of the engine and then burned.
Either way, the lubricating oil contained in the blowby gas is lost to the
engine.

Photo 7-1 Even now, a typical shop counter serves as a gas station in greater Paris: The characters "HUILE" can no longer be found on signboard (May 1979).

Therefore, oil consumption may be reduced by having the piston ring press harder against the cylinder so as to wipe all the oil from the cylinder wall. In so doing, however, the oil film between the rings and wall will become very thin, increasing the risk of seizure. The tightrope between the reduction of oil consumption and the prevention of seizure is a difficult one to walk.

Fig. 7-4 shows actual oil consumption data. Note that the oil consumption first increases, decreases to a certain point, and then slowly increases. Why does the oil consumption show this trend?

Fig. 7-5 shows the same trend, along with sketches of the piston, piston ring, and cylinder. In the initial period, the rings and cylinder are adjusting their mutual fit by a wear process known as the "break-in" process. During break-in, oil consumption may be high. Then, with break-in complete, wear begins to reduce the depth of the grooves in the cylinder, thereby reducing the volume of oil retained in the grooves. Consequently, oil consumption decreases. However, as this process continues, the wear is eventually

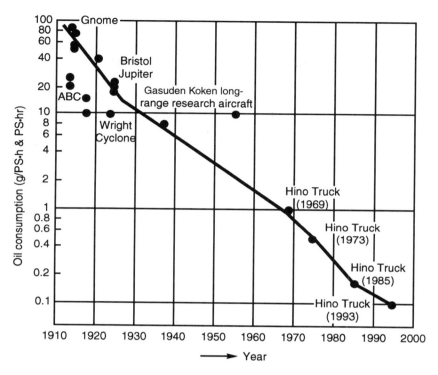

Fig. 7-2 Reduction of engine oil consumption.

enough to cause an increase in blowby, and oil consumption begins to increase. This trend continues to the end of the engine's life.

Two Key Factors to Extending Engine Life

The life of an engine does not depend exclusively on the pistons and cylinders. However, just as man has critical diseases, the engine has critical factors that determine its life. These factors include the pistons and cylinders (Appendix A7). Research on these parts determines how well the crisis in the initial and final periods of engine use can be managed and how long the engine can be used with a minimal maintenance cost throughout the life.

The crosshatching in the cylinder bore is finished by honing. The grooves are normally crossed with each other rather than made parallel. Hence, they are called "crosshatch." The crossing angle and depth of grooves are set at the optimum values as determined by each manufacturer's study, so they are different among manufacturers. The exact date that this particular concept was

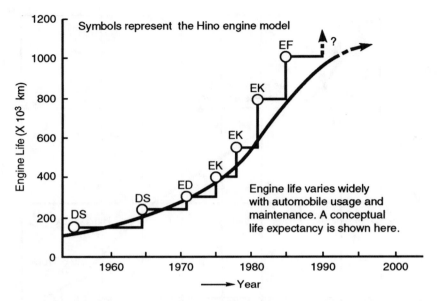

Fig. 7-3 Prolongation of engine life: The life of an engine is becoming longer as steadily as human life. (Note: Engine life varies widely with automobile usage and maintenance. A conceptual life expectancy is shown here.)

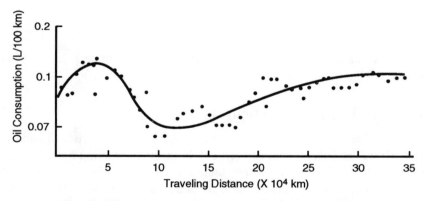

Fig. 7-4 Transition in oil consumption of truck engine.

established in the automotive industry is unknown, but this information is contained in the 1934 edition of Devillers' book[7-2] which is regarded as the Old Testament for the designers of the internal-combustion engine. Hence, the date of establishment must have been earlier than 1934 (Fig. 7-6).

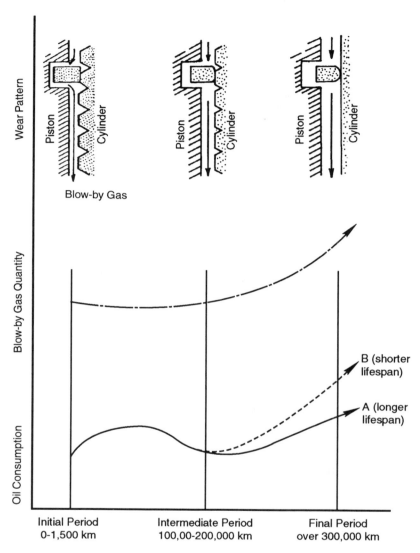

Fig. 7-5 Oil consumption and progress of wear.

However, the great improvement in oil consumption as a result of cylinder surface finish came to be recognized around 1957. Particularly in the United States, improvement progressed rapidly.[7-3] One day circa 1960, a customer complained to a serviceman about excessive oil consumption. The customer owned a V8-engine passenger car that traveled only 650 km per liter of oil. Even though the 1957 model usually consumed a liter of oil

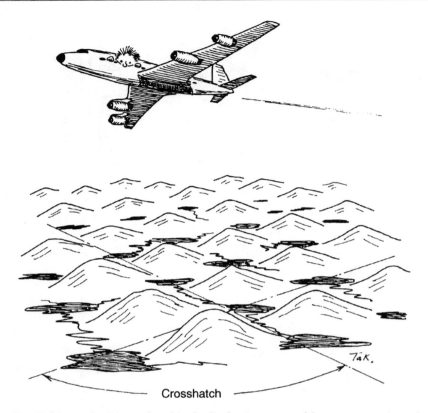

Crosshatch

Fig. 7-6 Inner face (crosshatch) of cylinder is comparable to a succession of mountains and lakes: Rebuilding of this "country" is the major subject on engine life.

every 400 km, the car owner complained that his car was using more oil than previously. In response to the customer's unfounded complaints, the serviceman substantially improved oil consumption by replacing all the piston rings with new ones. However, the customer still complained. To improve oil consumption even further, the serviceman carefully rehoned the cylinder to a much finer finish. Amazingly, this simple procedure instantly improved oil consumption to 1200 km per liter of oil.[7-3]

In 1971, the U.S. International Harvester Company announced that a simultaneous improvement was made on both oil consumption and engine life by applying an inner face finishing method called "plateau honing" to the newly developed 300/400 model engines.[7-4] The essence of this method is a productive realization of the serviceman's earlier attempts. Fig. 7-7 provides a microscopic cross-sectional view of the cylinder liner surface. After the crosshatching is ground into the cylinder liner, then the vertices of the crosshatch are finished flat by honing. The flattening of the top of the hill reduces the total amount of the remaining oil, and sufficient oil is supplied from the foot of the hill to prevent seizure. The "S" in the figure denotes the height of peak. 1S indicates approximately 0.001 millimeter.

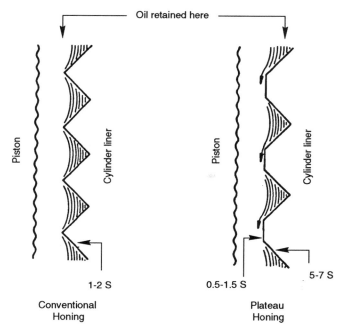

Fig. 7-7 Improved method of cylinder liner surface finish.

In recent years, even further refinement of the inner surface finishing process has been attempted to reduce oil consumption and extend engine life.

Appendix A7 Critical "Diseases" in Engine Life

Fig. A7-1 lists the lubricant-related problems on commercial vehicle diesel engines as reported at the 1976 Society of Automotive Engineers symposium.[7-5] The circled problems are related to piston, piston ring, and cylinder. Their importance is visualized here. The significance index in the figure is a weighting factor that results in a higher value when the problem occurred at a shorter mileage.

In contrast, Fig. A7-2 re-examines the problems that significantly affect the life of today's diesel engine for heavy-duty trucks. Even though the engine's

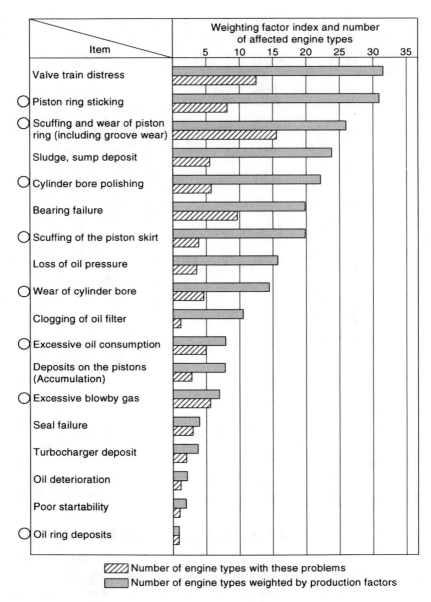

Fig. A7-1 Example of critical "diseases" in engine life (1976).[7-5]

average life has, in general, been extended substantially, really significant
changes have not been made on the major problems affecting the engine

life. Problems involving friction and lubrication (tribology) in the cylinder area still greatly affect the engine.

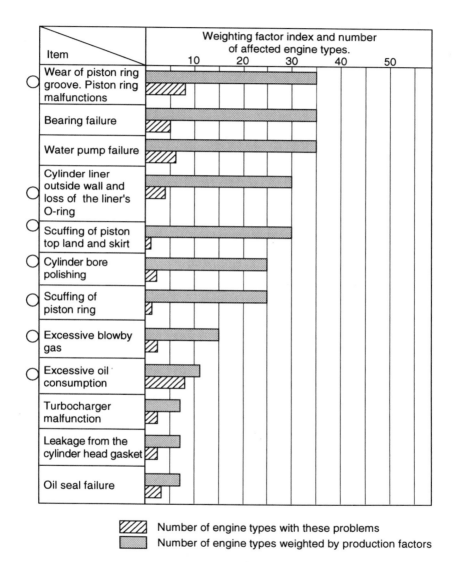

Fig. A7-2 Example of critical "diseases" in engine life (1987).

Chapter 8

Engine Life and Cylinder

Fateful struggle for power increase.

Life of Aircraft and Automotive Engines

The first naval aircraft engine was purchased from the Wright brothers in 1909 and is now exhibited at the Pensacola Naval Aviation Museum in Florida in the United States. When we look carefully at the engine, two large cracks are noticeable on the crankcase (engine body). Although of the same 4000 cm^3 displacement as the one used in the famous 1903 First Flight, this engine has a marking of 39 hp. This horsepower rating is a threefold increase from the 13-hp rating of the engine used in the initial flight. The cracks tell the fate of this engine, in which the output must have been increased at the expense of reliability (service life). I have no data on the cumulative operation time of this engine, but I can easily imagine how harrowing this engine was for those pilots who risked their lives each time they flew it (Photo 8-1).

In this early engine era, cars would break down on the road so often that drivers gave little thought to the lifespan of the engine. Since cars would often die while on the road, drivers always had to be ready to diagnose and repair the problem. These on-road problems were most often the result of the carburetor and electrical wiring.[8-1] Therefore, the true lifetime of the engine in those days cannot be estimated exactly. In the same year that the Navy bought the Wright brothers' engine, Louis Bleriot's monoplane with the Anzani engine made it through, albeit barely, that vital 38 minutes when it crossed the Dover Channel. According to legend, a sudden and violent squall saved his plane from overheating (Fig. 8-1, Photo 8-2).

*Photo 8-1 Wright's biplane engine: Crankcase has large cracks at two locations,
where a patch is attached (bottom center of photo, U.S. Naval Aircraft Museum).*

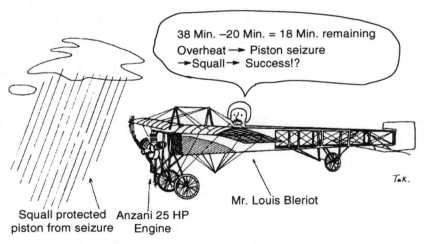

*Fig. 8-1 Louis Bleriot crosses the Strait of Dover (1909): The Anzani 2800-cm^3,
25-PS engine was on the verge of seizing.*

During World War I, it was proudly stated that the aircraft engines such as
the Rolls-Royce were overhauled only every 150 hours.[8-1] However, the

Photo 8-2 Anzani engine of Bleriot's monoplane: Presently exhibited at an aircraft museum in Paris.

overhauling interval was reportedly increased to about 300 hours near the end of this war.[8-2] The number of times that each engine was overhauled is not clear. As we neared World War II, it was said that the first overhaul occurred after 500 to 700 hours of operation; after undergoing several overhauls, the engine was removed from service. However, operating conditions are different among warplanes, and the exigencies of war determine the time and amount of engine maintenance. Hence, the real conditions of engine overhaul are not known.

Since World War II, unexpected engine failures have been rare, and the real lifespan of the engine is more easily determined. During the early Japanese engine development, automobile engines were most frequently used in taxis rather than private automobiles. Around 1955, this typical taxi engine was overhauled at 70,000 to 80,000 km, increasing to 120,000 to 150,000 km in the 1960s. Today, a taxi engine can go about 300,000 km or more before an overhaul is needed.[8-3] The previously mentioned aircraft engine lifetime in the World Wars cannot be correlated to that of a car engine; however, for information only, it may be estimated to be about 30,000 to 50,000 km.

During the 1960s, commercial vehicles, particularly heavy-duty trucks, had an overhaul interval of 120,000 to 150,000 km. In more recent years, these trucks commonly travel 1 million km between overhauls.

When an engine does need repair, the most frequent cause is excessive oil consumption due to the wear of the pistons, piston rings, and cylinders. As shown in Fig. 8-2, the years have seen a constant improvement in the rate of oil consumption (i.e., the number of kilometers per liter of oil has been increasing) so as to meet the users' demands. At the same time, the output power of trucks has been rising steadily as shown in Fig. 8-3, making the improved oil consumption even more remarkable.

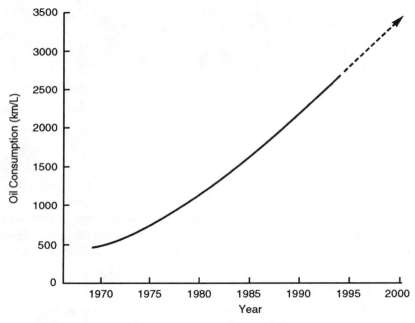

Fig. 8-2 Transition in oil consumption (km/L)(large truck).

Invention of Boron Cylinder Liner

Let me provide an example from postwar history of how the automotive industry has responded to the user's demands to reduce oil consumption and extend the service life of the truck engine. From 1963 to 1965, Hino Motors had a program to extend the service life of the engine. This program was code named the "EL committee," taking the initial letters of Engine and Life. The program was originally developed by the head of the engine

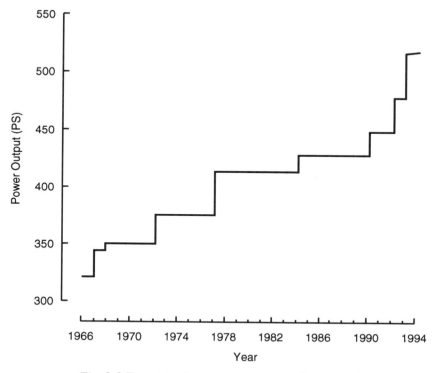

Fig. 8-3 Transition in maximum output of large truck.

design department, Mr. Iwasaki, and subsequently carried on by his successor, Mr. Sekiguchi. This program used the technique of failure analysis. The approach of the project team is summarized in Fig. 8-4. As the most basic step, dust was prevented from entering the engine. Then, coolant temperature control was improved because cylinder wear increases rapidly when the cylinder wall temperature is outside the 80°-150°C [8-4] temperature range.

Since that time, the condition of the cylinder bore and the alignment between the piston and piston ring have been considered important in preventing piston seizure. The most significant result at this time may be a boron (boron cast-iron) cylinder liner. Fig. 8-5 is the result of a boron cylinder liner wear test. Note that the extremely heavy wear of the chromium-plated liner was due to an improper shape of oil retention grooves on the surface and does not represent a general case. The use of the boron cylinder liner and other measures shown in Fig. 8-4 has greatly increased the engine life.

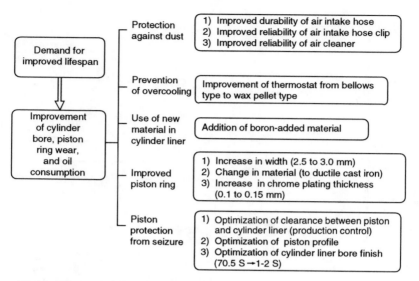

Fig. 8-4 Factors determining engine life and methods for improvement.

The composition of boron cast-iron is sketched in Fig. 8-6.[8-5] The compound containing boron carbide shown in this figure is called "special steadite." This steadite plays a central role in resisting wear. Its inventor, Dr. Tsutomu Takao[8-5], explains:

"Because the hardened steadite due to the presence of special steadite has a strong wear resistance, the wear lags slightly behind that of other areas. That is, when observing the frictional face, it appears that the special steadite forms the first sliding surface, and the pearlite and graphite at the base, which are lower in hardness, form the second sliding surface at a slightly lower level since the progress of wear is a little faster. Therefore, the opposing material in friction can continue to move on the special steadite safely with a reduced friction while receiving lubricant from the recess. Even when the opposing material is a hard chromium-plated surface, the boron cast-iron slides on the cemented hard compound of the first sliding surface, while receiving lubricant from the second sliding surface. Therefore, wear resistance is further enhanced. This resistance is based on the same principle as a 17- or 18-jewel watch, in which the shaft, made of an extremely hard steel, slides over the hard jewels accurately without wearing for a long time unless oil has run out."

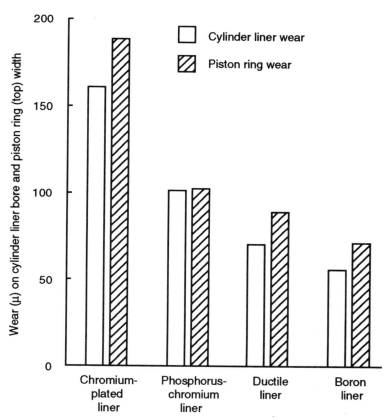

Fig. 8-5 Difference in wear due to the cylinder liner material; because of the use of a boron cylinder liner, engine life has been extended substantially (Model DS-50 engine, 2000 rpm, 3/4 load, 200-hr operation, dust charge JIS Class 8: 150 g, JIS Class 2: 15 g).

Main Factors in Extending Engine Life

Even though the boron cylinder liner was an important technological invention, Dr. R. Munro lists the following major factors in achieving today's engine life from a macroscopic viewpoint.[8-6]

1945 to 1950: Invention of lubricant with detergent additive and widespread use of Lo-ex piston material (aluminum alloy with a small expansion coefficient)

1955 to 1960: Invention of chromium-plated piston ring

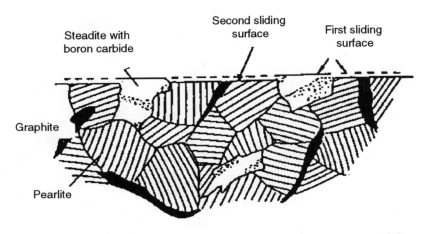

Fig. 8-6 Composition of boron cast-iron (section of cylinder bore).[(8-5)]

1960 to 1965: Invention of Alfin, a nickel wear-resistant piston ring insert (use of a nickel alloy piston ring insert to prevent groove wear)

1968 to 1970: Use of plateau honing on the cylinder liner. (The lifetime of the Hino engine has increased as shown in Fig. 7-3. Its factors may be traced with time as listed below, referring to the Munro approach.)

1965 to 1970: Adoption of boron cylinder liner

1970 to 1975: Adoption of direct fuel-injection diesel engine

1975 to 1980: Improvement on thermal load and sealed material (O- rings, for example, composed of polymeric material)

1980 to 1985: Improvement of cooling system

In the future, engine life will become even longer due to the development of new materials, the use of failure analysis techniques, and other electronic advancements.

Chapter 9

Another Genius, Sadi Carnot

A flash of scholarly insight during a student's military service. He conceives a good idea as a result of his review of earlier work. The spirit of "Tannisho."

Unrealizable Carnot's Cycle

The idea of improving engine efficiency by compressing the gas prior to combustion originated from Beau de Rochas as discussed earlier. However, 38 years before Beau de Rochas completed his work and 52 years before the completion of the Otto engine, Sadi Carnot predicted the same effect theoretically. In 1824, in his book entitled *Study on the Power of Fire and an Engine Suitable for Generating This Power*[9-1], the 28-year-old Carnot developed a theory that led to the principle of Carnot's cycle.

Through his analyses on the cylinder, in which air is confined, and the piston, Carnot came up with the following idea: Assuming that a heat engine has no losses during the cycle and that it works in reverse (called Carnot's cycle composed by isothermal and adiabatic change), the engine's maximum efficiency is determined by the difference between the maximum and minimum temperatures; the efficiency will never reach 100%. When this statement is applied to a current-day engine, the maximum efficiency of a heat engine is expressed by dividing the difference between heat quantity input to the working fluid (gas) and the heat quantity released to the atmosphere. In the Otto cycle, for example, the efficiency is determined by dividing the difference between the cylinder peak gas temperature and the exhaust gas temperature or compressed gas temperature and atmospheric temperature (see Appendix A4). Therefore, the actual available efficiency of the internal-combustion engine is far from the maximum efficiency of the Carnot cycle due to an irreversible cycle with various losses.

Today, research efforts are continuing with the goal of increasing engine efficiency by even 1%, thereby improving fuel consumption. Fig. 9-1 illustrates the slight improvements that have been made in raising the efficiency of combustion. The solid line at the top of the figure represents the Carnot cycle and corresponds to the case in which there is no loss at all. (The adiabatic engine shown in Fig. 9-1 is discussed in more detail in the next chapter.) We are now attempting to achieve a target that has been set by a 28-year- old youth over 150 years ago. In one sense, as Carnot stated, we are continuing efforts to increase the difference between the given and the delivered heat quantities while minimizing heat losses to non-work factors. However, Carnot's efficiency level can never be reached. The ideal engine and the cycle conceived by Carnot, named "Carnot's cycle," have been examined by many workers in the engineering field. The research has indicated that the ideal engine could never be realized because of the principle of heat known as the "Second Law of Thermodynamics."

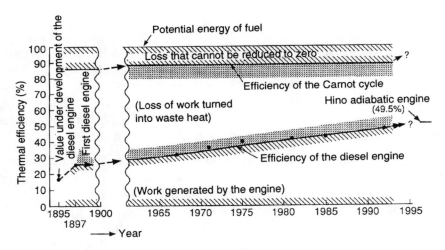

Fig. 9-1 Engine efficiency on the rise, though gradually, with loss gradually decreasing: Carnot's cycle was calculated assuming combustion and atmospheric temperatures to be 2300°C and 15°C, respectively. At the time that the diesel engine was invented, combustion temperature was lower than it is now.

Even with the understanding that the ideal engine will never be reached, readers may be surprised at the enormous amount of wasted energy. Fig. 9-1 shows that, as a rough estimate, only one-third of the energy consumed results in actual work, one-third is lost in heat exhaust, and the last third is absorbed by the coolant heat. The loss of all this energy is the reason that the car exhaust, the radiator, the engine, and the radiator are hot. Fig. 9-1 also illustrates the gradual reduction in heat loss that has been made (refer to Appendices A9 and A11).

Carnot's Excellent Idea

Because it was widely used during his time, Carnot studied the steam engine. He was surprised to find that, with steam as the medium, there were boundaries to the differences in the highest and lowest temperatures. Based on this finding, Carnot explained that he would need to build an engine that compressed the air it used before ignition. Carnot's work later provided the basis for the internal-combustion engine. In addition, Carnot predicted the eventual demise of steam locomotives, which happened only a few decades ago (Photo 9-1). This demise is natural since a steam locomotive can convert to useful work only about 10% of the fuel energy supplied; the remaining 90% is wasted. Surprisingly, the steam engine has outlived just about any other kind of engine. Attempts to use the steam engine for aircraft were made as late as 1933. Even in recent years, the use of the steam engine in the automobile has been considered as a possible answer to the internal-combustion engine's noxious exhaust emissions problem (see Appendix A15-1).

Carnot's publications reveal another surprising fact. He listed many of the desirable attributes of the engine in much the same order as we do today, that is, fuel consumption, reliability, lifespan, size (weight), and cost.

Carnot was reported to have said,

> "Through proper evaluation on the convenience of an engine and the realizable economy, it is necessary to distinguish the primary factors from the secondary ones, and to keep the primary factors in balance so that the best result is achievable by the simplest method. Development personnel should satisfy this requirement and should lead the work done by the related divisions and subordinates so that all staffmembers cooperate to achieve the goal."[9-2]

In effect, Carnot described an engine development group as it functions today. As an automotive engineer, I was relieved to note that even a genius such as Carnot did not concern himself with air pollution due to exhaust gas. As a result, he has fewer evaluation items than we have today. As I read

Photo 9-1 [Top] The Canadian national railways' Model 6400 locomotive, which hauled the trains reserved for King George V and Queen Elizabeth, is now sitting quietly (Ottawa National Museum of Science and Technology).
[Bottom] The king of the expressways, the tractor truck.

through Carnot's book, I was surprised to learn that Carnot had carefully organized and used efficiently the experimental results obtained by earlier workers such as J. Gay-Lussac and J. Dolton. This review of earlier work shows that even a genius cannot have an idea just by daydreaming. This book is impressive among those written in his century. From it, we can learn a basic rule: When working to solve a problem, we should study and review the results obtained by earlier workers in the field, organize the data, and then make our decision. If we just sit in a quiet room to think without studying earlier work, then only the Sandman will come rather than a new idea.

Writing Between Military Services

According to his biography, Carnot had been drafted into Napoleon's army as a student soldier when he was a student of Ecole Polytechnique. He later served in the military again and was discharged in 1828. His book was published in 1824, so it must have been written between his stints in the military. I admire Carnot for his positive attitude in understanding and solving his technological problems even under the adverse conditions of an army at war (Fig. 9-2). His theory remained obscure for a long time, finally receiving recognition after it was analyzed, edited, and published by his schoolmate, E. Clapeylon, and still later by William Thomson. This instance shows the importance of making sure people fully understand one's thoughts or concepts before asking them to accept it. This understanding by one's peers will be particularly difficult if the ideas are beyond the accepted realm of thought.

As an aside, it was said that when Carnot was a science student, his classmates teasingly said that the symbol for entropy, S, was taken from the initial letter S of Carnot's first name, Sadi.[9-3]

Finally, I would like to introduce a thought that was among those written by Carnot. The question asked by Carnot was, "If God is the source of ultimate good, then why does He punish sinners for all eternity?" In the 12th Century book *Tannisho*, the famous Japanese Buddhist monk Shinran said, "Even a happy, good man can go to heaven. Then, why not a bad man who has had a bitter experience in this world?" Carnot, a genius who died of cholera at the age of 36, may have gone to heaven to determine the answer to the Shinran's question for himself.

The average lifetime of a European at the beginning of the 19th Century was about 30 years. Carnot cannot be said to have died at an early age. Since his time, the human lifespan has been extended considerably. Major

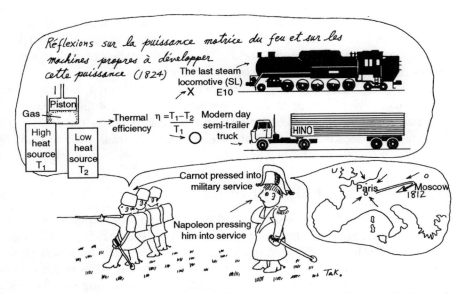

Fig. 9-2 Carnot participated in the 1814 battle in Vincennes. He was discharged from the military in 1828.

factors in extending the human lifespan include Jenner's discovery of the smallpox vaccination[9-4] and the improved quality of life due to the Industrial Revolution. As indicated earlier, the invention of the engine set off the Industrial Revolution, which served as one of the triggers for extending the lifespan of man.

Note: One day in 1979, I visited the Ecole Polytechnique, where Carnot had studied, to honor his achievement. To my disappointment, the gate was barred to visitors. A young man leaving the facilities said, "This is now a military school. The present Ecole Polytechnique is located in a suburb of Paris" (Photo 9-2).

Appendix A9 *Exergie* and *Anergie* in Engine

Even if the activation of a heat engine is reversible between a high heat source T_1 and a low heat source T_2, the maximum thermal efficiency η_t is determined by Carnot's theorem as follows:

$$\eta_t = (T_1 - T_2)/T_1$$

The efficiency of an actual heat engine is always smaller than this η_t value according to the Second Law of Thermodynamics; that is, heat cannot be

Photo 9-2 Main gate of Paris Ecole Polytechnique, Carnot's alma mater. It has been converted to a military school.

transmitted from a low-temperature state to a high- temperature state. In effect, a reversible engine cannot exist. Therefore, the portion of energy Q_1 (heat quantity) usable for work is always determined by the atmospheric temperature T_2 at which the heat engine operates, which means that the efficiency can never exceed the η_t value.

If some energy cannot be utilized throughout an intended process, it should be separated, and only the actual usable energy should be considered in the improvement of efficiency. Z. Rant thought this methodology to be more reasonable. The usable energy has been called *Exergie* (German term meaning available energy) and the unusable energy has been called *Anergie* (German term meaning unavailable energy).[9-5] In other words, the method of expressing the thermal efficiency is based on the energy inherent in the fuel (also called the efficiency according to the First Law of Thermodynamics). This method can follow the flow of energy in other than engine output, but cannot determine how a decrease in energy reduces output, or whether energy can be removed efficiently. Therefore, it was proposed that consideration be made on the efficiency based on the maximum energy obtainable according to Carnot's theorem (also called the efficiency according to the Second Law of Thermodynamics).

In Fig. A9-1, *Anergie* is defined as the loss that will never become zero. *Exergie* equals the difference given by subtracting the *Anergie* from 100%.

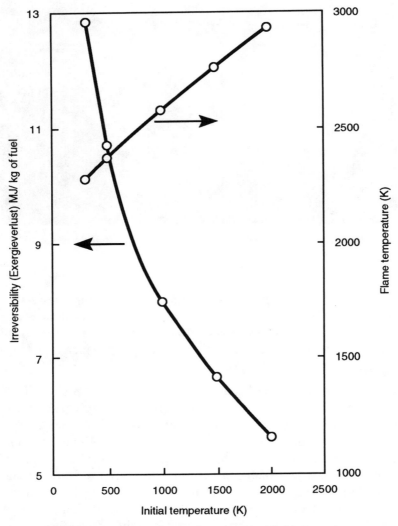

Fig. A9-1 Example of exergieverlust *in adiabatic engine.*

To enhance engine efficiency, it is necessary to maximize the available energy and minimize the loss from *Exergie* (called *Exergieverlust* or irreversibility). When replacing effective work, work obtained from the Carnot engine and atmospheric temperature with W, W_{max}, and T_1, the following equation holds:

$$W = W_{max} - T_1 \Delta S$$

where ΔS represents a change in entropy, which can be expressed as:

$$\Delta S = \Delta S_1 + (S_2 - S_1) \geq 0$$

where ΔS_1 stands for an increase in surrounding entropy, and S_2 and S_1 denote entropy values of a working material before and after change.

Fig. A9-1 shows an example of the study on how *Exergieverlust* (irreversibility) changes when the temperature at the start of combustion rises due to the method of heat insulation in an adiabatic engine.[9-6]

Chapter 10

Carnot's Dream, Adiabatic Engine (I)

Lesson from the battle in Nomonhan and an adiabatic engine.
The net energy of a vehicle is the same as paycheck.

❦

Oil Shock and Enforcement of the Clean Air Act

In 1975, the United States Energy Research and Development Agency (ERDA) approved a regulation that directed domestic car manufacturers to develop automobiles that would decrease fuel consumption by 30-50% for passenger cars, 23% for trucks, and 20% for buses in 10 years, namely by the year 1985.

The year 1975 was also the year that the Muskie Act, also called the Clean Air Act (a regulation proposed by Senator Muskie for reducing automobile exhaust to one-tenth), was scheduled to go into effect in the United States. Since 1970 when the Clean Air Act had been first enacted, the world's automotive engineers said this rate would be impossible to achieve. However, the 1973 Arab oil embargo suddenly forced everyone to realize the scarcity of oil. Still, despite the best efforts of automotive engineers, the technological barriers against the reduction of exhaust emissions were difficult to overcome. In particular, it was felt that a reduction in exhaust emission would inherently result in an increase in fuel consumption.

The United States had placed a high priority on fuel conservation because of national defense. Partly because of this policy, enforcement of the Muskie Act was postponed in 1973, 1974, 1975, and 1977. Even in 1980, only California was planning to begin enforcing the law in 1982. Japan in 1978 had set its emission regulation at nearly the same level as that proposed by Muskie, so the automobile and related industries began their efforts to meet the regulation. Then, in the United States, the federal regulation was enforced in 1981 with a regulation value of 1 gram/mile for nitrogen oxides (NO_x). It was finally decided that Muskie's limit of 0.4 gram/mile would be enforced during 1994. However, since then, a regulation level of 0.2 gram/mile has been proposed beginning in 2003. Further, California has established even stricter regulations that require a gradual decrease in the emission of those organic compounds that cause a photochemical reaction, namely nonmethane organic groups (NMOG), besides nitrogen oxides from 1994, and the introduction of the determined number of nonpolluting automobiles with no constituents to be regulated from 1998.

Diesel engines for heavy-duty trucks have also faced severe restrictions. In California, it was decided to limit the total emission of nitrogen oxides (NO_x) together with hydrocarbon (HC) to 5 grams/hp-hr from 1975. Even though the regulation was enacted in 1980, it was not scheduled to be enforced until 1983. Later, the federal government decided that a NO_x limit of 6 grams/hp-hr would be enforced in all the states beginning in 1990. In Japan, NO_x limits of about the same level had already been enforced since 1983. Note, however, that a federal NO_x limit of 4.0 grams/hp-hr or less, along with limits on particulate emissions, is scheduled to take effect in 1998. The feasibility of no-emissions vehicles is currently being examined.

Idea of Adiabatic Engine

Let's return to our discussion of 1975. During that time and under the governmental regulation background discussed earlier, American automotive engineers, particularly those specializing in truck engines, began looking for ways to reduce the energy wasted on exhaust emissions. The most promising of these methods involved the adiabatic engine. As we noted earlier, one-third of the fuel's energy is lost in cooling and another third is lost through the exhaust gas. The adiabatic engine is based on the idea of recovering and utilizing this lost energy.

In crossing the Straits of Dover, a fortunate squall prevented the Anzani engine in the Bleriot monoplane from seizing. Recalling this fact may help in understanding the heat concept. In an uncooled engine, not only can the piston and cylinder cause catastrophic seizures, but the other components of the engine may be thermally damaged. Heat damage, even if it does not happen suddenly, will shorten the engine's lifespan. As noted in Chapter 8, improved engine cooling can prolong the lifespan. Good cooling results in superb automobiles and airplanes, while poor cooling results in unsatisfactory products, which may affect even the life of a nation. Because of this importance, many people have attempted to improve the cooling capabilities of engines even since the beginning of the engine.

One of the people who accepted the challenge of reducing the cooling loss was Roy Kamo, a Japanese-American engineer who worked for the Cummins Engine Company. Using ceramic material, Kamo produced a piston, cylinder, cylinder head, and intake/exhaust valves. Since these parts could tolerate extremely high temperatures, the engine ran without a cooling liquid.

However, reducing the necessity for cooling alone does not improve engine efficiency. As the temperature of the uncooled cylinder rises, so does the temperature of the combustion gases. This increased temperature in the combustion gases raises the exhaust temperature, permitting even more heat to pass from the engine through the exhaust valve. To improve engine efficiency, this waste exhaust energy must produce useful work. Even conventional engines result in wasted energy in the exhaust gases. For instance, exhaust pipes in the World War II Japanese Zero fighter were individually mounted so as to face the rear (Photo 10-1) so that the thrust produced by the exhaust gas, however minor, could be used to increase speed.

Photo 10-1 Zero fighter model 52: Its exhaust pipes were extended from the engine cylinders (actually, 12 exhaust pipes from 14 cylinders) to use the exhaust gas energy to increase its speed.

The energy used by the engine during the intake and exhaust strokes can be substantially reduced by a centrifugal air compressor that supplies compressed air to the cylinder during the intake stroke, driven by a turbine powered by the energy of the exhaust gas. This process is known as "exhaust gas turbocharging."

As noted earlier, the exhaust gas energy increases in the Kamo adiabatic engine. Substantial energy is left in the exhaust gas even after driving the air compressor. Therefore, the exhaust gas is directed toward a second turbine, and the shaft of this turbine is geared to the engine crankshaft to add to the engine power. Even after passing through two turbines, the exhaust gas is still hot. So, the gas is used to heat water to generate steam, and this steam is used to rotate a steam turbine that is coupled to the engine crankshaft.

Fig. 10-1 illustrates each step of this exhaust gas utilization. As shown, the Kamo adiabatic engine eliminates both the heat radiation and the heat collected by the coolant, thereby increasing the exhaust temperature (energy). In this way, the exhaust gas energy is completely used.

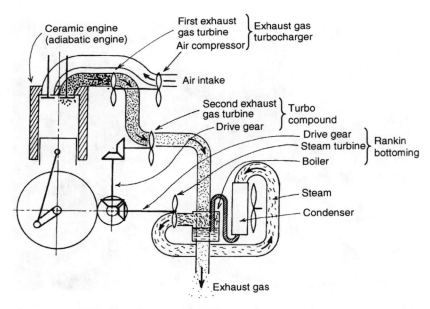

Fig. 10-1 Concept of adiabatic compound engine.

An engine consisting of a base engine coupled with an auxiliary engine (like the Kamo engine) is called a "compound engine." Fig. 10-2 shows how thermal efficiency is improved by using a compound engine. When examining the values shown in Fig. 10-2, notice that the adiabatic engine does not significantly reduce the cooling loss (from 29% to 25%). This minimal reduction is because bearings and other sliding parts must still be cooled by the lubricating oil, even though a separate coolant becomes unnecessary. It is understandable that efforts to reduce energy loss transmitted to the coolant instead reduce the loss of energy escaping with the exhaust gas (refer to Appendix A10).

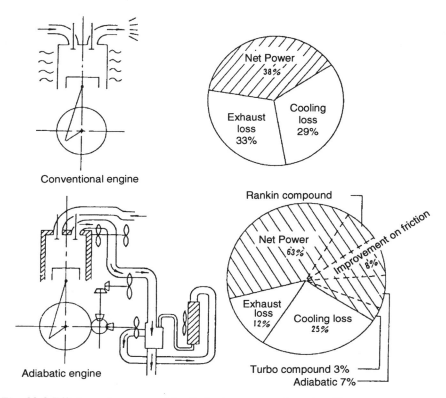

Fig. 10-2 Efficiency increase with adiabatic compound engine: Net power increases significantly from 38% to 63%.

War and Development of Scientific Technology

Much of the cost for the Cummins Engine Company research into the adiabatic engine was picked up by the U.S. Army. The primary research objective was to eliminate the need for the radiator louver in a battle tank. When an adiabatic engine is used in a tank, the risk of enemy bullets entering the tank through such a louver is eliminated. Of course, other advantages of an adiabatic engine include reduced fuel consumption, increased cruising range, and increased operability in hot regions.[10-1]

In 1939, a border dispute occurred between Manchuria (present-day northeastern area of China) and North Mongolia (present-day Mongolian People's Republic). Then, Japan and the Soviet Union, which supported Manchuria and North Mongolia, respectively, fought at Nomonhan. One battle in this conflict was The Battle of the River Khalkin. During this battle, the Japanese Army was unable to overcome the U.S.S.R.'s newest BT tanks. The Japanese Army finally adopted, as its sole defensive measure, a closeup attack in which Molotov cocktails were thrown into the louver of the tank radiator (refer to Fig. 10-3 and Chapter 25).

Fig. 10-3 The louver for cooling air is the most vulnerable point of the tank.[10-2]

Those who still remember this miserable battle can understand why the U.S. Army supported the Cummins research so as to eliminate the vulnerable louver. It is unfortunate that the advances of scientific technology have been so closely related to wars. Professor Yasushi Tanasawa has regarded this relation as the dark side of scientific technology and described it as follows: "War is an instinctive 'karma' of mankind. Technology is a most powerful collaborator in wars and sometimes may become a prime mover....Science seeks truth and places 'human love' at the center. I am amazed at how easily science can expose its dark side."[4-1] Fortunately, Japan has been able to avoid war for a long time. Not only engineers, but people in general, should always recognize and confront the "karma" of mankind.

I have strayed from my subject. Mr. Kamo is not a war-loving person, but rather an engineer who has devoted himself to conserving energy. He is also a humanist who enjoys growing radishes in his garden after he comes home each day. Mr. Kamo's garden covers more than an acre (4047 m^2) in his back yard. He even bought a used tractor to cultivate his radish field (Photo 10-2). Even after his mandatory retirement from Cummins Engine Company, Kamo has dreamed about the adiabatic engine. He established a company called Adiabatics, Inc., and has continued his research (Photo 10-3).

Photo 10-2 Mr. Kamo, who dreams of an adiabatic engine, holds the radish grown from the seeds sent from Japan.

Photo 10-3 Adiabatics, Inc. (AIDA) founded by Mr. Kamo; Mrs. May Kamo is shown at left.

Basis of Energy Saving

An adiabatic engine is the closest engine yet to achieving Carnot's ideal engine of 150 years ago. Will the adiabatic engine ever be perfected? The successful use of the adiabatic engine is not in the immediate future because of the many uncertainties that remain to be solved.

Even after a valid concept has been conceived, a newly developed technological product usually requires years to be commonly accepted. For instance, the now-popular automatic transmission required 16 years from its invention in 1930 until it was commonly accepted; the helicopter, which now flies over cities routinely, required 37 years from its 1904 invention to be accepted.[10-3]

By the way, for conserving energy, using the engine output efficiently has the same value as enhancing the engine's efficiency. Fig. 10-4 illustrates the process by which the fuel energy is gradually eroded until it finally reaches the tires. When following this process, I know I am not the only person who sighs over all the miscellaneous deductions that result in a substantial reduction in assets. Think of all those people who open their pay envelopes to find deduction after deduction taken from their paychecks.

Just as the net salary is a small percentage of the total, the final effective energy, that is, energy available to turn the wheels on the road, is only about

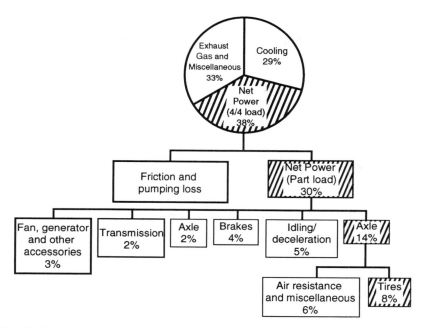

Fig. 10-4 Automotive energy distribution is similar to the withholdings taken from the salary check as shown on the check stub in the pay envelope (approximate values estimated on diesel truck engine referring to Pinkus' data): Net energy may be as small as 8%.

8% of the fuel energy. Thus, to conserve energy, it is obvious that every source of energy usage, however slight, must be minimized.

Appendix A10 Heat Loss in Theoretical Cycle and Recovery of Exhaust Gas Energy

In the theoretical cycle, loss due to cooling is not taken into account, so the heat loss is attributable solely to the exhaust gas. Fig. A10-1 illustrates the Otto cycle. Even though the engine still has pressure P_4 at the bottom dead center, the stroke ends there. Therefore, energy Q_2 at that pressure is discharged.

To recover this energy, the capacity is increased to allow a further expansion of the gas until the atmospheric pressure P_1 is reached, whereby the energy corresponding to the area 1-4-4" can be recovered. However, an increase in capacity means a larger engine and a larger loss due to friction. Therefore, improved fuel consumption is not really expected in practice. In this case,

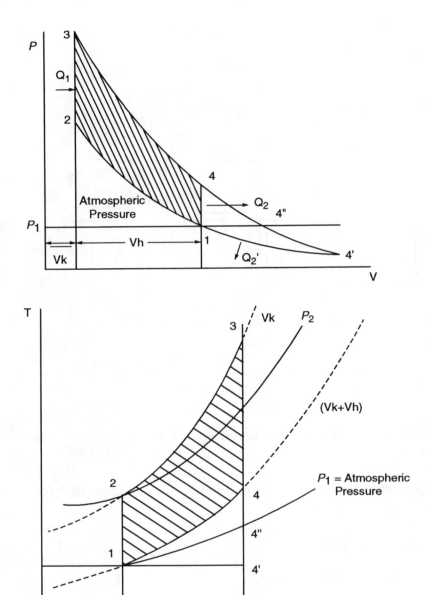

Fig. A10-1 Exhaust loss on Otto cycle.

the energy can easily be recovered by using a velocity-type turbine instead of a positive displacement machine. The concept of an adiabatic engine is dependent on the two-stage use of the exhaust gas turbine for supercharging the air compressor and driving a gear train from the crankshaft in a compound engine. The reason for this use is that the P_4 value actually takes 5 to 8 atm as a maximum value of pulsation, so two turbines are intended to utilize the pressure difference efficiently.

Even after this cycle, the temperature at point 4" is still higher than the atmospheric temperature. If the gas can be subjected to an adiabatic expansion up to the atmospheric temperature, that is, if it can be expanded to 4' and then compressed to point 1 at that temperature (or heat Q_2' can be radiated by isothermal compression), the energy corresponding to the area 1-4"-4' can be recovered. However, the realization of this idea is extremely difficult because isothermal compression is nearly impossible.

The goal of the Rankin bottoming cycle is to generate steam by using the steam energy in the 1-4"-4' diagram to rotate the steam turbine or steam engine, thereby recovering the energy. When checking the T-S (temperature-entropy) diagram, the energy still possessed by exhaust gas at the atmospheric pressure can be understood more clearly.

Chapter 11

Carnot's Dream, Adiabatic Engine (II)

Can the dream of both low environmental pollution and low fuel consumption be realized? Use of insulating materials encourages improvement on combustion.

✂

Challenge by Isuzu and Hino

In parallel with the American approach to the adiabatic engine, Japanese automakers Isuzu and Hino are vigorously promoting the adiabatic engine based on different concepts. One of the more significant differences between the two concepts is the use of ceramics. Isuzu uses monolithic ceramics, or a unit construction of ceramics for the cylinder liner, piston, etc., while Hino uses a composite material, or ceramics composite, with an iron base. Since the monolithic ceramics is low in thermal conductivity, it has better heat insulation than the composite material. Hino uses the composite material because it places a greater importance on heat resistance than on heat insulation, namely, the temperature increase induced by heat insulation sometimes damages engine components. Therefore, the heat-resistant characteristics of their materials should be considered simultaneously in order to recover more exhaust heat energy. To use the exhaust heat energy, Hino extracts power from the exhaust with a turbine connected to the crankshaft. Isuzu, on the other hand, is generating electricity with the turbine using a high-speed generator.[11-1,11-2] Isuzu and Hino are competing against each other to create a better engine for all.

Since 1981, Hino Motors has been researching the adiabatic engine to determine as early as possible the best way to conserve energy. Success is dependent on the idea that combustion, and the resulting exhaust emissions, can be improved through the use of heat-insulating material. Improved combustion in the diesel engine has historically been one of the more important goals. Of course, in recent years, engine manufacturers have also been pressured to reduce exhaust emissions even further.

As indicated in earlier chapters, Japan has historically imposed tougher standards on diesel engine exhaust emissions than other countries. Recently, however, it has been suspected that a carcinogen is contained in the exhaust gas particulates from diesel engines. This possibility has increased the need to reduce the diesel particulates. In the United States, the particulates on passenger cars and light trucks were regulated in 1982 and on large diesel engines in 1988. In Japan, all diesel engines were regulated in 1993 and 1994, depending on the vehicle model.

However, particulates and NO_x have an inverse relationship, that is, when reducing one, the other will generally increase. Though the efforts to reduce the NO_x level have had priority so far in Japan, the necessity to reduce particulate levels cannot be ignored. Researchers in Japan are now concentrating research efforts on improving combustion, which should aid the inverse relationship. Searching for this improvement on combustion constitutes an important background for pursuing the use of heat-insulating or heat-resisting materials such as ceramics for adiabatic engines. Photo 11-1 shows the late Prince Takamatsu eagerly asking questions on Hino's adiabatic engine exhibited at the 1985 Tokyo Motor Show; Photo 11-2 shows the Hino adiabatic turbo compound engine during the 1987 Tokyo Motor Show. In both engines, the exhaust gas energy from the turbocharger is recovered with the turbine and transmitted to the crankshaft.

Revival of Compound Engine

A Swiss engineer, Alfred Büchi, first conceived of a compound engine. In 1905, he coupled the turbine with the air compressor by extending the crankshaft. In effect, Büchi hit upon the idea of the present turbocharger and compound engine at the same time (refer to Appendix A11-1). However, the compound engine had to wait until 1952, that is, after World War II, for its full-fledged application in the form of the 3400-hp Wright Turbocompound R3350 aircraft engine. It was an exquisite design and a fitting commemoration to the finale of piston aircraft engines. This engine powered some of the last aircraft before the start of the jet age: the Lockheed Constellation and the Douglas DC7. Photo 11-3 shows the power trains from the turbine to the crankshaft of this compound engine. It can be seen that a fluid coupling and a reduction gear are combined to transmit the high rotation of the turbine smoothly to the crankshaft. The fluid coupling was considered essential for

Photo 11-1 Late Prince Takamatsu asking astute questions about the Hino adiabatic engine at the 1985 Tokyo Motor Show. (Hino's ex-chairman of board Yamamoto is to the right of the prince, president Fukazawa is facing the prince, and the author is to the left of Fukazawa.)

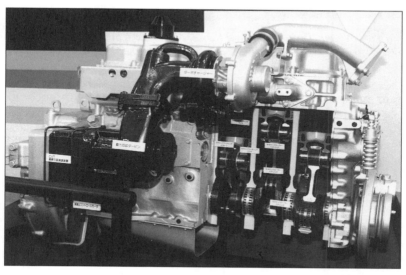

Photo 11-2 Hino's adiabatic turbo compound engine exhibited at the 1987 Tokyo Motor Show. Combustion chamber semiadiabatic, cylinder area not cooled, and ceramic roller bearing used for crankshaft.

Photo 11-3 Wright Turbocompound R3350 aircraft engine block for transmitting power from turbine to crankshaft.

the turbocompound, and it has been used in all subsequent turbocompound engines (see Photo 11-4).

Hino was the first company to use a continuously variable power transmission (CVT) to couple the turbine and the crankshaft. The CVT eliminates fluid loss and enhances its efficiency. Also, a ceramic roller bearing has been utilized for the crankshaft, valve gear, and other components so as to reduce frictional loss even further. The use of a roller bearing not only reduces the loss due to bearing but also eliminates the need to power a lubricating oil pump, which would be required if plane bearings were used, as is done in the crankshaft bearings of conventional design. This is because the plane bearing requires a more lubricous oil than the roller bearing. These effects are obvious at part-load conditions. Fig. 11-1 illustrates the hydraulic coupling, the CVT mounting, and the efficiency enhancement at full-load conditions. The improved combustion achieved with this engine was first presented at the 1986 SAE Annual Congress, and the concept received

Photo 11-4 Lockheed Constellation with the Wright Turbocompound R3350 engine. This plane was put into service in the final stage of World War II and used until the 1970s through constant improvement. It once served as a special plane for Eisenhower and MacArthur (Lackland Air Force Base).

interest from researchers around the world (Photo 11-5). This interest was because the two points below had become obvious. It was initially believed that fuel consumption could be improved by reducing heat losses through the use of an adiabatic engine. However, according to the result of Hino's experiments: (1) fuel consumption actually increased, and (2) it was caused by a change in combustion. In particular, the second point, namely a change in combustion characteristics, had not been previously considered to be so important. The fact that combustion characteristics are quite changeable by use of a heat-insulating material hints that combustion can achieve low emission and low fuel consumption depending on the combination of fuel injection conditions, combustion chamber shape, and other elements (see Appendix A11-2). This hint is given because the experimental results include an improvement of fuel consumption in some limited conditions, as described later. The results of this research bloomed in 1993 as a low-environmental pollution engine with the world's highest thermal efficiency of 46% for automotive diesel engines. The heart of this technology lies in the fact that an innovative piston achieved an adiabatic effect close to the optimum level and an ingenious turbocharger utilized exhaust gas energy more efficiently (see Appendix A11-3).

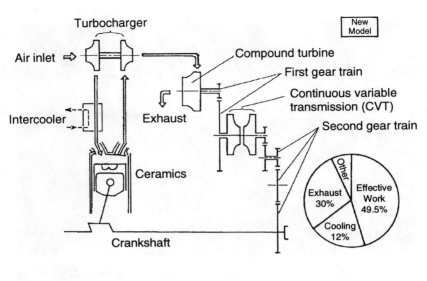

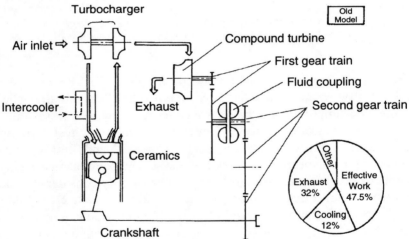

Fig. 11-1 Improvement process of Hino's adiabatic engine: Efficiency enhanced by 2% with the use of the continuous variable transmission (CVT) instead of coupling fluid.

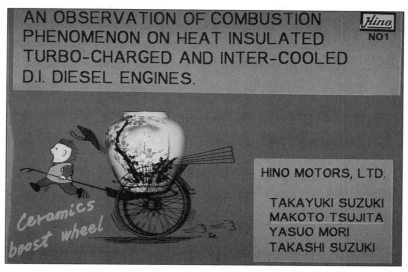

Photo 11-5 First slide of presentation for the 1986 SAE Annual Congress (Paper No. 861187): The result of combustion analysis on adiabatic engine was presented for the first time at this meeting.

Appendix A11-1 Founder of Compound Engine

Fig. A11-1 illustrates the engine conceived by Alfred Büchi. The left side of this figure is an axial flow compressor. A four-stroke-cycle diesel engine is provided to the right of a large bearing at the center. To the right of the engine, an axial flow turbine is directly coupled to the engine crankshaft. Although the operation was not performed successfully according to the original idea, this engine is the beginning of the compound engine, and it is also the origin of the turbocharger.

Appendix A11-2 Combustion Phenomenon on Heat-Insulated Engine

The Hino heat-insulated engine is based on the Model EP100 engine. Engine "adiabaticity" depends on where the ceramic material is applied to the engine combustion chamber, as shown in Fig. A11-2. Adiabaticity is a quantity defined by the following equation:

$$\text{Adiabaticity } A = \frac{Q_o - Q_i}{Q_o \times 100\%}$$

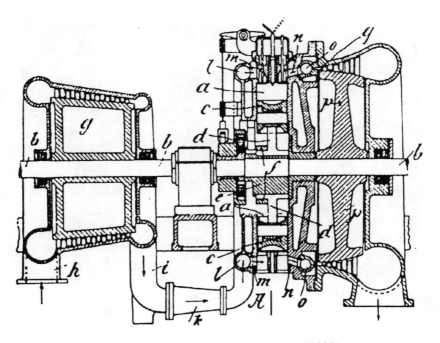

Fig. A11-1 Büchi's compound engine (1905).

where

    Q_o = Heat loss from noninsulated engine

    Q_i = Heat loss from insulated engine

Fig. A11-3 shows a change in the fuel consumption when changing its adiabaticity. According to the Hino experimental result, the fuel consumption ratio was at its best with an adiabaticity of about 20%. In this case, however, the NO_x was assumed to be constant. Although this figure compares the Hino experimental results with the preceding studies shown by the other lines, it signifies that the change of the combustion characteristics would not be adequate to predict the change of the fuel consumption. Fig. A11-4 compares the combustion characteristics between the engine with the maximum adiabaticity (50% in this case) and a conventional-based engine (adiabaticity of 0%). This illustration shows a measured value called the rate of heat release (ROHR). The ROHR is the amount of heat generated by combustion per unit of time (or per unit of crankshaft rotation). Tracing the ROHR curves in the figure reveals that, in the case of the higher adiabaticity engine, fuel is ignited very shortly after it is injected. The initial increase of the ROHR curve indicates ignition, and it nearly coincides with the start of

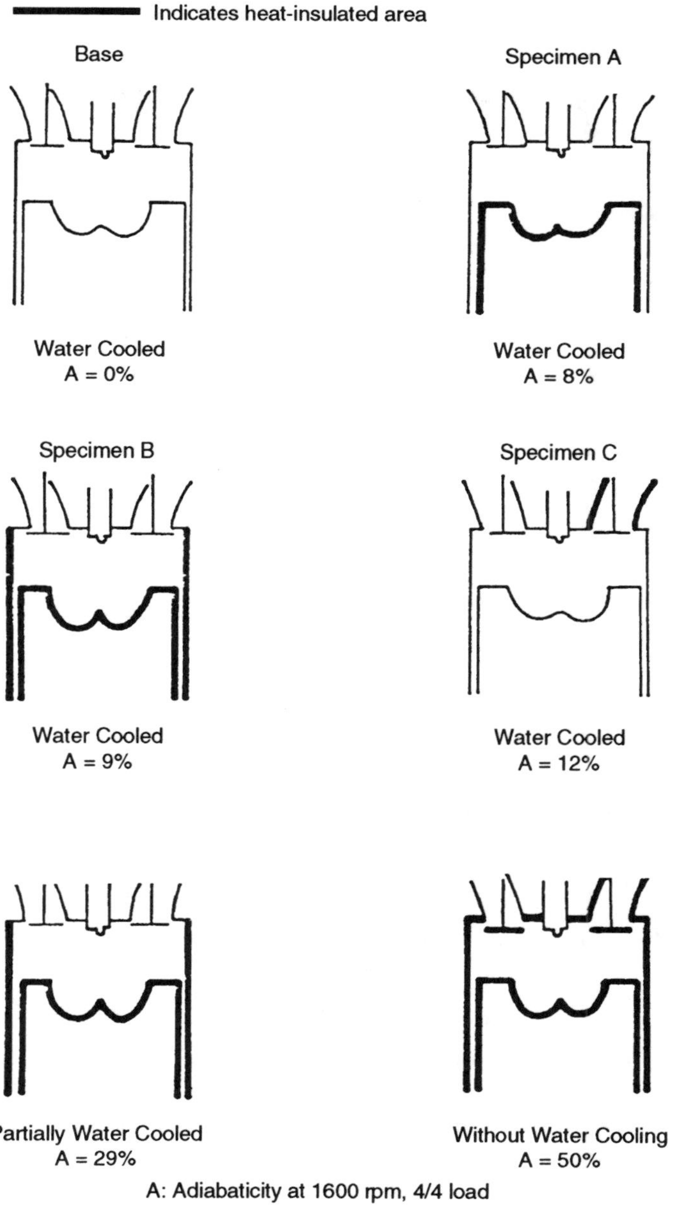

Fig. A11-2 *Several kinds of heat insulation applied to test engine.*

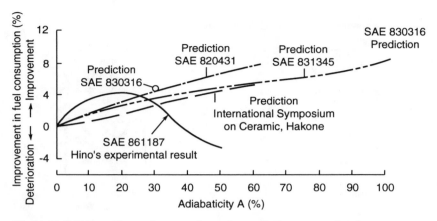

Fig. A11-3 Comparison of research results on fuel consumption improvement
of heat-insulated engine.

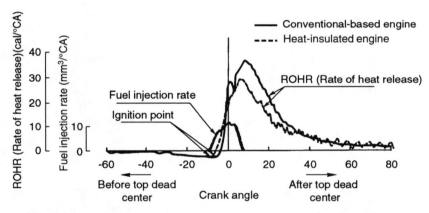

Fig. A11-4 Comparison of conventional-based engine and heat-insulated engine in
combustion analysis (1600 rpm, 4/4 load).

fuel injection. Quick ignition precludes much fuel evaporation and mixing
with air, hence subsequent ROHR is slower than the conventional engine.
Lower ROHR produces higher fuel consumption. Therefore, the start of
combustion is important to engine manufacturers. A slow start will produce
a discouraging result.

The time from the start of fuel injection to ignition is called ignition delay,
and it exerts a strong influence over the subsequent combustion. Fuel does
not ignite the moment it is injected. Ignition occurs only after fuel droplets
mix with air and droplets are heated up to the self-ignition temperature by the

surrounding hot air. Taking the period of ignition delay into account, fuel is injected so that maximum pressure is reached after the piston has passed slightly beyond the top dead center (TDC) to effectively obtain mechanical work. In general, fuel injection starts before the piston reaches the top of the cylinder or TDC. The fuel injection timing refers to the start point of fuel injection in crank angles (°CA). The injection timing for maximum efficiency, however, produces a high combustion temperature, that is, a high level of NO_x. For NO_x reduction, the combustion temperature must be lowered, which, in turn, calls for retardation of injection timing (meaning that injection starts after the piston comes closer to the TDC). In the conventional engine, the ignition delay is shortened by retardation of injection timing which gives a lower level of ROHR with lower combustion temperature.

However, this shortening of the ignition delay is saturated with further retardation of the injection timing as shown in the upper graph of Fig. A11-5. This saturation means that further reduction of NO_x is difficult. On the other hand, the ignition delay has a dominant effect for the combustion period. Therefore, the controlling of the combustion period is essential for low-NO_x, low-particulate emission without deterioration of the ignition delay period.

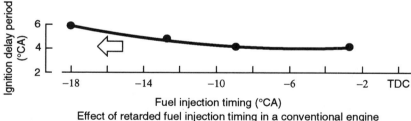

Effect of retarded fuel injection timing in a conventional engine

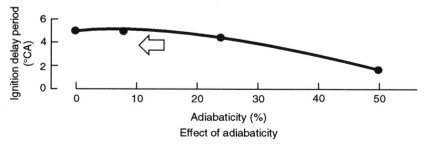

Effect of adiabaticity

Fig. A11-5 Comparison of ignition delay period.

The ignition delay of a heat-insulated engine, however, can be changed with the change in adiabaticity as shown in the lower graph of Fig. A11-5. This figure hints that the ignition delay period after their saturation can be controllable with the optimum selection of adiabaticity. Further, even though the ignition delay of a heat-insulated engine was over-shortened (adiabaticity > 20%), it can be seen that there is still a possibility of further control of ignition delay by adjusting the application of heat-insulated material even more, perhaps with the optimization of other combustion characteristics. Finding this further control will be a significant achievement for combustion control for low-emission engines.

Appendix A11-3 Fruit of Research on Heat-Insulated Engine

The research on the heat-insulated compound engine has given some ideas for improving the engine itself. It was felt that a more efficient recovery of exhaust gas energy should be achieved through the optimization of adiabaticity and the turbocharger should be improved before continuing to a more complicated and expensive compound engine.

First, it was found that the adiabaticity increases just by changing the piston material from an aluminum alloy to cast iron, and the efficiency can be improved by smoothing the flow into the turbine of a turbocharger. As a result of refinements on intake and exhaust valves, valve gear, and other components, the Model P11C engine was newly completed as an improved version of the Model EP100 engine. The new Model P11C engine could achieve a thermal efficiency of 46% as mentioned previously (Fig. 9-1). Fig. A11-6 shows the structure of the piston made of ductile cast iron (special high-strength cast iron) that has almost the same weight as aluminum alloy. Fig. A11-7 shows the structure of a new turbocharger with the mixed flow turbine.[11-3]

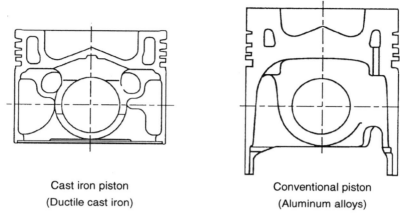

Cast iron piston   Conventional piston
(Ductile cast iron)   (Aluminum alloys)

Fig. A11-6 Small and thin ductile piston as light as an aluminum piston.

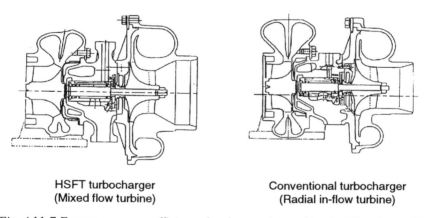

HSFT turbocharger   Conventional turbocharger
(Mixed flow turbine)   (Radial in-flow turbine)

Fig. A11-7 Energy-recovery efficiency has been enhanced by the Hino Super Flow Turbine (HSFT), which causes exhaust gas to enter smoothly in the oblique direction.

Chapter 12

Otto is Also a Pioneer in the Use of Exhaust Gas Energy

Recurrence of failure? EHV vehicle. Evaluate the preceding example according to basics. Live technological history dispersed.

✄

Historic EHV Engine

Not too long ago, billionaire William Harrah organized the world's greatest automobile collection in Reno, Nevada. The city of Reno is noted for its air races and its gambling. Though this museum currently has much fewer than its original 1500 exhibits, one automobile with a double expansion engine was among the exhibited vehicles. In an engine, the exhaust gas is discharged still at a rather high pressure and temperature. If the gas is introduced into another cylinder and expanded again, the energy remaining in the exhaust can be utilized more efficiently. This concept resulted in the double expansion engine.

The double expansion engine was built by the Connecticut-based EHV Company in 1906. As shown in Photo 12-1, the engine has three cylinders. Of these cylinders, the two on the outside are high-pressure actuating cylinders. The third cylinder in the center serves as the low-pressure over-expansion cylinder. Intake air flows into the outer cylinders, and exhaust gas comes out through the central cylinder. The high-pressure cylinders function in the usual four-stroke cycle, and the low-pressure cylinder operates in a two-stroke cycle since it receives exhaust gas in turn from the outer cylinders. According to the exhibited display, this quiet and odorless engine had an excellent fuel consumption. The car may indeed have been quiet and

Photo 12-1 Double expansion gasoline engine vehicle unveiled by EHV in 1906 (Harrah Automobile Collection).

odorless; however, its reputed good fuel consumption is questionable. This questionable fuel consumption is because Otto manufactured and sold an engine similar to this one in 1879, only three years after he completed the first four-stroke-cycle engine, and the disgruntled owner returned the engine because of poor performance.

Idea Bought by Sugar Company

This engine was designed by Gottlieb Daimler in accordance with the theoretical calculations of H. Güldner. The Deutz Gas Motoren GmbH, now the KHD Company, manufactured the engine and designated it the "Otto four-stroke-cycle compound engine" (Appendix A12).

Pfeifer und Rangen GmbH, a sugar company located in the Rhineland, Germany, which is known for its Moselle wine, enthusiastically bought the engine. To their disappointment, however, the engine constantly needed repairs and had poor fuel consumption. Finally, the buyer returned the engine to the manufacturer.

Professor F. Sass, in explaining the reason for the poor gas consumption, states that the exhaust gas that moves from the high-pressure cylinders to the low-pressure cylinder has a temperature up to 1000°C (compared to 800°C in a conventional gasoline engine). When this port and valve area is cooled, the valuable energy in the exhaust gas has a large loss. Further, the little remaining energy is consumed as friction loss of the large, low-pressure cylinder. Professor Sass deplored discarding this historic engine because of limited floor space in the museum, even though it was preserved until 1925.[1-2] The engine was discarded even in Germany, where technological products are highly valued, not to speak of the situation in Japan in which all products are easily tossed aside.

How did the American company EHV interpret this event? In the Daimler design, a slide valve (in which a plate slides to open or close the port) is used for air intake and exhaust. It can be easily imagined that the extremely hot exhaust gas would cause the slide valve to seize. EHV replaced the slide valve with a poppet valve (mushroom-shaped usual valve). However, it is entirely probable that even a poppet valve would not work well in an automotive engine. Unlike Otto's stationary engine, an automotive engine must function while traveling at high speeds. Also an automotive engine undergoes partial load far more frequently than it does a full load. This occurrence means that additional friction of the low-pressure cylinder would result in even more performance deterioration.

A relatively minor defect that is obvious may conceal an even greater defect because the seeker stops looking after he finds what he thinks may be the cause of the problem. The history of this EHV vehicle reminds us that all items that are being evaluated should be thoroughly checked before making any changes.

Idea of Double Expansion

Englishmen Jonathan Hornblower and Arthur Woolf thought of the double expansion process in 1781, five years after Watt completed his steam engine. Ironically, Watt sued the two men for patent infringement. Hornblower and Woolf lost their case because they were unable to properly explain their double expansion theory to the court.[12-1] Making people understand a new idea objectively is difficult, but it is necessary for the future development of technology. In 1845, William McNaught completed a steam engine that was dependent on double expansion after he improved Hornblower's design.

For the reader's information, the first Japanese-made steam locomotive completed in 1893 was dependent on this double expansion concept. The engine was supervised in its construction by the brothers F.H. and R.F. Trevithick, grandchildren of Richard Trevithick, the steam locomotive inventor. I understand that this double expansion steam locomotive was 20% more economical than its preceding single expansion type[12-2] (Photo 12-2). Now that the double expansion engine is a reality, it is natural to think that a triple expansion engine would be feasible. In fact, the triple expansion concept has been put into practical use as a steam engine. Even though this engine is said to have been first manufactured by the German company, Ferdinand Schichau, in 1883, an actual example has been preserved at the Massachusetts Institute of Technology. This engine is the Troy engine manufactured in 1909. According to historical records, this type of triple expansion engine was used in many ships (Photo 12-3).

End of the Harrah Museum and Its Miraculous Revival

Finally, I want to comment on the closing of the Harrah Museum. (Mr. Harrah preferred the term collection rather than museum.) One night in 1978 in the barroom of a Kyoto hotel, I overheard the conversation of an American sitting next to me. He indicated that the world's greatest automobile museum had become extremely difficult and expensive to maintain, and it might close down. I heard his story with some doubt, but it was true. Mr. Harrah, who had been called the Emperor of Casino, had died suddenly on June 30, 1978, as a result of unsuccessful surgery. Although the disease had been detected during a routine examination, he, according to rumor, delayed his surgery because of his tight business schedule. After his death, his company changed direction.

Photo 12-2 First Japanese-made steam locomotive Model 860 (old model 221)
(1893) (a replica exhibited at the 1985 World Fair).

Photo 12-3 Triple expansion engine TROY: 140 PS/350 RPM, 254-mm stroke, bores
are 152.4, 241.3, and 381 mm from the first stage.

To pay the huge inheritance tax, the museum was sold to the Holiday Corporation (Holiday Inn). This company auctioned off most of the collection in three sales held in 1984, and the remaining exhibits were eventually dispersed.

During the 30 years of the collection's existence, Mr. Harrah had restored his vehicles to showroom condition. This extensive restoration had cost huge sums of money. In the museum, the vehicles had been displayed in chronological order categorized according to the manufacturer so that an explanation could be given alongside the actual displays of technological proliferation, including both success and failures (Photo 12-4). The entire collection was disbursed, melting away like snow in spring. I wonder who bought the EHV vehicle.

Photo 12-4 Exhibition in Harrah Museum: Harrah's automobile collection, organized and maintained over a 30-year period with a great expense, was dispersed through three auctions. Was this sale caused by the inheritance tax? (Ford Trimotor called Tin Goose is at the far end.)

Fortunately, the automotive collection was later revived when the William Harrah Foundation was established to rebuild the museum. The Foundation was headed by the then Nevada state governor, Robert List. The Holiday Corporation contributed 175 unsold vehicles and historical documents to the Foundation. Thanks to the strong support of the Reno, Nevada, city government, a 9450 m^2 building was completed to house the museum, which reopened on November 5, 1989. The number of exhibited vehicles had been greatly reduced from the 1400 units that Harrah had in his collection to a little over 200 vehicles and displays. However, the historical settings had been faithfully reproduced, with the 20th Century being arranged into four time zones. The overall display is excellent, attracting visitors into each time zone. I cannot help but admire the Americans for their resourcefulness and creativity (Photo 12-5).

Photo 12-5 Streets in the 1930s reproduced in museum: The 1935 Duesenberg V8, 504-hp coupé is parked casually (National Automobile Museum).

Appendix A12 Otto's Double Expansion Engine

Fig. A12-1 shows a cross-sectional view of the Otto double expansion engine. In the figure, a_1 and a_2 indicate the high-pressure cylinders; b, the low-pressure cylinder; d_1 and d_2, the exhaust valves of the high-pressure cylinders; and e, the exhaust valve of the low-pressure cylinder. With this design, the area 4-4"-1 in Fig. A10-1 was intended to be utilized. Even though the slide valve may have been the most obvious flaw in this design, a more profound error in the design probably exists as well.

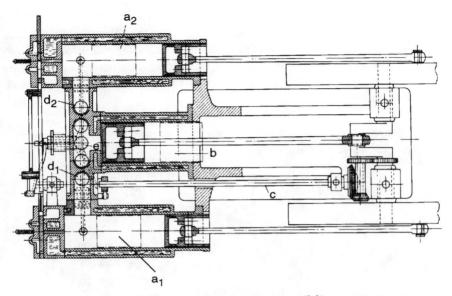

Fig. A12-1 Otto's double expansion engine (1879)[1-2]: a_1 and a_2 indicate
high-pressure cylinders; b, low-pressure cylinder; c, driveshaft for slide valve; d_1
and d_2, exhaust valves of high-pressure cylinders; and e, exhaust valve of
low-pressure cylinder (Sass).

Chapter 13

Problem of Cooling (I)

The cooling design led to bankruptcy. The rise and fall of the prestigious Curtiss Company.

Renovation of Curtiss

One month before the outbreak of the Pacific War in 1941, I saw in the November issue of the Japanese magazine, *Kohku Asahi*, a photograph of a nice-looking, twin-float biplane made in the United States, with a nattily dressed individual standing on its float. This man was responsible for an air raid on Tokyo in that he was the first pilot to launch twin-engine, long-range Army bombers from an aircraft carrier instead of the conventional carrier-borne aircraft. This feat was beyond my imagination, since I was just a junior high school student at the time. The man was J.H. Doolittle, and the seaplane shown in the magazine was the Curtiss Model R3C-2, which was powered by the Curtiss-manufactured 600-hp engine. In 1925, the Curtiss Model R3C-2 plane, piloted by Doolittle, won the Schneider Trophy race, defeating the strong English and Italian rivals in the process (Fig. 13-1).

The plane has been exhibited at the Smithsonian Museum in Washington, D.C. In viewing the plane at the Smithsonian, my first surprise was its main wings. These wings were covered with brass sheets, unlike the canvas-covered wings popular at that time. After unsuccessful efforts to minimize the parasitic drag of the radiator in the slipstream, the Curtiss Company designed the wing surfaces to serve as a radiator, thereby eliminating radiator drag.

Glenn H. Curtiss played a leading role in the manufacture of this seaplane. He had opened a bicycle shop while he was still in his teens. When he turned 23, he began manufacturing motorcycles. During the world's first

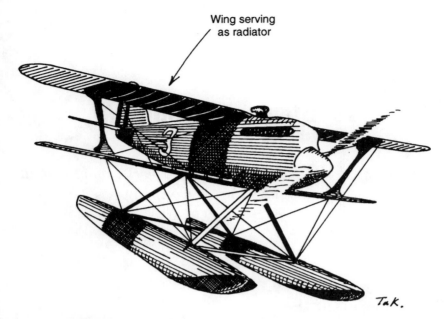

Fig. 13-1 Doolittle's Curtiss R3C-2 plane (1925): Doolittle calculated the optimum propeller pitch for the race course (optimum transmission gear ratio in terms of car).

turned 23, he began manufacturing motorcycles. During the world's first flight contest held in 1909, Curtiss piloted his plane to victory. Later, he founded the Curtiss Airplane & Motor Company. He is an American counterpart of the Japanese entrepreneur Soichiro Honda. I have already mentioned the 39-hp engine that the U.S. Navy bought from the Wright brothers in 1909 (Photo 8-1). The next year, Curtiss manufactured the engine shown in Photo 13-1. The reader may be amazed to see such an innovative and different design after only one year. The Curtiss Company prospered through World War I until the beginning of World War II. However, soon after Curtiss died in 1930, his company stumbled and began to wane.

What Caused the Prestigious Company to Decline?

In 1941, the year that the Pacific War began, the foremost fighter of the U.S. Army was the Curtiss Model P40. This model originated back to 1935 when the base Model P36 was designed. Officially used by the U.S. Army in 1938, the Model P38 had the first retractable tail wheel and main landing gear in the world. The Model P36 was adopted as its main fighter by almost all the Allied Powers including England, France, Canada, Norway, Finland,

Photo 13-1 The 1910 Curtiss engine (144-mm bore, 101.6-mm stroke, V8, 80 PS): A remarkable progress from the 1909 Wright engine is confirmed.

Thailand, and China (Photo 13-2). This period represented the highest point of Curtiss' prosperity. The P40 was designed by converting the P36 engine from air cooling to liquid cooling. Then, following the trend, more power was required. The design was changed again to a large output engine. However, the optimistic attitude of the design staff in making this design proved to be disastrous for the company.

The top sketch in Fig. 13-2 shows the design in question. A large radiator is hung easily under the engine. The design of the North American Model P51 fighter used at the same time as the P40 fighter is shown in the bottom sketch of Fig. 13-2. The maximum speeds of these aircraft, both of which used the same Rolls-Royce "Merlin" engine, are noted on the left side of the figure. The superiority of the P51 fighter over the Curtiss P40 model cannot

*Photo 13-2 Curtiss P36 for export to Thailand: Fixed landing gear was used instead
of retractable gears. In today's terminology, Curtiss responded to diversification
(Royal Thai Air Force Museum).*

be disputed. Near the end of World War II, the North American P51 fighters
flew over Japan as though they owned the sky. By this time, the production
of the Curtiss P40 had already been discontinued.

This difference in performance between the two aircraft cannot be attributed
solely to the radiator design. Obviously a great deal of attention was given
to refining each component of the P51 aircraft to ensure its maximum performance. The path of the airflow through the P51 radiator was not
achieved only by a clever design staff, but as a result of repeated experiments and persistence by the project team.

Subsequently, the Curtiss Company improved the design and produced prototype models one after another. Fig. 13-3 is an example of one of the new
designs. Although the design was finally completed, the war was winding
down. As a result, the military never ordered any of the planes, and Curtiss
never put the aircraft into production.

The Curtiss engineering style was not staid or old-fashioned as evident
from the grace and elegance of the aircraft produced for final manufacture
in Fig. 13-3. The capabilities of the design staff are evident in the exquisite
design of the Curtiss R3C-2 racer and in the design shown in Fig. 13-3.
However, the Curtiss Company was never able to recover and return to
prosperity.

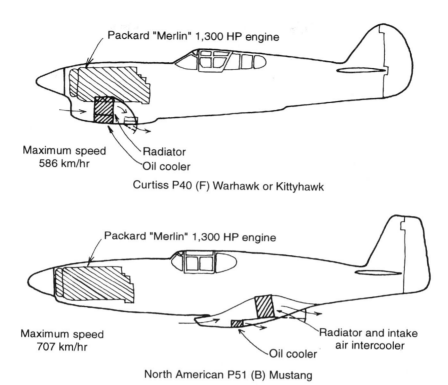

Curtiss P40 (F) Warhawk or Kittyhawk

North American P51 (B) Mustang

Fig. 13-2 [Top] Curtiss P40(F) Warhawk or Kittyhawk with a maximum speed of 586 km/h. [Bottom] North American P51(B) Mustang with a maximum speed of 707 km/h; an excellent engine could be either poor work or fine work, depending on the design of the cooling system. Poor work is a result of easy thinking, while fine work is the fruit of sharp thinking.

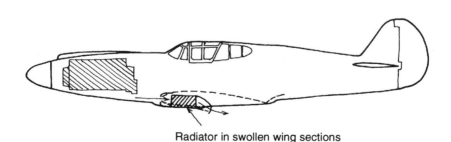

Radiator in swollen wing sections

Fig. 13-3 P40(Q) reborn with elegant style, unfortunately too late to be manufactured in time to aid the war effort.

The P40 conversion to a large output engine was finished in 1941, while the P51 design had been completed in 1940, a year earlier. At this time, the Curtiss Company should have re-examined the superb design of the North American plane. It may be pointed out first that the Curtiss project team failed to keep up with the state of the art, and the team also lacked a firm direction in the design. It appeared that the team had no focused company goals or objectives, and it lacked conviction and determination. The engineering staff lacked a spirit of innovation, and they were afraid to take risks. These shortcomings contributed to the final decline of the Curtiss aircraft company.

The Bradley Air Museum in Connecticut exhibits a strange-shaped aircraft with a front-mounted piston engine powering a propeller and a jet engine under the fuselage. Its sign reads, "The last aircraft made by Curtiss in 1945." After a long vacillation as to whether the jet engine or the piston engine would be used in the future, company officials decided not to decide, instead mounting both engines on a single plane. This lack of decisiveness was another step in the fatal decline of this once prosperous and innovative company (Photo 13-3).

Photo 13-3 Curtiss Model XF15C-1 fighter (1945): Despite its past glory, the Curtiss aircraft company did not survive this last plane (Bradley Air Museum).

As mentioned earlier, Doolittle made the first air raid on Tokyo as the leader of a squadron of B25 bombers. The planes dropped their destructive loads, and flew safely away, while looking down on the panic-stricken Japanese military. Doolittle passed away in 1993. I greatly admire his theoretical thinking, his tact, his decisiveness, and his courage. I pray that his soul may rest in peace.

Chapter 14

Talk About Oil Cooler

Intuition results in good designs, and this intuition is born of persistence and determination. Without these traits, a superior design can never be accomplished. Persistence even in the face of setbacks and obstacles may result in a masterpiece.

�֎

Control of Combustion

Attempts to eliminate exhaust emissions from the diesel engine have continued, mainly targeting nitrogen oxides (NO_x), as mentioned before. Nitrogen binds easier with oxygen at higher temperatures, thus creating more NO_x emissions. One method of reducing these emissions is to lower the combustion temperature.

In diesel engines, fuel is injected into the cylinder when the piston approaches the TDC (i.e., top dead center, the uppermost point of movement of the piston). By retarding the injection of the fuel into the combustion chamber as much as possible, the NO_x emission can be reduced. With retarded injection timing, when the pressure reaches its peak, the piston has already begun its downward stroke. Thus, the maximum pressure (and hence temperature) will not rise as high. However, the engine efficiency will also drop because much of the burning occurred late in the exhaust stroke and contributed little to the power output. One way to keep the engine efficiency from falling is to complete the combustion in a shorter time. This shorter combustion period can be achieved by mixing the fuel injected into the combustion chamber quickly with the air.

A bonfire burns well when it is fanned because the air is circulated, the fuel-air mixing increases, and fresh air is supplied to the point of combustion. This same phenomenon occurs in an engine. The air inside the cylinder is circulated by causing the inflow air to swirl turbulently as much as possible. Then the fuel droplets will also be more thoroughly mixed with the air, and combustion will be completed in a shorter time (Fig. 14-1). In many ongoing studies to determine optimum combustion airflow patterns, the air in the cylinder is observed with the same visual technique originally pioneered by Otto. In addition to visual observation, Hino Motors has studied engine turbulence with newly developed instruments such as a hot-wire anemometer in the 1970s and, later, the laser Doppler velocimeter. These ongoing studies have shown that the turbulence in the cylinder could be greatly increased by changing the shape of the intake air port (inlet).

Fig. 14-1 Greater turbulence means earlier end. Stronger disturbance is the key to accelerated combustion.[14-1]

Further, it was seen that the thermal efficiency could be enhanced far greater than the conventional engine through various combinations of this turbulence and suitable fuel injection conditions, etc. The incorporation of all these factors into a single concept resulted in the Hino Micro Mixing System (HMMS), the details of which are described later.

Efficiency Enhancement of Oil Cooler

When the fuel and air within the combustion chamber are rapidly mixed so as to accelerate the combustion, the chamber wall temperature is greatly increased. This increase is because the heat in the hot gas is transmitted to the wall faster. Therefore, the thermal load increases and some damage might be expected, much as a room would be damaged by rough-housing children. Since the wall temperature rises, the water and oil temperatures both rise. Therefore, the radiator to cool the water and the oil cooler to cool the oil must both be enlarged. The oil cooler of a truck engine is usually mounted on the side of the engine and is cooled by coolant. However, the engine is designed with an extremely small space.

Increasing a cooler by even 5 mm is a difficult modification for the engine. In a modern truck, the cab, which has the driver's seat, is positioned directly above the engine to increase load capacity. As a result, the engine, radiator, steering gear, and other equipment must be installed in a shallow space beneath the cab floor.

Examples of the numerous small improvements necessary to improve and enhance the oil cooler are shown in Fig. 14-2. The figure traces a series of improvements by changing the shape, position, etc., of the baffle plate to increase the efficiency of the oil cooler mounted on the side face of the engine. The uppermost sketch in this figure shows the top and side views of the original design. Although coolant enters from the left and exits from the right, part of the coolant bypasses the oil cooler for cooling the cylinder because the cooler is mounted on the side of the engine. Before the engine was configured to reduce the NO_x, the oil temperature had been 111°C, but it rose to 114°C after the NO_x reduction modification because of the retarded injection timing. The temperature rise is only 3°, but it is sufficient to shorten the engine lifetime by tens of thousands of kilometers.

The increase in temperature could easily be reduced by expanding the oil cooler. Increasing the width of the cooler would require that the vehicle frame be widened. This structural change in the vehicle is significant enough to be compared to an operation on the human backbone. Thus, instead of major structural changes, baffle plates of varying shapes and configurations were placed in the cooler case. All these experiments were

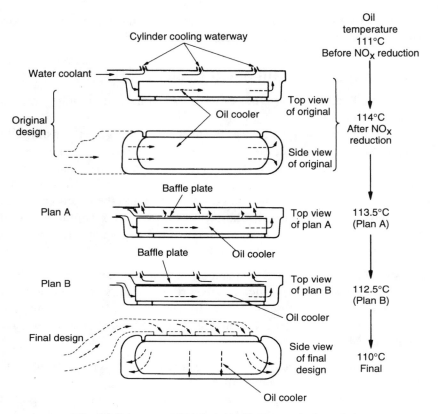

Fig. 14-2 Attempts to enhance efficiency of oil cooler.

unsuccessful, so the oil temperature could not be decreased significantly. Fig. 14-2 shows two examples in which the temperature dropped slightly.

The bottom sketch of the figure shows a breakthrough design, in which the coolant is introduced from the top rather than the side as previously was the case. Although this modification was minor, this intuitive idea proved to be of great importance when all other conditions affecting the cooler are realized. Thanks to this intuition, the oil temperature can be decreased to even less than before the NO_x reduction configuration. The Curtiss P40 design that I criticized in the previous chapter used the second poorest idea in this figure. The Curtiss engineers felt restrained to the conventional position of the radiator being placed under the engine. They did not have an intuition of shifting the radiator to a more effective position. For example, in the oil cooler shown in Fig. 14-2, the engine compartment would have had to be enlarged if the engineers had not had the intuition of circulating the coolant from the top rather than the side.

A design that lacks intuition can be considered poor work. This sense of intuition cannot flow if everyone in the group remains silent. Intuition is not something found in reference books. Only when the problem is struggled with repeatedly for a long time will intuition finally surface. The excellence of a design supported by careful thought and adequate consideration will be obvious to the observer.

Chapter 15

Discussion of the Hino Micro Mixing System

Has the method to reduce NO$_x$ on the diesel engine been found?
What mechanism does it have?

Indirect or Direct Fuel Injection?

In 1971, I met with Dr. A. Scheiterlein at the AVL research laboratory in Austria. The Hino Company had to take immediate steps to minimize exhaust gas emission from the diesel engine. I wanted to discuss possible solutions with him.

The NO$_x$ emission from a diesel engine can be reduced by retarding the fuel injection timing as mentioned before. However, this delay entails a significant rise in exhaust smoke density, preventing its practical use. How else could NO$_x$ be reduced?

Diesel Engine Manufacturers Worldwide Were at a Loss

With indirect fuel injection, NO$_x$ emission is extremely low from the start, and the exhaust particulate level (black smoke) does not increase rapidly. Many in the diesel engine industry felt that indirect fuel injection was the best solution to the NO$_x$ problem. Indirect fuel injection refers to a system in which a small prechamber is provided to the combustion chamber. The fuel is injected in the prechamber, and a small part is ignited; the rest of the fuel is burned in the main chamber outside the prechamber. Chapter 32 (Fig. 32-2) discusses this method in more detail.

The direct fuel injection system is one in which the fuel is injected directly into the main combustion chamber. Hino Motors had switched its main product engine from the indirect injection configuration to the direct injection configuration a few years earlier. Hino had felt that the indirect injection engine, because of its high thermal load (locally high temperature), could not meet the increasingly severe lifespan requirements demanded by rapidly expanding highways. Must the direct injection engine be abolished again?

A possible explanation for the indirect injection engine emitting less NO_x results from theoretical calculations performed by H.K. Newhall, then of Wisconsin University. Newhall had based the calculations on a principle of the Zeldovich Mechanism for the first time and, from its reaction temperature, estimated the amount of NO generated. He proved that significantly less NO_x is emitted from an indirect injection engine (Appendix A15-1). Dr. Scheiterlein maintained that the direct injection engine could also result in reduced emissions. What was the basis of his assertion? I wanted to know what his idea was. However, Scheiterlein was also a businessman. His only reply to my questioning was that he would make such an engine after AVL had a contract with Hino. He would not divulge any more information about his possible method.

Search for Mysterious Port

On my way back to Japan, I went over the conversation that we had at our meeting. I also remembered the remarks of other AVL researchers at the evening social that was held when I visited AVL. One of them muttered to me, "Mehr Vorkammer als Direkte! (after all, indirect injection engine is better)." They had no idea of Scheiterlein's concept. Only Scheiterlein knew a possible solution to the NO_x problem. Even though I had traveled as far as Stuttgart, I canceled my return flight to Japan and returned to AVL. I questioned Scheiterlein closely.

Finally, he dropped some veiled hints about his proposed method (Fig. 15-1). During his examination of engines made around the world, he had found only one whose exhaust smoke had not blackened further when the fuel injection timing was retarded. He apparently did not know why the smoke had not increased. However, he said, "You should do the same as that engine." Which engine? "The Steyr 120 mm × 120 mm (cylinder bore × piston stroke)!" I immediately flew back to Japan.

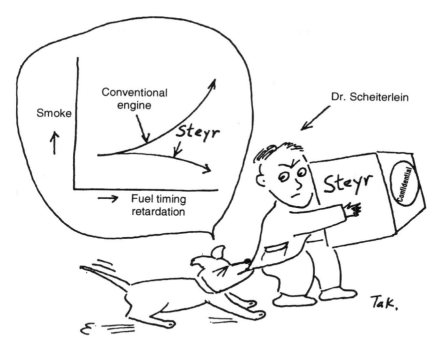

Fig. 15-1 A hint given after pressing Dr. Scheiterlein.

To discover the secret of the Steyr engine, I worked in the laboratory around the clock. Then one night, I detected an airflow that was peculiar to this engine. The intake air port of this engine caused the air flowing into the cylinder to separate into a main and some substreams. These air currents collided with each other in the cylinder.

The collision caused the combustion speed to increase significantly. The exhaust smoke did not blacken even though the NO_x emission had been reduced. Thus, the problem could be solved by improving the shape of the port and finding a suitable combustion system (fuel injection line, combustion chamber, etc.).

Appendix A15-1 NO_x Emission from Direct and Indirect Injection Engines

In the early 1970s, a Wisconsin University group analyzed theoretically both the direct injection and the indirect injection engine. The study indicated that the indirect injection engine emitted less NO_x because of its combustion mechanism.

When a third substance is produced as a result of the reaction between two other substances, a variety of reactions are repeated before equilibrium is finally reached. For the nitrogen (N) and oxygen (O) process to produce NO, he adopted the following elementary reactions (called the Zeldovich Mechanism) proposed by H.K. Zeldovich:

$$N_2 + O \Leftrightarrow NO + N$$
$$N + O_2 \Leftrightarrow NO + O$$

Fig. A15-1 was prepared to illustrate how pressure and temperature influence NO generation. From these results, it is understandable that an external-combustion engine is far more advantageous than the internal-combustion engine. Because of this fact, the steam engine or Stirling engine has temporarily drawn attention. (Refer to Chapter 39.)

An explanation of the differences between the direct injection and the indirect injection engines can be perceived from the result shown in Fig. A15-2. The abscissa is the fuel/air ratio divided by the stoichiometric fuel/air ratio (the equivalence ratio). Along the ordinate, the time for NO generation under a certain condition has been calculated. In the case of indirect injection, the fuel is ignited at an extremely fuel-rich condition (approximately 1.2 in equivalence ratio, i.e., right side of the figure) in the prechamber at first, and the main combustion is made in the main chamber at a lean condition (upper left corner of the figure). This procedure is called a two-step combustion[15-1], that is, the combustion jumps from the right to the left side of the figure.

Since the direct injection engine has a fuel injector nozzle on an open combustion chamber, the combustion went from the stoichiometric area to the lean zone continuously, but not as a two-step combustion process. The figure shows the mean equivalence ratio for DI combustion. As shown in the figure, the indirect injection has a much longer NO generation time than direct injection, signifying that NO emission is less.

Appendix A15-2 In-Cylinder Air Turbulence and HMMS

Several attempts were made to measure the air turbulence in a cylinder. However, at that time, none of the studies clarified the relationship between air turbulence and combustion. Through several clever experiments, Hino Motors demonstrated the air turbulence relationship with combustion, and reported it at the 1980 SAE Annual Congress in Detroit, Michigan. The paper created a great sensation.

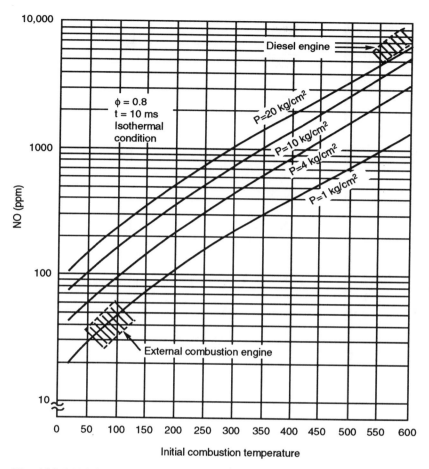

Fig. A15-1 NO formation versus initial combustion temperature and ambient pressure (conceptual diagram drawn by plotting each datum of external combustion engine and diesel engine on the result of the Newhall calculation).

How can air turbulence in a cylinder be measured? At that time, a current was passed through a very thin (5-μm diameter) platinum-rhodium alloy wire, called a hot-wire anemometer. The wire was placed in the airflow to measure its velocity fluctuation. Even though the wire was heated by an electric current, it was cooled when air flowed by and around it at a high velocity. To keep the wire temperature constant, a larger current was passed through the wire. That is, the wire temperature could be kept constant by passing a current in proportion to the velocity of airflow.

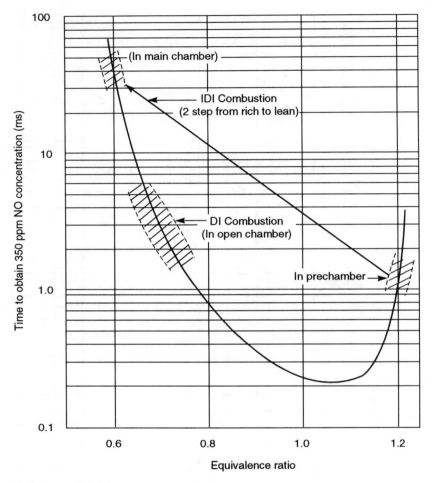

Fig. A15-2 Equivalence ratio and NO formation time (drawn by plotting each concept of DI and IDI on the result of the Newhall calculation).

Using this principle, air turbulence can be measured according to a change in the current flowing through the wire. However, only an irregular change can be known from a single measurement. Therefore, air turbulence was measured at each frequency of fluctuation, and the frequency was shown by the wave number, a value equivalent to the vibration frequency divided by the mean velocity. Since circular frequency and mean velocity are given by $2\pi n$ (Hz) and U (m/s), respectively, wave number K can be expressed by the following equation:

$$K = 2\pi n/U$$

where:

U = Mean velocity of air moving in the cylinder (m/s)
n = Frequency of fluctuations in air velocity

In some experiments, air was flowed through both the conventional intake air port and Hino's HMMS port at a certain flow rate, and the turbulence of the air was measured in a simulated engine cylinder. It was found that the turbulent energy produced by the HMMS port was the larger as described later (Fig. A15-5). High-speed motion pictures of the combustion produced by the two systems, using an engine with a quartz piston, show the difference distinctly. A special method called "Schlieren photography" was used, in which changes in gas density can be photographed. Schlieren photographs show that a stronger air turbulence clearly shows a better mixing with the fuel injected through the fuel injection nozzle, and therefore a faster flame propagation. Fig. A15-3 visually illustrates the combustion flame development. It is understandable that combustion develops at a very high speed using the HMMS intake air port, which is used to increase the turbulence in the cylinder.[15-2]

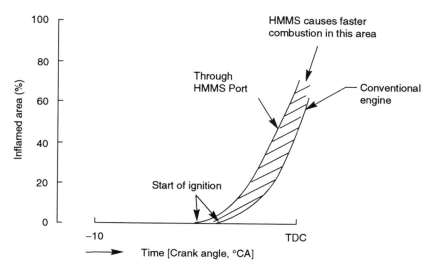

Fig. A15-3 Combustion development: When comparing the flame-developing area in the combustion chamber, the HMMS is much faster in burning. This phenomenon resembles that of a fire expanding when fanned by strong winds.

In addition, Fig. A15-4 shows that the HMMS allows a much shorter combustion period, and, therefore, a higher thermal efficiency and a lower fuel consumption. Note that photographing the inside of a combustion chamber of a gasoline engine with a high-speed camera has been used for a long time in the automotive industry; however, photographing the entire combustion chamber of a diesel engine, particularly with a quartz piston, had seldom been attempted because of the high combustion pressure in the diesel

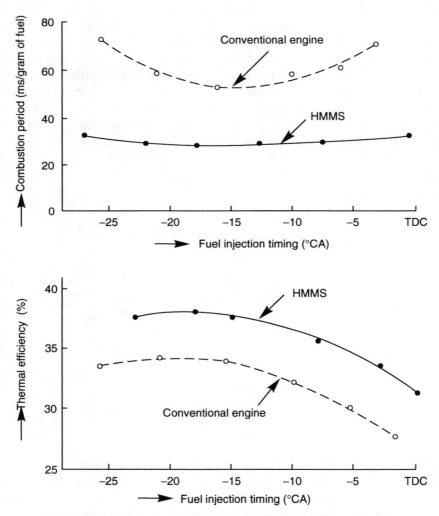

Fig. A15-4 Comparison of combustion period and thermal efficiency (2400 rpm, 4/4 load).

engine. Hino Motors was the first in the world to successfully photograph the combustion process *in situ* (refer to Chapter 23).

Appendix A15-3 Hypothesis of HMMS

In flows that are originally laminar, turbulence arises from instabilities at higher speeds. A common source of energy for turbulent velocity fluctuations is shear (by distortion) in the mean flow. The turbulent energy of the in-cylinder air motion was measured with a stationary flow-test rig as described previously. It was not measured on the engine during actual combustion. Why is such a turbulence effective for engine combustion? Even now, the answer is not known with any certainty. However, a partial consideration concerning diesel combustion is provided below.

Some time is required for ignition to occur after fuel injection. This *ignition delay period* is the time required for the fuel droplets to be heated by the surrounding air, the fuel and air to mix with each other under an ignition-facilitating condition at the evaporation point, and the fuel to reach its self-ignition temperature. The delay time is approximately 0.5 ms at an engine speed of 2400 rpm and 1 ms at 1000 rpm.

After this ignition delay, the injected fuel during this delay period burns simultaneously, which is called premixed burning. After the premixed burning, the combustion known as diffusion burning is followed by the rate of fuel injection, which is still continued. Therefore, generally, diesel combustion has two peaks on the ROHR curve; these peaks are known as the premixed burning and diffusion burning (see the ROHR curve in Fig. A11-4). The time from the beginning of diffusion burning to its peak on the ROHR is about 0.5 ms for an engine speed of 2400 rpm and about 2.5 ms for 1000 rpm. If the air turbulence is to be effective, it must occur during the ignition delay period or during the time beginning with diffusion burning and ending with its peak of ROHR, that is, 0.5-2.5 ms (or, in other words, the period from the beginning of fuel injection to the peak of diffusion combustion).

On the other hand, though it depends on the stroke of the engine, the mean airflow velocity (U) in the cylinder can be assumed roughly the same as piston speed:

$$U = 12 \text{ m/s at 2400 rpm}$$
$$U = 4 \text{ m/s at 1000 rpm}$$

If the engine intake air has a swirl motion in the cylinder, then it will be a rotational flow. The accompanied flow with piston motion is an axial flow, and, though not exact, can be roughly assumed to be twice that of the rotational flow, that is, 24 and 8 m/s.

The swirling motion assists in the distribution of the fuel droplet during injection without considering the time period. The turbulent effect should be considered during ignition delay or from the beginning of the diffusion burning to the peak of its ROHR since the turbulence must affect the swing motion in the limited time period (swing the fuel droplets for instance).

Therefore, the corresponding wave number of both the ignition delay period and the period from beginning of diffusion burning to the peak of it may be determined as follows:

Ignition delay period
At 2400 rpm, assuming that 0.5 ms approximates 2000 Hz:
Wave number = $2\pi n/U = (2\pi \times 2000)/(12$ [no swirl] to 24 [swirl ratio 2]) = 1050 to 530
At 1000 rpm, assuming that 1 ms equals 1000 Hz:
Wave number = $2\pi n/U = (2\pi \times 1000)/(4$ to 8) = 1570 to 780

Period from beginning of diffusion to peak of its ROHR
At 2400 rpm, the period is 0.5 ms,
Wave number = 1050 to 530
At 1000 rpm, assuming that 2.5 ms approximates 400 Hz:
Wave number = $2\pi n/U = (2\pi \times 400)/(4$ to 8) = 630 to 310

In conclusion, the wave number of the subject turbulence is approximately 300 to 1500 or more (when considering the period from the beginning of the injection to the peak of the ROHR of diffusion burning, it is about 200 at a minimum, using the same method of estimation).

If the fuel droplets are swung once in the left to right direction within these periods, the wave number becomes twice as large as previously stated. Here we must call on the theory of Russian mathematician A.N. Kolmogorov. During his extensive research on hydrodynamics, he stated in his Hypothesis of Local Isotrophy concerning the size of an eddy that turbulent energy has the following characteristics with respect to wave number under a certain hypothesis; that is, the turbulent energy can be divided into the ranges defined below.

First, the large-eddy range, one of low-frequency fluctuations, is a range in which eddies are formed due to the distortion of a fluid. The small-eddy range, one of high-frequency fluctuations, is one in which the energy of all eddies is finally dissipated as heat due to the viscous resistance of the fluid, that is, the eddies disappear. The area between these two ranges is called the inertial subrange, in which the energies of the large eddies arrive in order and move to the small-eddy range. In other words, the eddies in this range discharge energy, but do not attenuate because the energy is replenished. The turbulent energy in this inertial subrange is proportional to the -5/3 power of the wave number; that is, this theory is expressed by the following:[15-3]

$$E(K) = \alpha\varepsilon^{2/3} \times K^{-5/3}$$

where

K = Wave number
ε = Dissipation coefficient
α = Constant

Each of these turbulent energy levels was rewritten on a logarithmic scale for both the HMMS and the conventional engine. The portion exactly proportional to -5/3 power appeared, in which the HMMS had a large energy as shown in Fig. A15-5.[15-4] The relevant wave number coincided with the value estimated at the specified combustion period. In the HMMS, the turbulent energy is large in the inertial subrange during the intake stroke, and it remains large throughout the compression stroke. As a result, the fuel droplets or evaporated portion vibrates, facilitating its mixture with the air. Today, this premise is still regarded as a supposition, and the Kolmogorov theory that supports this supposition is based on yet another supposition. As indicated earlier in this book, only after a supposition is verified through strict and repeated experiments will it become a principle or theorem. However, rather than not progressing at all before a perfect theory is proven, it is advisable to move ahead with only a hypothesis and to prove the theorem later.

Even the Carnot theorem mentioned in Chapter 9 remained a working and unproven supposition for 20 years until Thomson postulated a theorem (later proven by Lord Kelvin).

Appendix A15-4 Turbulence Generation Mechanism in HMMS

Photo A15-1 is a photograph of an observation of the HMMS process. In this process, the air flowing in through the intake port is separated into the main flow and the subflow, and they collide with each other in the cylinder. Fig. A15-6 shows sketches of the same observation as a comparison with

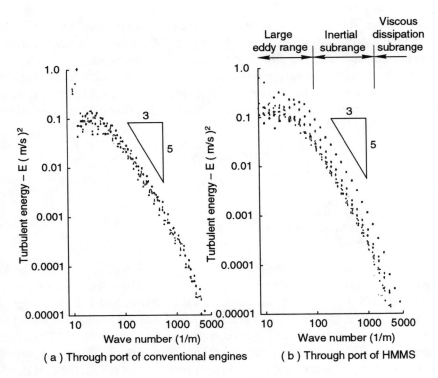

Fig. A15-5 Comparison of the spectrum of turbulent energy: The effective wave number that corresponds to the estimated value at specified combustion periods follows the Kolmogorov -5/3 law.

the conventional engine, including the intake air port. It can be seen that the unique shape of the port serves the important directions of the two flows in the case of the HMMS. When studying the turbulence formation mechanism through a more detailed examination and measurement, it can be surmised that the subflow, which has a velocity different from that of the main flow, collides with the main flow. A turbulence results because of the differences in velocity between the two flows as shown in Fig. A15-7. The turbulent energy is difficult to attenuate according to Kolmogorov's hypothesis. As a result, it is believed that the mixing of injected fuel jet with the air during the last part of the compression stroke is facilitated, thus improving the combustion process.[15-5]

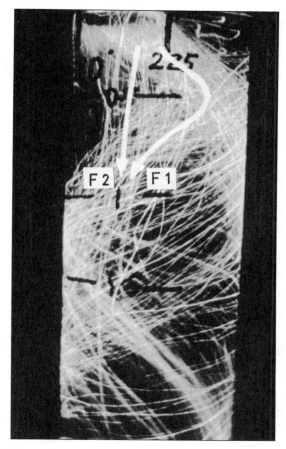

Photo A15-1 Subflow (F2) is formed by breaking away from the main flow (F1), and they collide with each other.

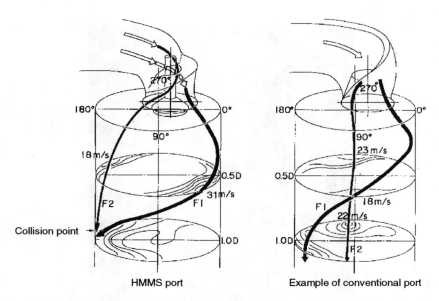

HMMS port   Example of conventional port

Fig. A15-6 Flow pattern of HMMS compared to the pattern of a conventional engine.

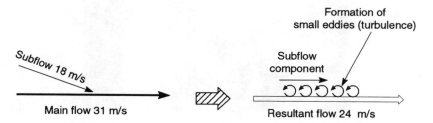

Fig. A15-7 Two different velocity flows collide with each other to create a turbulence.
This turbulence improves combustion.

Chapter 16

Problem of Cooling (II)

The Contessa owed its success to Michelotti's sulking. The Ki-83 was a success because of a belief.

�֍

Michelotti's Rejection

During World War II, the technology gap between Japan and the Western countries had greatly widened, not only in the automotive field but in all other manufacturing fields. After the war, many Japanese automobile manufacturers attempted to transfer automotive technology from European countries or the United States. As part of this technology transfer, Hino Motors had initiated a contract in 1953 with Regie Renault (the Renault Corporation of France) for the licensed production of his 750 cm^3 compact passenger car Renault 4CV. By 1957, Hino had completed the technology transfer sufficiently to have completely domestic production. Four years later, in 1961, Hino had developed, independently of Renault, its own 900 cm^3 passenger car, the Contessa 900. This car was still similar in concept to the Renault 4CV; however, the successor to the Contessa 900, the Contessa 1300, had a completely new concept, even though it did have a rear-engine rear drive (R-R), the same as the Renault 4CV. This chapter tells the story of the development of the cooling system for the Contessa 1300, with its enlarged water-cooled rear engine.

In April 1961, on the same day the Contessa 900 arrived at the dealers to be sold, Hino Motors sent a letter to the Italian designer, G. Michelotti. Hino management had decided that Michelotti would design the next Hino passenger car, the Contessa 1300. The Hino-determined design conditions were detailed in the letter. The Contessa 1300 would need expanded cooling capacity to service the larger engine. Since I had been placed in charge of the engine, I unilaterally added the requirement that a cooling air intake area of about 1500 cm^2 be provided facing the front. Michelotti was a world-famous automobile designer; even though the requirement was a severe one, I expected that Michelotti would provide a beautiful solution. Finally his eagerly awaited design arrived. The design appeared to have successfully captured the essence of the ideal small-sized passenger car in both proportion and details. What about the air intake that I had specified? An extremely large air intake protruded from the side of the rear fender (Photo 16-1). My great expectations from Michelotti had been shattered by this large protrusion on the rear of the vehicle. Not even considering the poor aesthetics of the design, this extruded rear structure could easily have hit obstacles, resulting in a hazard to the vehicle. Because of Michelotti's response to my request, the overall design was a failure. This poor design had to be interpreted as Michelotti's repudiation of my requirement. What was I to do? (See Photo 16-2.)

Photo 16-1 Contessa 1300 prototype No. 1: One view of the model shipped to Japan. The air intake protrudes on the rear (Courtesy of E. Michelotti).

At about this same time, one of Hino's staff, Fujisawa, had just returned from a European trip to complete the details of the Contessa 1300. Fujisawa provided information about the new Renault Model R8 automobile that had been unveiled at the Geneva Show. The Model R8 had also adopted the water-cooled rear engine, but the cooling air intake was not on the side at all. Instead, the air entered through a grille on the top rear of the body. The

Photo 16-2 Michelotti had provided the Contessa 900 Sprint (1963) with an elegant-style air intake. A similar design was expected for the Contessa 1300.

radiator was also located at the rear of the body. Because of the radical design of the Renault vehicle, the Hino design staff had to re-examine the very basis of its cooling design.

Regie Renault Getting Nervous

By the way, the Contessa 900 had inherited its radiator configuration directly from the Renault 4CV car as shown in Fig. 16-1. Regie Renault had become concerned about Hino's Contessa 900, which appeared only three years after the production of the 4CV car in Japan. Renault suspected that the Contessa was a duplicate of the Renault car, and it sent technicians to investigate this possibility. The Hino staff was also greatly concerned about the accusation since it had to prove that the Contessa 900 was not copied from the Renault model, nor was its radiator configuration a duplicate of the Renault method. It had to be proven that Hino had instead used a common and well-known method.

I still remember when I found in several publications the 1935 Benz Model 170H, which strongly resembled the Renault design. Thanks to these publications, I could successfully argue that the Contessa radiator installation was indeed a "well-known fact." About eight years after this incident, I

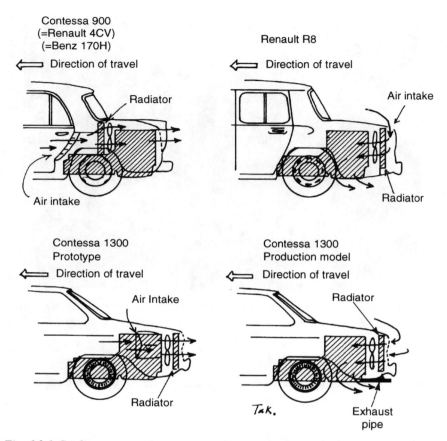

Fig. 16-1 Cooling system of a rear-mounted engine: The method originating from Benz 170H was reviewed by both originator Renault and Hino.

finally saw the 1935 Benz car exhibited at the Benz museum (Photo 16-3), and I was deeply moved because I had found the root of the Renault 4CV, the same vehicle discussed in the technical publications I had found so many years earlier.

According to some records[16-1], the first car with the rear-mounted engine and radiator configuration was a 1923 two-liter racing car (Fig. 16-2) designed by Dr. Hans Nibel. Nibel became the chief engineer of Benz in 1929. Then, in 1935, the design was incorporated into the Model 170H. Porsche then transferred this design into the Volkswagen automobile and then the Renault 4CV (Fig. 16-1, Photo 16-4).

Photo 16-3 Benz (1935): I was deeply moved when I happened to see the first of the rear-mounted engine, which I had finally found in literature after a great deal of effort. The H in the number 170H stands for H of Heck Motor (rear engine) (Benz Museum).

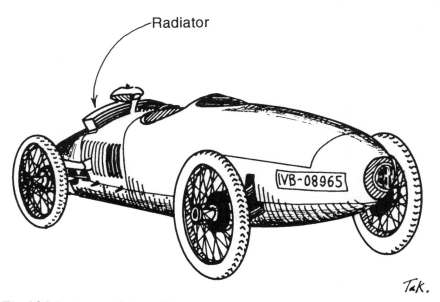

Fig. 16-2 Racing car designed by Hans Nibel in 1923. The Contessa may have been the root of this Benz.

Photo 16-4 [Top] Benz 170H: [Bottom] Renault 4CV: The son's rear end resembles that of its father.

Design of Engine Compartment

As stated earlier, the car layout had to be reviewed. With regard to this problem, Mr. Iwasaki, then division manager, instructed us: "Do not design the engine, but rather the engine compartment." This bit of advice was certainly appropriate for engine engineers. First, we looked at narrowing the air intake on the side and forcing the radiator slipstream to the rear of the car. However, the cooling was still insufficient, perhaps due to the fan's slipstream not being uniform. I felt some basic research was needed in the advantages of either a push or a suction fan. I suggested that Hino contract the research to a university, and the suggestion was accepted immediately. The basic research contract was awarded to the laboratory of Professor K. Komodori at the Keio University. Simultaneously, the Hino research staff continued to examine all possible layouts. The staff used wind tunnel tests to investigate the air pressure flow and distribution, particularly on the rear of the body (Appendix A16).

These studies found that the prototype's airflow, which used a push fan, was improved by sucking the cooling air from the rear face and discharging it under the floor. A baffle plate was added between the bumper and body to prevent the discharged air from returning to the rear face. In addition, the position of the exhaust pipe was adjusted so that the suction fan would not ingest the engine exhaust gas (see Fig. 16-1). Also, in an effort to lower the temperature in the engine compartment, the engine was inclined at a 30° angle. This inclination would minimize the length of exhaust pipe exposed in the engine compartment. These modifications were needed because a rear-mounted engine tended to overheat, especially during hot summer temperatures. The overheating could cause the fuel in the carburetor to boil after the engine stops and to spill over into the engine. The engine would then fail to start.

Coffee tastes best when the water boils over and soaks the coffee grounds. The process of liquid boiling over, whether in a coffee maker or a carburetor, is called "percolation." The percolation in an engine, however, is quite undesirable. To prevent this percolation phenomenon, a vent hole may be bored in the carburetor, which would be similar to boring a hole in a kettle. Some European-made cars had adopted this practice. However, this modification has a worst-case scenario of the boiled-over gasoline being ignited. Therefore, Hino decided not to use this method.

In a gasoline engine, the intake air pipe must be heated in cold weather; the exhaust pipe and intake air pipe (manifold) are usually brought into contact so that the incoming air would be warmed by contact with the exhaust air. This configuration results in the carburetor becoming extremely hot during hot weather, probably resulting in fuel percolation. To avoid this possibility in the Contessa, it was decided to have the engine coolant heat the intake manifold (air pipe) and to equip the carburetor with an electrical automatic choke to aid in starting and warming up in a cold climate. The Contessa was the first vehicle in Japan to use the electric automatic choke, a device to deliver a rich fuel blend to the carburetor because cold fuel is harder to evaporate. The choke also served to control the rise in warming water. Poor coolant circulation could result in a sporadic rise in the coolant temperature inside the engine, particularly during an uphill drive. To prevent the possibility of overheating, the water line from the engine to the radiator was led out from the front, rather than the rear, of the engine. Thus the newly modified Contessa 1300 engine compartment and layout were completed. Even under the hot sun at ambient temperatures of 40°-45°C, percolation did not occur; start and warm-up operations were smooth even in extremely cold climates (Photo 16-5).

Photo 16-5 Engine compartment unique to the Contessa 1300: The rear of Contessa was well designed without boring a hole in the top and side faces.

The Contessa 1300 was released in 1964, one year after a water-cooled, rear-engine-mounted car called the Hillman Imp was unveiled by the English Rootes group. The Hillman Imp was a popular car that sold quite well. However, the Hillman Imp suffered all the problems that Hino had worried about in developing the Contessa 1300. These problems included overheating, blowing out of the head gasket due to poor coolant circulation, and carburetor overflow, namely percolation. Other problems included failure of the pneumatic accelerator interlock device developed for the rear engine, premature clogging of air cleaner, and even engine fire. I was greatly relieved when I read the article on the Hillman Imp contained in the *Auto Car* journal.[16-2] I said to myself, "Michelotti's spitefulness ultimately led to a product that satisfied both function and style."

In January 1980, the automobile designer Michelotti, who is said to have designed the Contessa while sipping whiskey, passed away. As a small token of gratitude for his design of the Contessa, Hino Motors sent a large flower arrangement to his funeral. Also, Professor Komodori, who contributed greatly to the layout of the Contessa's cooling system, died in 1981. I first read about his death in the Journal of the Japanese Society of Mechanical Engineers. I was on a business trip to Europe at the time of his death. Both Michelotti and Komodori contributed to the design of a splendid car, and I pray that their souls rest in peace.

High-Speed Plane Ki-83

For background, I would like to introduce another example of a success due to spitefulness. In August 1945, shortly after the end of World War II, the U.S. Army occupying forces test flew a prototype of the Imperial Army fighter Ki-83, the last one remaining in Matsumoto, Japan. In this test flight, the plane (Fig. 16-3) reached speeds of 762 km/h. At that time, the world record of 754.97 km/h was held by the Messerschmitt in 1939. In 1969, 24 years after the Ki-83 test flight, this propeller plane speed record was broken by a specially modified race Grumman F8F, with a speed of 777.74 km/h (Photo 16-6).

Considering the probable poor mechanical condition of the Ki-83, we can imagine the excellence of the performance of this test model fighter. During the development of this fighter, the Imperial Army had demanded a two-seat design. Usually, the canopy on a two-person plane is rather large so as to accommodate both crew members. However, the chief designer (engineer Tomio Kubo, later president of Mitsubishi Motors) had his own opinion of the requirements of long-range fighters. Therefore, he designed one of the crew stations to be encased completely within the fuselage[16-3] (Fig. 16-4). In effect, the design was substantially one of a single-seat fighter. This design was probably made to spite the demands of the military. Every designer must always keep and cherish a vision of his design. The vision must be gradually fermented in his heart until it is established as a belief. Fermentation depends on continuous study, and the established belief some-

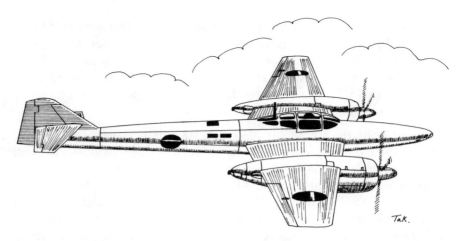

Fig. 16-3 The Japanese army fighter Ki-83: The Ki-83 took off from Matsumoto Airfield in August 1945. Piloted by a U.S. soldier, the plane was clocked at speeds of 762 km/h, breaking the current world's record of 755 km/h.

times entails some brooding. When this brooding finally results in a product, it is usually a real masterpiece. In March 1990, Mr. Tomio Kubo was buried with the sweet fragrance of Japanese plum blossoms in the air. On the day of his funeral, a quartet played Beethoven quietly in the background while friends and associates, who greatly respected him for the masterpiece and his mind, saw Mr. Kubo off.

Appendix A16 Contessa's Cooling System

Fig. A16-1 compares the wind velocity distribution at the front of the radiator between the push fan and suction fan. As shown by the Keio University study, it is obvious that the suction fan has a much higher uniformity and therefore a higher cooling efficiency. Fig. A16-2 traces the change in the engine compartment temperature after the engine has stopped. It is evident that temperature rise is less with the suction fan. A possible reason for this difference may be that the push fan promotes the entry of dust into the rear engine compartment from the ground. Thus, to dust-proof the engine compartment, the gap was minimized, which made it difficult to dissipate the hot air after the engine was stopped. Fig. A16-3 shows how engine heat radiation is decreased by minimizing the length of exposed exhaust pipe in the engine compartment. Although an even greater decrease in heat would have resulted in an engine inclination angle greater than 30°, this angle was selected for maintainability and other factors.

Photo 16-6 Grumman F8F plane developed to defeat the Zero fighter: With this plane
modified as a racer, Grumman broke the propeller plane's speed record in August
1969, held for 30 years by the Messerschmitt, with a speed of 777.7 km/h. A P51
propeller spinner and Douglas Skyraider propeller were used. To reduce weight, the
wing flaps and the hydraulic system were eliminated, and the landing gear was
modified to be retracted by a one-shot nitrogen gas charge and lowered by gravity
at the dive. Proper component selection and a thorough design ensured success
(Smithsonian Museum).

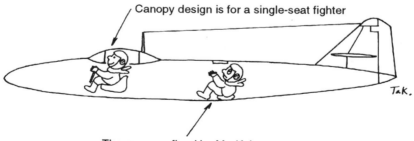

Fig. 16-4 Double-seat plane Ki-83 born from the belief in the superiority of single
seat: Brooding sublimates to a masterpiece.

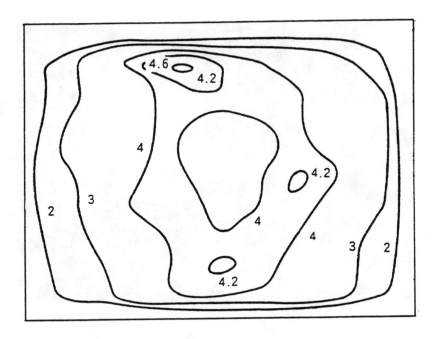

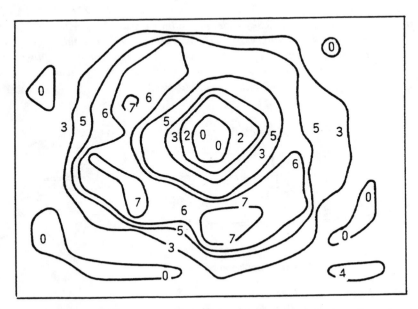

Fig. A16-1 Wind velocity distribution at front of radiator with push- and suction-type fans: [Top] Suction-type fan (with standard guide), 1930 rpm; [Bottom] Push-type fan (with standard guide), 1930 rpm (wind velocity in m/s).

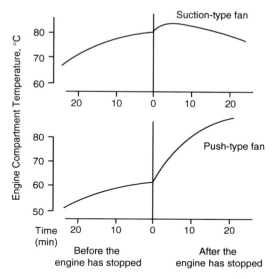

Fig. A16-2 Lapse of the engine compartment temperature with push- and suction-type fans.

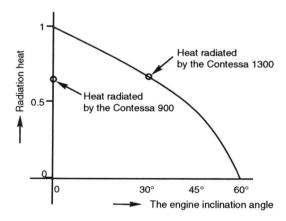

Fig. A16-3 Quantity of heat radiated into engine compartment from engine (with reference to heat radiation at engine inclination angle 0° represented by "1").

Chapter 17

Fate Depended on
Engine Compartment

Close calculation and persistence are indispensable for
completion. First, establish a firm basic concept.

✄

Water-Cooled Rear Engine Car Tucker

In one corner of the Harrah Museum, a 1948 three-headlamp car manufactured by Preston Thomas Tucker is exhibited (Photo 17-1). Most people may not stop to examine this car in detail, even though they may think the car to be mildly interesting. It was of great interest to me because this car has a rear engine and its cooling system is configured the same as the Contessa.

Fortunately, I was unaware of the existence of this car when I was developing the Contessa's engine compartment. I say "fortunately" because the exhibited car was not the car finally put into production. If I had studied it during the Contessa's development, it may have served as a red herring. Let us look more closely under the rear hood at the engine compartment (Photo 17-2). Excess space on both the left and right sides of the radiator could have permitted hot air to pass through the radiator and be recycled to the front, to be sucked in and passed through the radiator again. Since the fan seems to have been a suction fan, the exhaust gas emitted from as many as six exhaust pipes under the radiator would probably have been sucked into the radiator. All this dirt- and exhaust-laden air entering the carburetor from the engine compartment must have caused premature clogging of the air filter. As determined during the development of the Contessa, the air in a rear engine compartment contains approximately six times as much dust

Photo 17-1 Tucker with three headlamps and water-cooled rear engine (1948): This style was very elegant during Tucker's time (San Antonio Automobile Museum).

Photo 17-2 Engine compartment layout of the Tucker automobile: Very similar to the Contessa, but easy to overheat (Automobilorama Museum).

as a front engine compartment. As a result of this finding, the Contessa was designed to suck the air from the front of the car.

Every designer should learn from earlier work in the field, but he must not be mesmerized by it. Unless a designer thoroughly understands his or her design concept, it would be easy to overlook a fault in a flawed product. During that time, the United States led the world in automobile production, and every design originating from the United States was regarded as an "advanced design." If the Tucker automobile had been discussed in a widely distributed magazine, the design may have been simply copied. To have done so would have resulted in a failure. For example, in this model the grille on the rear fender is a dummy and the air vent is not open (Photo 17-1). In the initial stage of development, air was probably planned to be sucked through the fender, and a push fan was to have been used for the radiator. However, the push fan was probably changed to the rear suction fan because of excessive backflow into the radiator. Even this change did not resolve all its problems, so I think that even more modifications were made. This version of the Tucker car was discontinued after only 50 cars were produced (an additional 13 cars were hand-assembled by volunteers after the plant had shut down, but more about this later). The real reason that this car stopped production may never be known, nor may the real value of the technology be determined. It is noteworthy to realize that the designers of this car wanted to create nothing less than the "Car of the Future."[17-1,17-2]

Excess Idea Backfired

During World War II, Tucker designed and manufactured armored cars and turrets for torpedo boats, based on his patent. After the war was over, he enthusiastically turned his attention to manufacturing a new car. The basic design of his car was originated by a prewar racing associate H. Miller. Tucker's idea was to manufacture a 9.6-liter, 150-hp horizontally opposed six-cylinder engine with hydraulically opened and closed valves. The engine was placed transversely on the axis of the rear axle, and the rear wheels were to be driven by separate torque converters on the left and right. Some of Tucker's own concepts were also added to the vehicle design including: the fenders moving together with the wheel; independent torsion bar suspension; a third headlamp (called the Cyclops Eye) capable of changing direction in conjunction with the steering mechanism; the door's opening intersecting into the roof to allow easy entrance and exit; and elimination of the exterior rain gutters. Advanced safety features included a padded dash and a popout windshield that minimized breakage during an accident.

Alex Tremulis and others in his group eliminated some of the more advanced ideas that had insufficient mass production experience. The Miller engine was abandoned after the first five cars as being too large and complicated for a mass-produced car. Subsequent engines were then acquired from Air Cooled Motors, a descendant of the Franklin Automobile Company, which had once produced excellent cars. The Tucker car used engines descended from the Franklin 5.5L horizontal, opposed, air-cooled engine produced for the Bell Helicopter Company during World War II. The engine was modified for cars, and the cooling system was converted from air to water so as to make the cars easier to sell. The cooling system was also completely sealed. Attempts to install the engine directly on the axle were abandoned, and the rear-engine, rear-wheel-drive (R-R) was used based on the front-engine, front-wheel-drive (F-F) car transmission of a very successful car, the Cord. Excessive weight on the rear axle of an R-R car often results in steering instability. I personally feel that replacing the lightweight air-cooled engine that had extensive production experience with the much heavier water-cooled engine was a questionable decision.

The development period was only 1.5 years in that the design layout was frozen on Christmas Day of 1946 and production began in the summer of 1948. Tucker's company at this time was no bigger than a private management company; it was absurd to incorporate so many new ideas in its first car. In fact, fear of product immaturity caused the Tucker stock price to fall sharply.

Because of his financial collapse resulting from the sharp decline in his stock value, Tucker ceased production of his car. The failure of the Tucker company was said to be the result of a conspiracy by a rival automobile company or the bureaucracy of the regulatory agencies. However, the immaturity of his overall design could not be denied. Actually, I do not think that his extremely advanced design was even feasible at this time. For example, his design permanently sealed the engine coolant into the aluminum engine. This engine is still subject to corrosion even with the long-life coolant that had been developed only a few years ago. To have sealed the coolant system without this type of coolant was not realistic.

Tucker Car Likes Old Crow (Kentucky Bourbon)

The Tucker vehicle is said to have been one of the factors that triggered General Motors' development of its Corvair model. The Corvair vehicle always had problems with an uneven load distribution between the front and rear axles; that is, it had an overload on the rear axle (Photo 17-3). It was also reported that the Tucker car had problems with handling stability at higher speeds. If the Tucker vehicle had been mass-produced, and this handling stability problem had been generally known, the Corvair disaster probably would have been avoided. Of interest is the fact that cooling problems had never been reported with the Tucker model. Did its radiator have excess capacity? I don't know.

Photo 17-3 Corvair (1960): This vehicle made a spectacular debut with an elegant style and a unique engine compartment, but entailed a defect due to its poor handling stability because of excessive rear axle load.

However, it has been reported that vapor lock (a problem in which fuel fails to reach the engine because the engine and its engine compartment are overheated) caused a Tucker vehicle to stall while it was being driven to California to obtain some parts. According to some records, the engine trouble was solved when a mechanic poured five bottles of Old Crow (a Kentucky whiskey) into the gasoline tank. The engine returned to a more pleasant mood when the carburetor was cooled by the latent heat of vaporization of the alcohol when it evaporated. The vapor lock mentioned in the record may have been more precisely known as percolation. As mentioned earlier, percolation is an important problem that must be considered when developing a rear engine.[17-1]

As a matter of interest, the development of the Tucker car is said to have suffered a severe setback because of the death caused by extreme fatigue of a talented engineer named Jimmy Sakuyama, a Japanese graduate of Wisconsin University. His death was reported to have been a great personal loss for Tucker.

Chapter 18 introduces another failure in the development of an engine compartment.

Chapter 18

An Engine Compartment that Ruined the Third Reich

Although persistence is necessary, a change may be necessary on some occasions. Heinkel and then Fisher failed in engineering management.

Appearance of Four-Engine Strategic Bomber

After World War II began, it became evident that the four-engine strategic bomber prepared by the United States was extremely effective, and other countries promptly began development of this type of bomber. Originally designed by the Boeing Aircraft Company, the massive size of the Boeing plane resulted in a poor evaluation by the U.S. Army. In the meantime, Clairmontl Egtvedt, Boeing's chief engineer, had to overcome obstacles such as the crash of the prototype plane, the U.S. Army's cancellation of the development contract, and the Army's awarding of the bomber contract to Douglas Aircraft Company for the manufacture of its twin-engine B18 bomber. Despite a very vocal criticism of the cost of his bomber development program, Egtvedt eventually completed the bomber. Although correct engineering may see the needs of the future, it may not necessarily be accepted easily (Photo 18-1).

Just before the outbreak of World War II, Heinkel, in Germany, was continuing his development of a bomber with an excellent conception. To minimize air resistance, four engines were arranged into two nacelles, so that the bomber could be considered a twin-engine plane. During the last world war, a Japanese aircraft magazine had reported the conception of the new German bomber. The article commented that German air raids on the U.S.

Photo 18-1 The Boeing 299 as a prototype plane of B17: This plane had a bright future because of its successful 2100-mile flight from Seattle to Wright Field; however, shortly afterward, it crashed on October 30, 1935. The famed pilot Les Tower died in the accident, and the development contract with the U.S. army was canceled (Boeing Museum).

mainland would become possible, exposing the United States to a serious threat from the Atlantic coast in addition to the Japanese threat from the Pacific coast. An artist's conceptual illustration of the plane showing propellers both at front and rear from tandem-mounted four engines was printed without any real information about the "four engines that can be seen as twin engines" (Fig. 18-1).

Fig. 18-2 shows the actual configuration of the German bomber designated as the Heinkel He177 *Greif* (mysterious bird). Its engine was composed of two sets of inverted V12 cylinders coupled together as shown in Photo 18-2 and Fig. 18-3. The engine had a clever design. At the front, gears were merged so as to use a single propeller shaft. At the rear, a large rubber damper was sandwiched between two blocks and bolted together (Photo 18-2). However, configuring the engine compartment to dissipate efficiently the heat from the exhaust piping in each V block (Fig. 18-3) was extremely difficult. From the first flight on, the engines continually overheated. However, because the Germans were on the losing end of their war effort, bombers were desperately needed. Bomber production was continued even if they had

Fig. 18-1 Imaginative sketch of the Heinkel Greif bomber: According to the
information "Four-engine bomber looking like a twin-engine type excellent in
aerodynamics," such an imaginative sketch as this one was drawn in an
aircraft magazine. This design possibly would have avoided the problems
with the engine compartment.

Fig. 18-2 Heinkel Greif bomber: The real Greif mounted two units of 24-cylinder
engine, prepared by coupling two sets of inverted V12 cylinders. This engine
compartment layout was fatal to this plane.

no solutions to the problems. War records indicate as many as 1146 planes
were produced.

However, the engines' overheating prevented a successful air raid across the
Strait of Dover, just as Bleriot's monoplane had problems. On February 13,
1944, thirteen *Greif* bombers took off for an air raid on the British mainland. Of this squadron, eight turned around halfway into the mission
because of overheating. Of the four planes reaching the mainland, one was
shot down and the remaining three surrendered after jettisoning their bomb
loads into the sea.[18-1] It would seem that the danger of overheating made
carrying out the raid too risky.

Photo 18-2 For the Greif, a coupled engine assembled in which two sets of inverted V12 cylinders were used. Daimler-Benz Model DB610, 71.4L, 2980 PS/2800 rpm (Benz Museum).

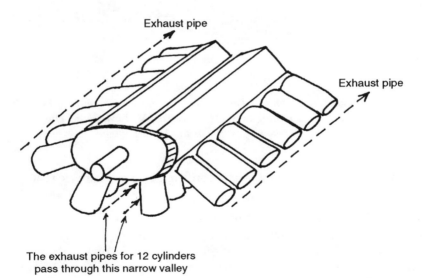

Exhaust pipe

Exhaust pipe

The exhaust pipes for 12 cylinders
pass through this narrow valley

Fig. 18-3 Idea sketch of coupled engine consisting of two sets of inverted V12 cylinders (24 cylinders in total).

In December 1969, I visited the KHD where I talked with Mr. Roggendorf. During World War II, he had been in the Benz factory developing the *Greif* engines. This engine was originally developed from the 12-cylinder Model DB600. After several modifications, the last model, Model DB610, coupled two of the 12-cylinder engines to make a 24-cylinder engine, which served as the basis of the *Greif* engine. Mr. Roggendorf had worked on all these engines. That evening, I talked with him about this Benz engine in detail at a restaurant near the Rhine River (Photo 18-3).

During our conversation, he said, "It can be said that overheating of this engine was attributable solely to poor ventilation in the engine compartment. Simply widening the open area at the front of the compartment may have improved the ventilation. However, widening the front of the plane fuselage would have increased the wind resistance, defeating the original purpose of the *Greif* design. Thus, the failure to resolve this serious design problem invited tragedy." To solve the problem, Heinkel reportedly proposed to the German Air Ministry that the plane be remodeled to an improved separate four-engine bomber configuration; that is, the wings had four separate engines mounted on them. Although his recommendation was rejected, the four-engine bomber remodeled from the twin-engine *Greif* was already planned as early as 1941. To my surprise, the detailed design of the four-engine bomber had been assigned to Farman, an aircraft manufacturing company in German-occupied France. The delay tactics of the French workers caused development to lag significantly behind schedule, so much so that the initial flight was carried out by the Allied Forces after the war, according to historical records.

A new design calls for an adventurous spirit and the willingness to take chances. However, when going on an adventure, contingencies should always be provided should the adventure fail. A development procedure must have some goals from the very beginning, and these goals should be incorporated into the management policy. A flaw in the basic policy such as hastily subcontracting a vital component of the war effort to the enemy was one factor that helped to defeat a country. This catastrophe was not a failure of engineering; rather it was a failure in engineering management. The engine nacelle with its engine compartment design that contributed to the defeat of the Third Reich is now resting quietly in the Smithsonian Museum. However, its sleek, compact form appears incapable of housing a huge V12 × 2 engine (Photo 18-4).

Photo 18-3 Meeting with Mr. Roggendorf: [Top] We talked about the past tragic engine on the banks of the Rhine River. [Bottom] Mr. Roggendorf sat at the right end, and the author stood behind him.

Photo 18-4 The nacelle included the inverted twin V12 engine, radiator, and oil cooler, was compact and elegant and helped defeat the Third Reich. (Nacelle for Daimler DB610, 2980 PS, V12 × 2, 24-cylinder engine for Heinkel HE177)

Lessons from Japan and United States Prototype Planes

The Japanese Imperial Navy also planned an airplane using the V12 × 2 engine. The high-speed reconnaissance airplane, Keiun, would have as its engine the Model Ha-70-10, made by Aichi Kohkuki according to the Benz design. Maximum speeds of 720 km/h or more were expected because of the planes's reduced wind resistance. However, the engine compartment caught fire during its maiden flight, and the plane had to make an emergency landing; this emergency landing marked the end of the Keiun project. This project was so short-lived because the Japanese engineers failed to examine the design of the engine compartment for themselves, instead relying completely on the design concept of the world-famous Heinkel. It is interesting to note that the United States had also at this time built a prototype plane with a similar design. The engine was the 2600-hp Allison Model V-3420. This coupled engine was a combination of two sets of V12 engines. At the tip of the extension driveshafts, which reminds me of the large tusks of an African elephant, a contrarotating propeller (two propellers rotating in opposite directions) is mounted (Photo 18-5). This coupled engine was mounted in the Fisher P75 plane, which was produced by General Motors. The General Motors factory had been hurriedly converted to an

Photo 18-5 Allison V-3420, 24-cylinder coupled engine, 2600 PS, reminds the author of the tusks of an African elephant (Bradley Air Museum).

aircraft factory after the start of World War II. This plane was reportedly discontinued after only six prototype units were produced. I wonder if the engine compartment of this plane also caught fire (Fig. 18-4).

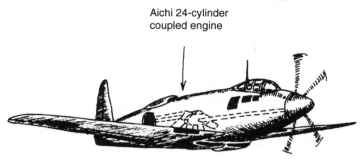

Aichi 24-cylinder
coupled engine

Discontinued development because
of fire inside the engine nacelle

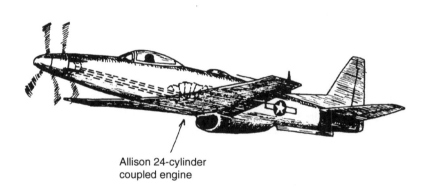

Allison 24-cylinder
coupled engine

Discontinued development after manufacture of six prototypes

Fig. 18-4 (Top) The Japanese Navy Keiun; (Bottom) The U.S. Army P75: Cooling of engine and inside the nacelle is a basic subject of layout design.

Though there is no written discussion of its engine compartment, the only remaining machine, the Fisher P75A Eagle, did have an elegant style (Photo 18-6). However, since the United States had only recently been drawn into World War II, a new plane was urgently needed. To minimize development time for the new XP75, already completed and proven components from other planes were used. For example, the wings had been used on the P40, the tail on the A24, and the landing gear on the F4U. Although the idea of using proven assemblies was good, additional emphasis should have been placed on the purpose of the plane. For example, the expected missions of the new plane should have been considered, and the

Photo 18-6 Fisher P75A Eagle with huge nose: Proven components were used to shorten the aircraft development time, but the random collection of components signifies that they are a rabble in spirit as well (U.S. Air Force Museum).

assemblies should have been designed with those missions in mind. Although several conceptual ideas may have all achieved the mission objectives, the appropriateness of using the previously developed components should have been considered only after the needs of the aircraft were determined. In another words, the mission requirements should have been the driving force for the design of the aircraft, not the fact that some components and assemblies were quickly available. It was ridiculous to have used the main wings of an unsatisfactory P40 aircraft. Even though the error in design was eventually realized, the experimental XP75 was reconfigured into P75A aircraft. The confusion that resulted from this plane was never fully resolved. Even though the P75 has an elegant nose with its sleek contrarotating propeller, we still see poor technology management in the rest of the plane's design.

Similar to the P75 effort, Japan also had an airplane whose development was initiated after the outbreak of the Pacific stage of World War II. However, this plane was completed in time to be used in actual service. The *Saiun,* manufactured by Nakajima Aircraft Works, was a carrier-based aircraft intended for high-speed secret aerial reconnaissance. As the war was drawing to an end, the *Saiun* was detected and pursued by

U.S. Navy aircraft during its reconnaissance of American military bases in the Mariana Islands. After the mission, the *Saiun* pilot telegraphed a message, "No enemy plane was able to overtake my plane." The people responsible for the design and production of the aircraft were overjoyed by the news because the seemingly unending string of defeats had caused their morale to plummet. Even though intended to be used only for reconnaissance, as many as 500 of this successful plane were manufactured.

In a post-war test by the U.S. military, this plane reached a maximum speed of 695 km/h. The high-performance capabilities of this plane can be seen from the extremely thin fuselage and the large-diameter propeller (Fig. 18-5). Although a variety of factors contributed to its success, the configuration of its main wings appears to have made the most significant contribution. One of the *Saiun* designers, Mr. Yasuo Naito, had statistically studied the characteristic values of as many as 300 airfoils that had been evaluated at the U.S. NACA in a study of the wing shape as a parameter. As a result of this analysis, a new laminar airfoil (airfoil with reduced resistance for use in a high-speed plane) was designed and adopted for the *Saiun*. It was reported that his firm did not have the high-speed test facilities necessary to test this new airfoil, so tests were performed in a high-speed wind tunnel at the Japanese Naval Aeronautical Engineering Center. The general plan of the *Saiun* was approved by the military in July 1942, the issuance of drawings began in September, and by December it was 90% completed. The maiden flight was May 15, 1943. These engineers had always been keeping up with technological advancements by reading pertinent technical journals and studying experimental data with enthusiasm and with tightly defined objectives. The dedication of these engineers paid off in the successful completion of this urgent project. This notable and rapid development is an event that every engineer should remember and compare to the poor P75 developmental efforts that used the 1930s P40 airfoil just because of an immediate need for the aircraft.[18-2]

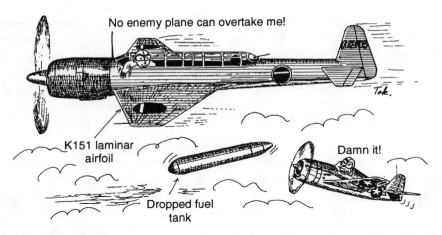

Fig. 18-5 Persistent research bore fruit, resulting in an excellent airfoil that made this plane faster than the enemy's.

Chapter 19

An Engine Compartment That Saved a Nation

Avro covered an engineering error through a prompt switchover. Engineering management should allow for minor errors beforehand.

✂

Development of Lancaster

Sitting proudly in the center of the Royal Air Force Museum in Hendon, located at the northern end of London, is the Avro *Lancaster* bomber with painted markers designating 170 successful bombing raids (Photo 19-1). In addition to the bombing raids, this model airplane has several other important World War II achievements to its credit. They include carrying two-thirds of the British bombs dropped on Germany; successfully dropping 10-ton bombs, the world's largest bomb at that time (contemporary Japanese heavy bomber had a maximum total on-board load of only 1 ton); and destroying the Möhne Dam during an ultralow 18-meter-altitude raid.

Noteworthy is that the development process of this plane was quite similar to that of the German's Heinkel *Greif* twin-engine bomber. It, too, was planned as a twin-engine plane with two coupled Rolls-Royce V 12-cylinder engines, each fabricated with an X-shaped coupling. The development of the *Manchester*, the predecessor to the *Lancaster*, was carried out by a design team headed by Roy Chadwick. Just as in the case of the *Greif* plane, the production was driven by urgency. Even before the first test plane was flown, the *Manchester* production line was set up and 1400 of the planes were ordered. However, this new X 24-cylinder engine (called the Rolls-Royce Vulture) often had trouble with the bearings in the connecting

Photo 19-1 This four-engine Lancaster *plane conducted a test flight only three days after the* Manchester *twin-engine bomber had made its debut. A backup for the adventurous work of the twin-engine bomber had been in preparation from the beginning. The twin-engine* Manchester *was discontinued after only 159 units were produced because the engine problems could not be solved (The Royal Air Force Museum).*

rod (perhaps as a result of metal fatigue). The configuration was extremely complicated, and it had a poor maintenance record. Even though the *Manchester* took off for numerous bombing raids, many of the planes failed to return, either because of engine trouble or being lost during combat (Photo 19-2).

Chadwick's Extraordinary Talent

The *Manchester* twin-engine bomber made its debut on February 24, 1941, in the Royal Air Force attack on Brest, Germany. On February 27, only three days later, an improved model with four Rolls-Royce engines of the usual V 12- cylinder configuration made its test flight. Chadwick had obviously been preparing a backup from the very beginning of his project. Surprisingly, though, he had also been planning a transport plane version of the bomber in parallel with the *Lancaster*. The transport plane, called the Avro *Yoke*, played a prominent role in transporting soldiers and weaponry. Transport is indispensable in wartime. Even though many bombers were hastily converted to transport airplanes during the war, the British Avro manufactured both bombers and transport airplanes from the same production line

Photo 19-2 Manchester *twin-engine bomber: One plane after another was lost because of problems with the Rolls-Royce Vulture X 24-cylinder engine.*

with an ample time margin. Thus, the *Manchester* twin-engine bomber was discontinued after only 159 units. The four-engine *Lancaster* was produced from the same assembly line as the *Manchester* and sent to the battle front in a steady stream.[19-1] I cannot help but admire Chadwick for his design philosophy, his engineering management, and his leadership. As a result of all these traits, the *Lancaster* sits proudly in a place of honor in the museum.

Chapter 20

Twin Beauties, Quadruplets and Their Early Death

Man repeats failure.

Bugatti, the Best Among Beauties

I doubt that any car in the world can surpass the beauty of the Bugatti. I hear that its horseshoe-shaped unique mask was a result of Bugatti's love for horses. The spirit of the Bugatti had been passed on to the son from his father. Its increasingly refined beauty has such a strong sense of continuity that one cannot feel any generation gap. The extreme beauty of the 1937 Atlantic coupe designed by the son could take your breath away (Photo 20-1). The Bugatti chassis is a work of art. Every panel shimmers with an iridescent glow. The beauty of the Bugatti is not limited to its exterior. Its engine is also a work of art. It is hard to believe that this slender engine could produce such a large amount of horsepower. All engineers should bear this sense of aesthetics in mind (Photo 20-2) when they are designing a project.

In 1930, a car named the Bucciali was also manufactured. Although the designer of the Bucciali is unknown, he obviously had a deep appreciation of Bugatti's work. Every panel in the Bucciali has the same iridescent sheen as the Bugatti. The Bucciali has a coupled engine with two sets of series eight cylinders (Photo 20-3). However, the Bugatti was the first car with a twin eight-cylinder engine, that is, 16 cylinders.

Photo 20-1 The 1937 Atlantic coupe, the most beautiful Bugatti (Harrah's Automobile Collection).

Photo 20-2 The 1930 Bugatti Royale engine: eight cylinders, 12.7L displacement, three-valve system, 250 PS/1700 rpm (Musée Francois, Schlumpf Collection).

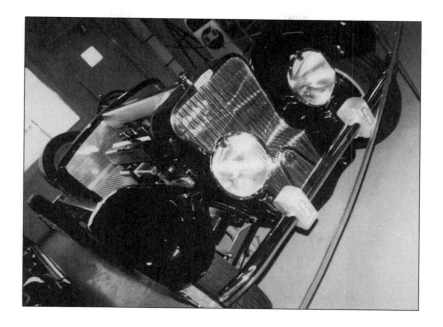

Photo 20-3 Bucciali's 1930 model coupled engine with eight cylinders × 2 = 16 cylinders: Every panel glitters like fish scales (Harrah's Automobile Collection).

Development of a Parallel Eight-Cylinder Coupled Engine

In 1915, during World War I, the French Army requested Bugatti to develop a liquid-cooled engine rivaling the Mercedes. Bugatti was of Italian origin, but he had moved to Paris to design a series eight-cylinder engine. After completing this engine, two of the eight-cylinder units were joined in parallel to make a twin engine. Then two crankshafts were coupled with a gear to receive the output, thereby resulting in a 16-cylinder engine (Photo 20-4).

Photo 20-4 Bugatti's coupled engine: 120-mm bore, 160-mm stroke, 16 cylinders, 420 PS (Musée de L'Air, Paris).

The U.S. Dusenberg Motor Corporation was awarded a contract to develop this parallel eight-cylinder twin engine. Harry Miller collaborated with Dusenberg at that time in building the engine. Later, Miller won the Indianapolis 500-mile race when he installed a centrifugal supercharger on the engine of his race car. However, the Dusenberg's engine was never put into practical use because the war ended before the engine was complete.

Yet, Bugatti had joined two sets of the twin engines, resulting in four eight-cylinder engines. These engines are placed in the shape of an "H" with two engines each at the top and bottom of the legs of the "H"; four crankshafts are coupled with a gear to receive the output (Photo 20-5). This huge engine was mounted on an airplane (Fig. 20-1) called the *Breguet-Leviathan*

Photo 20-5 Bugatti's quadruplet engine: 108-mm bore, 160-mm stroke, 32 cylinders, 47L displacement, 100 PS/2200 rpm (Musée de L'Air, Paris).

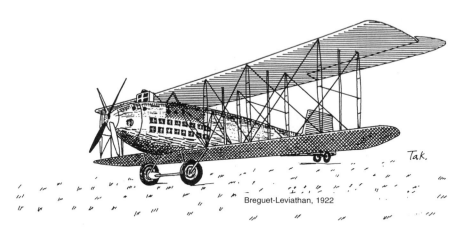

Breguet-Leviathan, 1922

Fig. 20-1 The Breguet-Leviathan (Sea Monster) using the Bugatti quadruplet engine (1922) (structural details include guesswork).

(Leviathan was a legendary monster inhabiting the Leviathan sea). Since a photograph of this plane has been found, it may have actually flown. However, the passenger cabin and all those in it were probably subjected to extreme heat and noise. Again mankind repeats a similar failure as exemplified by Bugatti and Breguet near the end of World War I, and by Heinkel near the end of World War II. To date, those Bugatti engines are carefully preserved in the Meudon Aeronautical Research Institute in a Paris suburb where Bugatti spent much of his time designing the engine. A possibility exists that the exhibit may be moved to Le Musee de L'Air at the Le Beurget airport (Photo 20-6).

Photo 20-6 Aeronautical research institute in which Bugatti designed his engine rivaling Mercedes: Later converted to a museum preserving his engine (author at front).

Chapter 21

Imitation of Porsche

Imitation is the basis of creation. True imitation begins when one has sympathy.

❃

Masterpiece Renault 4CV

As is well known in the music world, the fourth movement of Brahms' Symphony No. 1 is very similar to the fourth movement of Beethoven's Symphony No. 9. Historians also know well that Beethoven's Symphony No. 9 owed its musical character to Cherubini 32 years before the first performance of the Beethoven symphony. The music of Cherubini had impressed Beethoven deeply, and it remained in his heart and consciousness for years; similarly, Beethoven's movement deeply impressed Brahms' heart, where it found a foothold that resulted in the composition of another famous symphony. Designing machinery, including automobile and engines, undergoes a similar process. Masterpieces are always made by receiving impressions and taking inspiration from work that has gone before and incorporating them into one's own work. I have already explained that the Contessa was developed from the Renault 4CV automobile. As is well known, the Renault 4CV was completed shortly after World War II, thanks to a great car and engine designer, F. Porsche. Porsche had thoroughly examined and improved the design drawing of the Renault 4C while he was imprisoned as a war criminal. Some publications speculate that the car was Renault's attempt to thwart the French industrial minister, who wanted to produce a French version of the German Volkswagen (people's car). The Volkswagen, although yet to be manufactured, was originated by Adolph Hitler. The Renault 4CV, involved with Porsche, established a reputation during its own time as a masterpiece.

Birth of Volkswagen

You may notice that Porsche's masterpiece of the century, namely, the Volkswagen Beetle, had skillfully incorporated many of its forerunners' ideas in its structure. Adolph Hitler, who had established his administration in January 1933, visited that yea"s Berlin Auto Show. He strode directly to the Tatra display without even glancing at the other booths.

Hitler was a great admirer of the Tatra. At the booth, he met the Tatra designer, Hans Ledwinka, and talked about having driven the Tatra Twin on the one-million-kilometer political campaign he had made in Austria (Photo 21-1). The Tatra Twin was a small Czech-made car that had an 1100-cm^2, air-cooled, two-cylinder, 12-hp engine. The engine was bolted to the backbone tube chassis (structure for supporting the body with a backbone-shaped tube)(Fig. 21-1). Hitler listened carefully to the detailed explanation of the new Tatra with a rear-mounted V8 air-cooled engine. During that same evening, Ledwinka visited Hitler as requested and talked with him until well after 10 p.m. about the Tatra Twin. Just before Ledwinka left, Hitler reportedly said, "Our new German domestic car should have a strong air-cooled engine like the Tatra."[21-1]

Photo 21-1 Neighborhood of Dachstein: Austrian countryside around which Hitler conducted his campaign while driving the Tatra Twin.

Near the end of this same year Porsche completed his concept of the people's car and sent his first report to the Nazi transport minister. The second

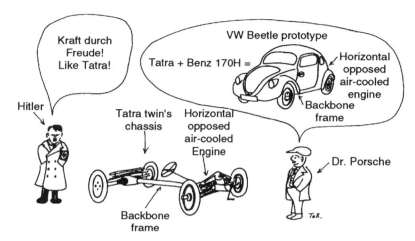

Fig. 21-1 Tatra's idea absorbed into Porsche's dream as if dissolved.

report was submitted in January 1934. Soon after, the famous Porsche-Hitler meeting took place at the Keiserhoff Hotel in Berlin, which eventually led to the origination of the Volkswagen. One suspects that Hitler must have said, "Make it like the Tatra."

The ground-breaking ceremony for the Volkswagen factory in Wolfsburg was held on May 26, 1938. Hitler was the keynote speaker and gave his speech as he stood beside a well-polished Volkswagen prototype. Even at this date, the Tatra company had informed the Volkswagen manufacturer of about ten instances of patent infringement discovered on the Volkswagen.

For instance, hanging the engine from the rear end of the backbone tube was a solution that Ledwinka, after great efforts, had devised to reduce the noise in a rear-engine car. Also the Tatra gearbox layout of the transmission and its system of cooling air ducts were both incorporated into the Volkswagen without any changes. Ledwinka had left his former employer, the Steyr Iron Works, in 1921. Porsche joined the Steyr Iron Works in 1929 and gained access to all of Ledwinka's design data.

As mentioned earlier, Porsche had been gaining experience on rear-engine cars since 1923. Porsche had been working with Dr. Hans Nibel at Daimler, designing the Benz 170H, its earlier model 130H, and so on. Porsche may have already solidified his concept of a new car based on all these valuable data, his own experience, and above all, his passion for a small-sized people's car. All these ingredients must have melded into the concept of the Volkswagen as a result of Hitler's direction and support.

A great work such as the Volkswagen could not have been created simply by stealing other ideas. Only after the ideas of Porsche's predecessors had been digested and merged with his own experience, when those parts that resonated most strongly with his own image were consolidated into a vision of what he wanted to create, did the masterpiece take shape on the draftsman's table.

Incidentally, Tatra tried to revive its patent-infringement claims after the war, but they seemed to have melted away and were never seriously considered by any court.

Chapter 22

Rolls-Royce Copying Daimler

Superb engine born from a plundered bride. Maybach quit, leaving a superb engine.

Long Story Deriving from a Stolen Engine

On August 4, 1914, England declared war against Germany. That same night, an English naval officer in civilian clothing stealthily carried away a used engine from the scrap yard of the Daimler distributor in Long Acre. A little over one month prior to the declaration of war, or on June 28, the Austrian Prince Ferdinand and his wife were assassinated by a Serbian. World War I broke out soon after the assassination (Photo 22-1). As a result, the German staff of the Daimler distributor had already been recalled to Germany. Not long after the midnight excursion, the engine was unpacked in the Rolls-Royce Derby factory, carefully disassembled, and sketched.

On July 5, shortly after the assassination, the France Grand Prix was held at Lyon. In this race, the Daimler Mercedes won a lopsided victory when it captured first through third places (Photo 22-2). The victorious Mercedes engine was completed as a result of Paul Daimler's devotion. This engine had an innovative structure with the world's first overhead camshaft (OHC) mechanism and with four valves and two spark plugs for each cylinder. The engine provided 115 hp at 2700 rpm.

Rolls-Royce staffmember W.O. Bentley was extremely impressed with the innovative design of the Mercedes engine. He promptly requested that his immediate superior W. Briggs obtain one of the engines to study its design. This scenario explains the background of the stealthy action described in the first paragraph of this chapter. An English Navy man was involved in this

Photo 22-1 Prince Ferdinand and his wife were assassinated in this car. The holes made by the Browning bullets remain unchanged on the body of the Graf and Stift (Wien military historical museum).

Photo 22-2 Mercedes swept first through third places in the France Grand Prix: Here the first-place winner, Christian Lautenschlager, is shown far ahead of the other cars (Benz Museum).

event because the Navy had commissioned Rolls-Royce to develop a 75- to 100-PS aircraft engine capable of competing with the Mercedes counterpart. This situation set off the imitation story of the century.[22-1]

Royce's Decision

The Lord Montagu National Motor Museum in England has spotlighted in the center of one of its darkened display rooms the Silver Ghost, a historically significant car (Photo 22-3). Our first impression of the display may be comparable to an encounter with the Venus de Milo similarly spotlighted in the Louvre Museum. The Silver Ghost had been manufactured by the Rolls-Royce Company, which had been founded by C.S. Rolls and Henry Royce. The engine of this particular car employed a side valve instead of the overhead valve mechanism that had been used in the preceding model (Fig. 22-1). Royce had made this change to reduce the engine noise as well as to increase its reliability. Royce believed that a simpler side valve mechanism was more reliable than the overhead mechanism because the manufacturing process available at that time could not provide a reliable and high-quality cylinder head gasket. The use of this side valve resulted in the Silver Ghost's gaining a reputation as having a superb automobile engine. This engine did have a problem with poor volumetric efficiency, that is, the

Photo 22-3 Rolls-Royce Silver Ghost 1909 model: Exhibited in the Lord Montagu National Motor Museum in England.

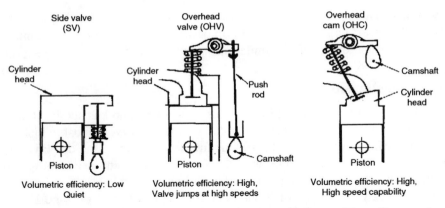

Fig. 22-1 Various valve drive methods: SV for Rolls-Royce Silver Ghost and overhead cam for the Mercedes race car.

feeding of the air/fuel mixture into the individual cylinders, that resulted in low output. To overcome this deficiency, Rolls-Royce incorporated the Mercedes' overhead cam mechanism into its new aero engine.[22-2]

To improve the volumetric efficiency of an engine, the size and opening of the intake valve must be maximized, which requires an overhead valve system. However, an overhead valve is encumbered with the extra weight of the pushrods and other necessary components (see Fig. 22-1). At high speed, inertia forces cause the valve to jump, eventually being damaged. To solve this problem, the camshaft was moved to the top of the cylinder head, and the pushrod was eliminated, enabling high-speed rotation. This configuration illustrates the principle of the overhead cam mechanism. In addition, to prevent valve jumping, Mercedes had halved the weight of the individual valves when it doubled the number of valves, creating a total of four intake and exhaust valves. To drive the overhead camshaft, Mercedes incorporated a vertical rod with bevel gears on both ends. The crankshaft rotated the lower bevel gear, transmitting the rotary motion to the upper bevel gear, then turning the overhead cam (Fig. 22-2).

This Mercedes concept was first incorporated into the Rolls-Royce Hawk aircraft engine (Photos 22-4, 22-5, and 22-6). The later superb Rolls-Royce Merlin engine is the result of the merger of the Rolls-Royce technology with the plundered Mercedes engine.

The German forces were astounded to find that the shot-down enemy fighters had an engine that closely resembled the German-made Mercedes engine. Angered by this blatant theft, Mercedes sent an invoice for a

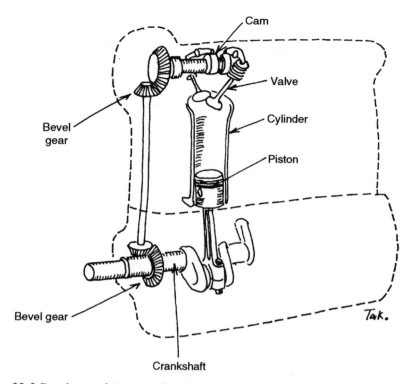

Fig. 22-2 Bevel gear-driven overhead cam (OHC): In the Mercedes, the crankshaft drove the camshaft through the use of the two bevel gears (two-valve type shown here).

patent-licensing fee to the Rolls-Royce company. This reaction was mild when compared to events that happened later during World War II. The Mercedes overhead cam design was also introduced into the Italian-made Fiat cars, and it served as the basis of the Russian tank engine described later. One of the Mercedes cars used in the 1914 Lyon Grand Prix was imported into the United States and was imitated, resulting in the Liberty aircraft engine. On April 7, 1922, the previously unknown Norwegian Sig Haugdahl established a world-record car speed of 180.3 mph (288.5 km/h) while driving a Wisconsin Special in the U.S. Daytona Beach race. This car incorporated the Wisconsin aircraft engine, which was also very similar to the Mercedes engine (Photo 22-7).

Photo 22-4 Six-cylinder engine of the Rolls-Royce Silver Ghost: Utilizing the design of the Mercedes engine (shown below) for the upper half of this photo, the Hawk aircraft engine was completed (Museo dell' Automobile Carlo Bescaretti).

Photo 22-5 Mercedes racing car engine: 115 PS/2700 rpm (Benz Museum).

Photo 22-6 Rolls-Royce Hawk aircraft engine: 100 PS/1500 rpm. I heard that the lower half had inherited the Silver Ghost design, but it seemed quite similar to the Mercedes.

Photo 22-7 Wisconsin Special driven by Sig Haugdahl: Displayed together with a strange mirror in a corner of the Automobilorama Museum.

Successors of Mercedes

This shaft-driven overhead cam design had been used in the engine of the 1906 Mercedes racing car. Of interest is the fact that in 1906, Mercedes had two racing engines: one with a 13L displacement and 100 hp, while the second had an 11L displacement and 125 hp. The first engine was the usual overhead valve type produced by Paul Daimler, while the second was a high-output overhead cam type built by Wilhelm Maybach (Photo 22-8). As is evident in the later models, the Maybach overhead cam system was later adopted for all the engines. However, the following year, 1907, Wilhelm Maybach left his position as chief engineer of the Daimler company, the maker of the Mercedes engine. Paul Daimler, the eldest son of Daimler's founder Gottlieb Daimler, was then appointed to the vacant position.

Photo 22-8 The 1906 Mercedes racing engine: Wilhelm Maybach left the Daimler Company as well as this superb engine. This overhead cam mechanism became standard for subsequent high-output engines (Benz museum).

This discussion brings to mind the fact that the exhaust valve open/close mechanism of Otto's first four-stroke cycle engine was also dependent on this shaft drive (see Photo 6-1). It seems that Maybach's first idea was revived here and underwent a rapid development.

Of some interest is the 1905 race car developed by American Carl Fisher, a co-founder of the Indianapolis Motor Speedway. Fisher made a race car that he named World Beater. This amazingly high 14L displacement[22-3] engine was air-cooled and had a camshaft drive bearing a remarkable resemblance to the 1906 Mercedes. However, the extremely large engine made this car too heavy. To meet the weight restrictions, holes were bored at numerous locations on the vehicle structure and the body shells were eliminated. Fisher probably obtained and utilized the Maybach idea in his engine (Fig. 22-3). The Rolls-Royce engine was later produced as the Merlin engine, and was manufactured in the United States through a license agreement with the Rolls-Royce company. This Merlin engine was used in all the major planes of the Allied Forces.

Fig. 22-3 Fisher's World Beater (1905): Because the 14L engine was extremely heavy, holes were bored at many locations in the structure of the car to stay within the weight limit. Even though the frames were stripped off, the car was still overweight. The designer lacked a sense of balance (drawn with reference to H. Helck: Great Auto Races [published by Asahi Shimbun]).

On the other hand, the Mercedes engine was developed to the Daimler 600 series engine. This engine was manufactured in both Japan and Italy through a license agreement and was used in all major planes on the Axis

Powers. Thus, fierce battles were fought between the two engine families during World War II. I wonder if I alone feel the karma in this story that seems as though the strife was among blood relatives.

As a note to the reader, I owe this story of intrigue and suspense involved in the imitation of the Rolls-Royce engine mainly to W.O. Bentley's book. However, the book[8-1] by A. Bird and I. Hallows fails to mention this event at all; surprisingly, even the name "Bentley" does not appear. I agree with Professor K. Tomizuka when he said that history is unreliable and sometimes depressing. Nevertheless, if in this depressing story, one can find inspiration on the lineage of a valuable piece of technology and be encouraged in one's own technical development, it becomes worthwhile.

Chapter 23

Talk About Knocking

Mercedes was successful in controlling the knocking, even though it was unintended. One of the great discoveries of the century was a result of persistent peeking.

✄

Knocking Phenomenon

The Mercedes engine was victorious in the French Grand Prix race. In this engine, the intake and exhaust valves were positioned at the top of the combustion chamber, avoiding the side valve mechanism. This design is effective because it increases the amount of mixture gas supplied to the cylinder (or volumetric efficiency) as previously described. Another advantage of this design is that it significantly improved the engine output process, that is, it unintentionally eliminated an abnormal combustion phenomenon called *knocking*. The term "unintentional" is used in this context because the knocking phenomenon was first identified in 1938. The fact that the Mercedes engine was equipped with two spark plugs, one on each side of the combustion chamber, resulted in an effective control of this adverse knocking phenomenon.

In March 1980, the U.S. Society of Automotive Engineers (SAE) celebrated its 75th anniversary. As one of the commemorative events of the annual meeting, Messrs. G.M. Rassweiler and L. Withrow were honored as the persons who had marked a milestone in the automotive engineering field. The paper on knocking, originally published in 1938, together with the first high-speed photographs of the knocking phenomenon, was reprinted.[23-1] In addition, Dr. Withrow was asked to deliver a commemorative address to the SAE. Even though Mr. Rassweiler had died earlier in 1978, his son was able to attend the meeting and he was introduced to the audience. The commemorative lecture was delivered in a small room attended only by those people associated with combustion study. This session was presided over by F.W. Bowdich, who had been a younger colleague of Dr. Withrow and who was renowned for his observation of the combustion chamber from the bottom for the first time. Withrow's lecture was a short one, presented as the first address at the Engine Fluid Motion and Combustion Diagnostics session. The session attendees were deeply moved.

When accelerating even a modern car, a knocking sound is emitted, a faint one in most cases. The sound is faint because the car has been designed to minimize the sound. As noted earlier, an increase in the compression ratio can enhance the thermal efficiency. Of course, now the output can also be improved, but the knocking phenomenon had prevented such an enhancement in the early stages of the gasoline engine development. When an engine is set to a higher compression ratio, the engine emits a noise as though it were being hit with a hammer. When the engine is set at wide open throttle, the noise steadily increases until the engine undergoes catastrophic failure. Although knocking was first noted around 1904, numerous studies[23-2] failed to determine the underlying cause of the sound. However, basic combustion research has revealed that when a fire is ignited at one end of a long pipe filled with combustible gas, the flame will propagate toward the other end at several meters per second. In some cases, however, the flame suddenly travels at an explosive speed of 1000 to 3500 meters per second. This phenomenon is called detonation. Before the knocking process was thoroughly understood, the detonation that had occurred in the engine combustion chamber was believed to have been knocking.

Kettering Permitted the Peeping

Rassweiler and others wanted to confirm visually the knocking phenomenon and had an idea of peeping into the combustion chamber via a hole in the chamber. They planned to photograph the combustion process with a high-speed camera through this observation port. In 1931, they presented their plan to their immediate superior, C.F. Kettering. In his lecture, Withrow explained their situation at that time: "Then, the American economy was in a severe recession. In that year, my company (General Motors) had undergone a large-scale layoff, and all expenditures had to be curtailed substantially. However, all our experimental plans, including an engine for photographing, would have been expensive. The Kodak high-speed camera alone cost $3000 at that time. The total research effort was estimated at $40,000. However, Kettering realized the necessity of this research project and authorized the effort. Today, the camera and engine can be synchronized easily, thanks to the development of electronic equipment. But at that time, we had to modify the mechanical systems of the engine and camera in order to synchronize them. Of course, they faced many problems while trying to see inside the combustion chamber. Improving the pressure meter, which required synchronizing the measures, was perhaps the greatest obstacle."

Dr. Withrow continued, "We swore to do three things in our research efforts. They were to (1) never give up, (2) do our best, and (3) make no recommendations!

"In 1937, the mechanics of the knocking phenomenon were captured with the high-speed camera, exposing its essence to mankind. The knocking phenomenon was not the same as the detonation process. Instead, we found that before normal propagation of flame can occur, self-ignition happens at multiple locations, caused by a group that randomly initiates combustion. Therefore, the entire combustion chamber is subjected to a rapid combustion, causing a sudden increase in pressure. As a result, combustion pressure oscillates the cylinder, causing the hammering noise. In the combustion chamber, there are factors that oppose normal action just as there are people of this kind in the human world (Fig. 23-1)." The research project of Rassweiler and his team was completed. Once the nature of knocking had been determined, the methods of controlling knocking could be established. Aiding in the suppression of knocking was the fuel additive (tetra ethyl lead), which also had been discovered by the same Kettering group. In consequence of this discovery, the compression ratio nearly doubled the previous value. Thus, two gallons of gasoline performed the same amount of work that had required three gallons before this project.[23-3] In the evening of January 14, 1938, the results of this remarkable research were announced at the Cadillac Hotel in Detroit, Michigan (Photo 23-1).

Dr. Withrow closed his lecture, again thanking Kettering for his understanding of the need to carry out their research. Then, Bowdich, who had followed Withrow's research with his own observation of the combustion process from under a heavy-duty quartz piston, presented Withrow with a Society of Automotive Engineers letter of appreciation and praised him as a great forerunner who left a precious milestone in the history of automotive engineering. The audience saw Withrow off with a standing ovation (Photo 23-2 and Fig. 23-2).

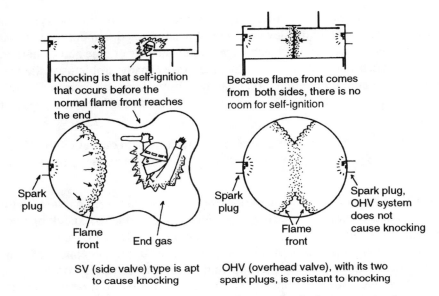

Knocking is that self-ignition that occurs before the normal flame front reaches the end

Because flame front comes from both sides, there is no room for self-ignition

Spark plug

Flame front   End gas

Spark plug

Flame front

Spark plug, OHV system does not cause knocking

SV (side valve) type is apt to cause knocking

OHV (overhead valve), with its two spark plugs, is resistant to knocking

Fig. 23-1 Knocking occurs due to Gewaltakt (student's demonstration by arm represents self-ignition) of end gas.

Controlling the Knocking

Knocking is an explosion of the last fuel-air mixture in the combustion chamber to burn (called the "end gas"). The end gas self-ignites before the flame front, initiated by the spark plug, reaches it. Therefore, knocking can be alleviated by making the combustion chamber more compact (for instance by abandoning the side valve system) so that the flame reaches the end of the combustion chamber earlier, as shown in Fig. 23-1. Combustion is completed even earlier when two spark plugs are used as was done in the Mercedes in the French Grand Prix (which was probably unintended for knock), so there is less chance of early self-ignition.

Thereafter, the two-spark-plug system was often used in aeroengines to control this knocking phenomenon in addition to improving reliability. Recently, the system has also been used for speeding up combustion and thereby improving fuel consumption (as in the Nissan NAPS).

As I noted previously, a diesel engine does not have a spark plug. Instead, a high compression ratio is used to compression-heat the air in the cylinder to about 600°C or higher. Fuel is then injected into the cylinder to bring about self-ignition. In the diesel engine, early self-ignition is not only desirable but essential to ignite the fuel soon after fuel injection begins. When this

Photo 23-1 The Detroit Cadillac Hotel was the site at which the true nature of the knocking phenomenon was first disclosed.

happens, the fuel injected subsequently burns as soon as it mixes with air, and combustion is smooth. If self-ignition is delayed, all the fuel injected up to the time of ignition will burn almost simultaneously, causing excessively high cylinder pressure (knocking). Therefore, in the diesel engine, early self-ignition is required, and late self-ignition causes knocking. In the gasoline engine, delayed self-ignition is required, and early self-ignition causes knocking.

In the usual diesel engine, self-ignition occurs when about 20% of the fuel in that injection cycle has been injected. Therefore, there is always a low-level knocking. This is the reason that a diesel engine emits a noisy sound. In a cold climate, the internal temperature of the cylinder is low, particularly in the morning. Therefore, self-ignition is delayed, the fuel is be ignited after a substantial fraction of all the fuel is injected, and engine knocking is loud. This process is called "diesel knock." Thus, in a single word, the difference between normal diesel combustion and diesel knock is only one of degree.

Photo 23-2 Dr. Withrow is delivering a lecture in honor of his late colleague Rassweiler and his former supervisor Kettering (February 1980).

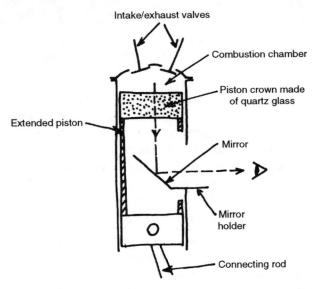

Fig. 23-2 Bowdich observed the inside of a combustion chamber from under the piston for the first time in 1960. This method is useful because, previously, the size of a window in the cylinder head would have been restricted by the intake and exhaust valves. In 1977, Hino Motors succeeded for the first time in applying this technique to a diesel engine, which has a combustion pressure twice as large as that of a gasoline engine.

Therefore, fuel that has been formulated to have a long ignition delay (a high octane number) is most undesirable for a diesel engine. The diesel engine calls for a low-octane fuel, but diesel fuels are rated by a different parameter, called cetane number. A cetane number measures how easily the fuel self-ignites, and a high cetane value is welcomed. Fuels with high cetane number have a low octane number. A poor student in the world of the gasoline engine becomes a bright student in the world of the diesel engine.

Victory as a Result of Teamwork

The ex-chairman of the General Motors board of directors, A.P. Sloan, said of Kettering, who gave approval for the research project done by Withrow and others, "He gave inspiration to all the senior members of our company, thereby leading our thought, imagination, and action until we have come to recognize the extreme importance of technological development. This is one of his greatest contributions to GM."

Also, Kettering said to his younger colleagues, "Industrial progress has no pause. We must always be entertaining questions on change, change, change."

Finally, let me tell an anecdote about Kettering. When Lindbergh succeeded in crossing the Atlantic Ocean in 1927, Kettering's wife said to him, "How wonderful! I heard that Lindbergh arranged everything by himself." Kettering responded, "[The flight] would have been more impressive if the success was achieved not by a single man, but by collaboration of many people."[23-3] (See Photo 23-3.)

Modern engineering has been finely divided into various fields, and a system has come to comprise many functions. So, a single engineer alone cannot complete anything. The development of a car or engine can be accomplished only by the collaboration of many people. The understanding of knocking and its suppression represents a victory for the team led by Kettering. I cannot help but praise Kettering for foretelling the end of one-man play in modern science and pointing out the importance of teamwork, and his team for persuading management through the encouragement of their colleagues.

Is Knocking Actually Detonation?

The study on knocking was carried on by many researchers after Withrow and Rassweiler, and more powerful high-speed cameras were used for subsequent studies. Rassweiler's team used a camera capable of exposing 5000

Photo 23-3 Lindbergh's plane Spirit of St. Louis *crossed the Atlantic Ocean for the first time (Ford Museum): However great a single man's work may be, it is not the essence of technological development. If the work had been accomplished through collaboration with many people, it would have been more significant (Kettering's words).*

frames per second. In 1949, Male of the U.S. NACA analyzed knocking using Schlieren photography at 500,000 frames per second and found a shock wave (a boundary wave, across which temperature, density, and pressure change suddenly due to a shock given to the air, and which usually propagates faster than acoustic velocity) due to the ignition of the end gas in the cylinder.

The phenomenon was called "detonation."[23-4] In a more recent study[23-5] not only the presence of the shock wave, but also its propagation over the noncombustion region accompanying a chemical reaction have been verified by using a laser wave for a high-speed camera (more exactly, laser shadowgraph). The term "detonation" is defined as a shock wave (more exactly detonation wave) that travels faster than sound and is sustained by the energy of the chemical reaction initiated by the temperature and pressure of the wave. Therefore, the phenomenon in question seems to be detonation.[23-4]

The person who first hypothesized that the knocking in an engine is detonation is unknown. This person's reason for using this term may have been that he believed combustion in an engine may suddenly change to detonation, as happens in the combustion experiment involving a pipe. However, after knocking was determined to be the result of end-gas ignition, detonation was considered to be inaccurate terminology. Thus, the word detonation was deleted from the famous textbook by L. Lichty and replaced with the expression engine knock.[23-6] Unlike the detonation in a pipe, the knocking phenomenon in an engine is a complicated one. Today, more exact research has been performed, and these studies indicate that, after the ignition of the end gas, the chemical reaction riding on the shock wave collides with the normal flame front. After the collision, only the shock wave crosses the flame front, propagates to the burned gas, and is reflected by the combustion chamber wall (photo 23-4). Therefore, calling both phenomena "detonation" appears to be inappropriate. I wonder what the exact term should be for the spontaneous combustion that partially accompanies detonation.

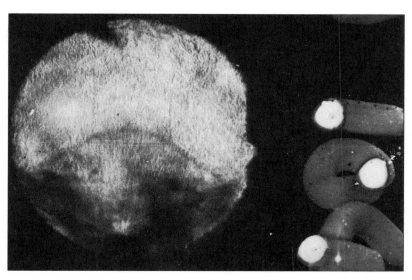

Photo 23-4 The engine's knocking phenomenon: The shock wave (crest at the center is the leading edge of this wave) generated due to the self-ignition of end gas crosses over the normal flame front and reverses after collision with the opposite combustion chamber wall[23-5] (Courtesy of the Toyota Central Research Laboratory).

Chapter 24

Energy Conservation and Tank Designer

Christie's idea of a front-engine/front-drive (F-F) is revived because of the oil crisis. The idea of F-F is needed to refine technical problems.

❧

Characteristics of X Car

In 1979, General Motors Corporation unveiled an innovative energy-saving passenger car called the "X Car." As mentioned earlier, the American car manufacturers were hurting badly because of the brisk sales of imported vehicles, particularly Japanese and European economy cars. As a result of the Arabian oil embargo, U.S. government regulations had imposed even tougher limits on fuel consumption. To regain its market share, the GM Corporation invested an enormous amount of money, $2.7 billion, to develop its X Car. The concept of this vehicle was derived from a thorough and systematic analysis of those factors that reduce fuel consumption, shown in Fig. 24-1. The basis of this reduced fuel consumption was weight reduction and optimization and loss minimization of the power plant and power train. The factors for increasing the paycheck explained previously (see Fig. 10-4) were also examined thoroughly, and a number of improvements were introduced. For example, the energy loss caused by oil splashing in the gearbox was reduced by changing the oil level in response to oil temperature.[24-1]

The most notable characteristic of the X Car is its front-wheel/front-engine drive. To ensure a comfortable amount of passenger space with the minimum vehicle weight, the front-engine/front-wheel (F-F) drive (a system in which the engine drives the front wheels without a driveshaft) was adopted

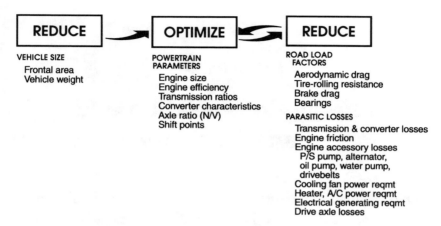

Fig. 24-1 Technical measures for reducing fuel consumption. [24-1]

with a V6 engine (or in-line four-cylinder engine, depending on car model) mounted transversely. By adopting this system, each X Car realized a substantial weight reduction of 360 kg or more (the X Car had an empty vehicle weight of about 1100 kg). [24-1] Later, the X Cars (Chevrolet Citation and others) were not always successful in regaining GM's market share because of manufacturing defects and other quality problems, but they did make the F-F system popular before their eventual disappearance from the marketplace.

Problem in F-F Use

The first front-engine/front-wheel-drive system was produced by the American John Walter Christie in 1904. Also, a prototype was attempted in 1899 by the Austrian Gräf, who designed the car for Prince Ferdinand of the Austria-Hungary Empire. [24-2] It seems that Christie's primary purpose was to increase the cornering speed on the race track by using the front drive. Among his F-F cars, the one made in 1906 attracted the greatest attention. In this car, a gigantic V4 engine with a 45.9L displacement was used. The World War II Zero fighter plane displaced only 28 liters (1100 hp). Even today, Hino Motors manufactures the world's largest automotive engine with only a 25L displacement. Christie's engine was placed transversely at the front of the car (as in the X Cars), and the front wheels were bolted directly to the crankshaft, as shown in Fig. 24-2. The American writer Arthur Lee Homan said," The V4 cylinder Christie car dashed around a dirt track like a torpedo boat in the raging ocean, while emitting a roar from the

Fig. 24-2 Christie front-wheel-drive car (1904): To reduce the drive loss in cornering (running along a curved course), Christie adopted the front drive and used a dual inner tire.

exhaust pipe." He also said, "This car was the most exciting thing in car races at that time. For ordinary travel, however, no one would have wanted such a beastly car."(22-3)

After some years, the F-F system was attempted by several makers, but they all encountered difficulties in the initial stage. One of the problems was front wheel shimmy (i.e., vibration of the front wheels). For instance, I heard that shimmy during high-speed cornering occurred on even the famous Citroën Big 6. Also, Hino Motors marketed an epochal F-F commercial car "Commerce" in 1960 shortly before releasing the Contessa 900. During the development of this car, the Hino engineers worked hard to eliminate a shimmy that occurred while driving downhill (Fig. 24-3). In both the Big 6 and the Commerce, the shimmy occurred because the constant velocity joint of the front wheels did not rotate at exactly constant speed while steering.

To adequately realize the F-F advantages, it is necessary to understand the numerous technical problems that accompany the F-F idea. An idea cannot be used practically while it still remains naked, that is, without its having undergone refining or a fine-tuning through a thorough review. After a staff member has conceived of a new idea, then management must discover and solve those problems that are involved in any new idea by thoroughly and painstakingly reviewing the possible program.

As an aside, the world's first four-wheel-drive vehicle was the "Blue Flyer," manufactured by Christie in 1905. Later, Christie moved on to design military tanks, which were as unique as his cars. The Union of Soviet Socialist

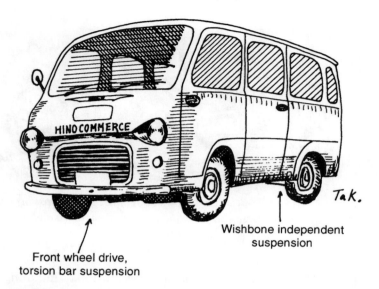

Wishbone independent
suspension

Front wheel drive,
torsion bar suspension

Fig. 24-3 Pioneer of the F-F system (one-box car) in Japan, Hino Commerce (1960): 24 PS, low-floor, capacity of 2 to 10 passengers, car design based on a unique idea.

Republics successfully manufactured Christie's tank by copying his designs. This story continues into the next chapter.

Chapter 25

Dead Copy Saved Nation

Christie's raw idea was borrowed and refined by Koshkin. Victory through a technical study while undergoing severe political disturbance.

Really Wonderful Christie Tank

I have earlier related a story in which the Japanese military could not counter the Soviet's newest BT tanks, which appeared suddenly at Nomonhan (see Fig. 10-3). This Soviet BT tank was actually a copy of the tank designed by the pioneer of the F-F system, John W. Christie. While Christie was in the U.S. military's transportation division during World War I (a position he held since 1916), Christie developed this tank, which was to be his last work. The Christie tank is said to have been the end result of a long period of development and evaluation.

During his design efforts, Christie's main concern was speed. He reasoned that if a tank had speed, it could encircle the enemy easily. Detouring around obstacles or enemy strongholds would be possible, and strategic points can be reached before the enemy. Christie had the idea of creating a tank that could travel either with or without tracks; conventional tank could not travel if the tracks were removed. Therefore, Christie's tank reached a speed of 103 km/h on a road with the tracks removed, and 64 km/h with the tracks mounted.

This emphasis on speed was beyond the understanding of tank specialists of other countries. At this time, most people thought that the best way to use tanks was as support for the infantry, whose soldiers were restricted to a necessarily slow pace of advance as they crawled on their stomachs to evade the enemy bullets. Christie, however, envisaged that future tank battles would be like the German-Soviet confrontation on the Soviet plain or the German-American/English tank battles in North Africa. His ideas were not those of an ordinary person. For comparison, the Japanese 89-type tank used in the Nomonhan (Battle of the River Khalkin) had a maximum speed of less than 26 km/h.

No one at the time appreciated Christie's concept of speed except for the Soviet Union. In 1931, the Soviet government purchased two of Christie's 10-ton tanks under the pretext of that they were agricultural tractors. The Soviets then duplicated these tractors, modified them into military tanks, and transported these tanks to Nomonhan. The only way the Japanese could retaliate against the new tanks was by using Molotov cocktails or fire bombs.

The duplication of the Christie tank and further development was carried out by Mikhail Koshkin. Immediately after the battle at Nomonhan, Koshkin replaced the gasoline engine with the diesel engine so as to reduce the hazard of fire with gasoline fuel. This modified tank was later developed into the T34 tank, which has been called the best tank of World War II (Photo 25-1).

Photo 25-1 Glorious T34 tank led the Soviet Union to victory: The tank now sits proudly at the gate of the Moscow war museum. Its achievement should be praised forever, together with its talented designer Koshkin, who foresaw the future trend of the market.

Appearance of the T34 Tank

In July 1941, five months before the Pearl Harbor attack, the German armored corps on the eastern front was terrified at the sudden appearance of the T34 tanks. Douglas Orgill, in his book[25-1], recalled, "One Soviet tank suddenly came out of the cornfield. It had a strange crouching shape. Immediately, several German army tanks fired at it, but without much success. The tank began maneuvering along a road between fields. At the end of that farm road, a German 37-mm antitank cannon was waiting for the tank. It began to rain shells on the approaching Soviet tank. The Soviet tank, unharmed, kept going into the German-held territory, crushing the antitank gun underneath its broad tracks." (See Photo 25-2.) The T34 tank, which thus appeared in the Russo-Germany war, did not burn when hit as easily as those tanks equipped with gasoline engines. Also, because the T34 tank had low fuel consumption, it could travel three to four times the distance of its German counterpart. Making use of its high speed, the T34 tank moved quickly on the Russian plains and eventually led the Soviet Union to victory.

Photo 25-2 The T34 tank appeared suddenly out of the woods: The sight of this tank bearing down on them terrified many German soldiers (The Patton Museum).

Lessons learned from the battle at Nomonhan, data from mechanized unit experiments, and practices evolved from those in England since 1927 were all carefully assimilated into the Soviet tank. Original analysis and research were also performed. The key points were to strengthen both the antitank firepower and the tank's armor.

Fig. 25-1 compares an increase in the thickness of armor plate between Germany and Soviet Union, both countries leading the world in tank production at that time. From this figure, we can see that the Soviet tank quality was progressing faster than that of Germany. The figure is also impressive in view of the Soviet history. The so-called great purge in the Red Army continued from 1937 to 1939, during which time high-ranking and foresighted officers such as General Tukhachevsky were all dismissed or executed. During this period, Koshkin and his team continued to improve tank technology. When the purge was over, they had developed the new T34 tank. This purge is said to have been ordered by Stalin, who labeled the "tankman sitting in an iron box and looking down on the general public as a tool of imperialism and bourgeoisism afraid of the proletariat's power."[25-2]

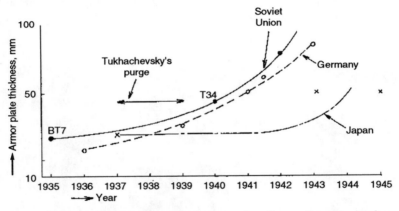

Fig. 25-1 Increase in thickness of armor plate for medium-size tank.

Difference Between the Russian and Japanese Engineering Staffs

The design of the diesel engine in the T34 tank is commonly credited to J. Vikhman and T. Chupakhin. However, this engine was in fact a copy of the Fiat aeroengine. Nevertheless, the improvements made on the T34 tank were the result of studies from Christie's excellent design; lessons learned from the battlefield (market need in today's terminology) were taken into the design immediately; and the competitors' designs were examined and dexterously combined (benchmark activity) to complete the final product, as illustrated in Fig. 25-2. This process should be learned by every designer.

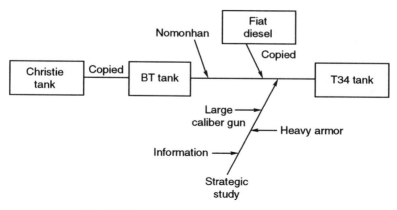

Fig. 25-2 Process of T34 tank development.

The author of *T34 Tank*, D. Orgill, comments, "The T34 was born of people who could visualize the battlefield of the 20th Century [market trend at present]. They were not geniuses but ordinary people. The T34 was the product of normal people with foresight."[25-2]

Let us look at Fig. 25-2 again. What a miserable situation the Japanese tanks were in! In contrast with the Soviet Union, which rapidly learned from the Battle of Nomonhan (the River Khalkin), the Japanese military failed to learn anything from the battle and reactions were slow. Mr. Kohtaro Katogawa, who was associated with the Japanese army tank development and knew the exact situation at that time, explained: "The military staff did not have much understanding of tank operation; partly because there was no one who dared to lead or champion it, weaponry study did not progress significantly as it was influenced by the China Incident, which had no anti-tank battles." He added with disappointment, "The improvement of the 75-mm tank cannon was incredibly slow, taking a full five years."[25-2]

In spite of the Japanese Army's having no political purge such as did the Soviet army, the Japanese tank research work slowed to a halt. On the other hand, the Russian research activities continued in spite of the hardships imposed by the political purge. These reactions show the differences in the commitment of the Japanese and Soviet engineering staff. The difference in devotion and positive thinking for research work between the Soviet Union and Japan resulted in a large technology gap.

Chapter 26

The Enigma of the T34 Tank

Goal-oriented production engineering staff and flexible quality control. The 1930s version of the COCOM (Coordinating Committee for Export to Communist Areas) affair.

✄

Excellent Soviet Union Engineering Staff

When we travel westward beyond Southampton, England, which was the last stop on the tragic voyage of the luxury liner Titanic, we will arrive at the Bovington Camp. In its museum, the T34 tank, taken apart for analysis, has been carefully preserved.

Museum goers are surprised at the sophisticated engineering embodied in the B2 (also called V2) diesel engine used in the T34 tank. The B2 diesel engine, which is said to have been copied from a Fiat, has a double overhead cam (DOHC) and 12 cylinders arranged in a V, as shown in Photo 26-1. The distributing device located between the cylinder banks acts as a pump to inject the air used by the engine directly into the cylinders. This air is used to start the engine in cold weather. When the engine is started, the pump delivers compressed air into the cylinders to increase the compression ratio and temperature. Though the B2 is undoubtedly copied from Fiat, its features have been blended well with the Soviet design (Photo 26-2). The 12-cylinder fuel injection pump at the center of the engine is of the well-known Robert Bosch type, but it was produced in the Soviet Union.

At the time of World War II, Germany, which should have led the world in diesel engine technology, used Maybach's gasoline engine in its tanks. The difference in fuel consumption between the gasoline and diesel engines resulted in a wide variation in the cruising ranges between the German tanks

Photo 26-1 B2 (or V2) type diesel engine for T34 tank: The distributing device at the front is used to inject air directly into the cylinders (Tank museum).

and those of its enemies (Photo 26-3). Given this historic background, a Hitler request that Japan provide the diesel engines for German tanks may be more believable. The engine ordered by Hitler was the Japanese military-standard Type 100, manufactured by the forerunner of Hino Motors, and other companies (Photo 26-4). The data in Appendix A26 show that the Russian B2 had a far better rate of fuel consumption than did the Type 100 engine. The preserved Soviet B2 diesel engine excels in workmanship and appearance. Further, the Soviet Union's tank production reached 24,000 units or more in 1943.[25-2] The Japanese annual tank production, on the other hand, peaked at about 1300 units in 1942.[26-2] This Soviet production level could not have been achieved if it were not for the close working relationship between the design engineers and the production engineers.

The differences in tank production between Japan and the Soviet Union were significant. For example, Japan was satisfied with riveting 20-mm-thick carbonized steel armor plate, which is made by quenching and hardening a steel plate in a carbon atmosphere for an increase in hardness. The Soviets, however, punched 45-mm-thick steel plates with a large press machine.[26-1] The Soviets also adopted a cast steel tank turret 50 mm or more in thickness. The manufacturing process of this thick cast steel turrent was troubled by the inclusion of a large cavity in the front of the turrent, which made the turrent vulnerable to enemy fire. However, the Soviets

Photo 26-2 The Fiat AN1 aerodiesel engine (1930): The compressed air distributor for starting is the same system as that of the B2 used in the T34 tank. Bore × stroke = 140 × 180, six cylinders, 16.6L displacement, for AN1 reconnaissance plane (Fiat Museum).

revised their manufacturing process so that the inclusion was formed on the rear of the T34 turret. This change in position was valuable in that the stronger front of the turret received the brunt of the attack, while the more vulnerable back side received only minimal hits (Photo 26-5). This idea and the casting plan to accomplish it should be admired. Inflexible thinking will not result in such a high-quality standard and could result in failure for the entire plan.

*Photo 26-3 T34 was a "Güte Machine": On a late autumn afternoon, a gentleman
past middle age gazed at the T34 until sunset. A former German tankman,
Mr. Scheitel, said to me, "This tank with a diesel engine had a range of 300 km. Our
Tiger tank with a gasoline engine ran short of fuel at 150 km. That point was the end
of the battle. This was a 'Güte Machine.'" (Military History Museum in Vienna)*

Why Was the Christie Tank Sold?

Military experts acknowledge that the T34 tank developed from the Christie
tank was far better than its contemporary U.S. Sherman tank. In fact, in
1950 the T34 tanks pushed the United Nations forces to the tip of the
Korean peninsula.[26-3] Why then had the Christie tank been sold to the
Soviet Union? During the east-west Cold War, such an arrangement would
have violated the COCOM (Coordinating Committee for Export to Communist Areas) agreement, which was an agreement of western countries
restricting the export of advanced technologies etc. to Communist countries,
concluded in 1949 (Photo 26-6).

During World War I, the U.S. Army had given a contract to J. Walter
Christie for the manufacture of an artillery tractor. Christie closed his Front
Drive Motors, an automotive production company that he had established in
1915, and then devoted himself exclusively to the study and assembly of
tanks. He designed and built a high-speed tank and, later, a prototype
amphibious tank. Although both vehicles satisfactorily passed all acceptance criteria established by the U.S. Army, the tanks were not accepted by

Photo 26-4 Type 100 diesel engine used in many vehicles of the old Japanese military: There was a wide range of versions from an in-line six-cylinder 130 hp to V12-cylinder 300 hp with supercharger. The place in which the fuel injection pipe of each cylinder is accommodated is a prechamber. Cooling air is sucked from around the prechamber and discharged to the opposite side after cooling the cylinders (preserved in Hino Motors).

the conservative and narrow-minded Army officers. Between the first Army test in 1919 and the year 1930, the Army bought only eight tanks (1928 model) despite Christie's devotion, and the blood, sweat, and tears that went into his tanks. It cost Christie $35,000 to assemble each unit of the 1928 model, and his selling price was about $83,000 per tank. However, the Army replied that it had a budget of only $15,000 per tank. As Christie agonized over this impasse with the U.S. Army, the Polish government approached him with an offer of $30,000 per unit and a fee of $90,000 for manufacturing rights.

Then came the Soviet Union. Taking advantage of the stalemated negotiations between Christie and the U.S. Army, the Soviets successfully purchased Christie's tanks for $55,000 each. To meet export restrictions, the cannons were removed, and the tank was registered as an "agricultural tractor." On Christmas Eve of 1930, a ship laden with two Christie tanks departed Pier No. 6 of Staten Island. The Soviet's shopping expedition had nabbed one of the best bargains of the century!

Photo 26-5 Cast steel turret of T34 tank: Internal shrinkage cavities inherent to cast steel are absent on the bullet-receiving front, but cavities up to 20-mm diameter are seen on the back side. This design maintains an adequate product quality for a specific purpose. Quality control is unimaginable from stiff thinking (Tank museum).

Photo 26-6 U.S. Sherman tank: Pushed back to the tip of the Korean peninsula by the Soviet Union's T34 tank developed from the Christie tank, which was originated in the United States (Patton Museum).

This "tractor" mounted the V12 Hispano Suiza 750-hp aeroengine, and had a cruising range up to 320 km, almost matching the range of the later T34. The Soviet B2 engine somewhat resembled this Hispano engine.

Christie Had Made a Mistake, but He Did Not Sell His Soul

During this time, Major Daikaki, a Japanese Army officer, also contacted Christie in an attempt to procure the Christie tanks. However, Christie did not even negotiate with Daikaki, reportedly because of his dislike of the Japanese. Yet, it cannot be denied that the Japanese Army had a foresighted officer.

The Christie tanks shipped to the Soviet Union were first converted into the Bystrokhodnii (Fast) Tank (BT) and later developed into the T34 tank, which eventually defeated Germany's armored corps. Hitler was taken off guard by the German Army's resounding defeat at the Eastern front. After he was informed that the Soviet T34 tank had originated from Christie, Hitler sent a confidential messenger to Christie. The messenger, a man named Stinnes, crossed the ocean in his yacht and offered Christie one million dollars to supervise the German tank production. He reportedly said to his son, "Selling my tanks to Russia was bad enough. The U.S. Army did not penalize me for this mistake. But if I sold my soul, nothing would be left."

The 1930s version of the Christie tank was manufactured by Morris Commercial Cars, Ltd., in England. Later, this tank developed into the cruiser tank A13 (Photo 26-7) which played an active role in the North African front. The A13 tank battled with the German armored corps led by Lieutenant General Rommel. The degree of development of the A13 was much less than that of the Soviet T34 tank. This development can be attributed to the difference in the basic concept of tank design and tactics used by the differing countries. Could this difference be attributed solely to Koshkin's leadership?

After the Russian sale of his tanks, Christie undertook a study of a flying tank. He was assisted by P. Tucker, who has been discussed earlier in this book. Christie's flying tank was a lightweight tank transported by an airplane with a rear engine system.[26-4] From his experience with Christie, we can see the background and connection that led Tucker to develop a rear-engine car.

Photo 26-7 England's 1941 cruiser tank, Crusader MKII: Christie suspension wheels are laid out the same as the T34, but the gun (40 mm) was powerless. Engine: Nuffield Liberty MKIII V12 water-cooled gasoline 340 PS (South African war museum).

Appendix A26 B2 (or V2) Diesel Engine for T34 Tank

The B2 diesel engine was composed of aluminum alloy and had a direct injection system with 60° V12 cylinders, overhead camshafts, 150-mm bore, 180-mm stroke on main connecting rod side, and 186.7-mm stroke on sub-connecting rod side. The subconnecting rod layout is shown in Fig A26-1. This diesel engine had a 38.8-L displacement and four valves with the fuel injection nozzle in the center of the cylinder and had a capability of producing 500 hp/1800 rpm, a maximum engine speed of 2000 rpm, and an output per displacement of 12.9 hp/liter. To my surprise, the fuel consumption was only about 170 g/PS-h. The Japanese diesel engine could not obtain this level before the 1970s. The water and oil pumps were positioned at the lowest level, so we can see attempts to minimize problems resulting from inadequate oil supply.

In contrast, the Japanese Type 100 diesel engine at that time was of a pre-combustion chamber design. Although details are unconfirmed, its fuel consumption was estimated to be above 200 g/PS-h. The Type 100 engine had the following specifications; 120-mm bore, 160-mm stroke, and 120-hp (11 hp/liter) with six cylinders. The largest engine in this series was a super-charged V12 (in trial manufacture) that delivered 300 hp.[26-5] However, it is

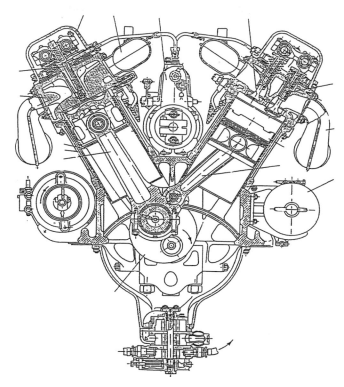

Fig. A26-1 B2 (V2) diesel engine: Oil and water pumps are located at the lower end of the engine. The designers were thinking of the survival of the engine even with battle damage or under extreme operating conditions (or to withstand abuse). However, the subconnecting rod system, direct-operated valve gear (intake/exhaust valves directly driven by camshaft), etc., are quite the same as those of the Fiat gasoline aeroengine.

worth mentioning that this diesel engine was air-cooled. In particular, the suction-type cooling from the prechamber side (port side), which was high in thermal load, was an excellent arrangement (Photo 26-4).

Chapter 27

Dream in Star-Shaped, Radial Engine (I)

An extraordinary idea in which a star is rotated. Marriage of rotary stars. Gnome-Rhone, a growth accomplished by throwing away pride.

What Is a Star-Shaped Engine (Radial Engine)?

In most companies, a new employee is assigned to a production site to gain some practical experience for some period of time. After undergoing such a period of orientation, I was assigned to the design division. One day, I could not locate a drawing easily in the drawing room, and I had to search in several other possible locations for the missing drawing. While searching, I happened to see the design drawing of an old star-shaped (radial) diesel engine. In a radial engine, the cylinders are provided in a radial pattern. This particular design was for a water-cooled engine rather than the air-cooling configuration usually employed for the radial cylinder layout. This particular engine was planned to be mounted on the Japanese Army's high-speed landing craft.

Although the expression "star" as used for a radial engine is a rather romantic one, the English term for this engine is actually "radial engine," reminding us of nothing other than machinery. I am impressed by the rich sensitivity of the person who called it "star." To my disappointment, he is not a Japanese, but perhaps he was a Frenchman. I suggest France because it appears to have been the earliest origin of the radial engine, even though the term "radial engine" is *moteur en etoile* in French and *stern-motor* in German, both identifying a star. Because of advanced development of other

engine configurations, we have almost no chance of seeing the radial engine
in the practical use. However, this engine developed explosively during
World War I. In World War II, the major aircraft engines were roughly classified into air-cooled radial engines and liquid-cooled engines with cylinders arranged in a V configuration. In the final stages of World War II, the
radial engine was used widely to obtain the highest power output. Even
after the war, the large output of the radial engine was unparalleled, and it
co-existed with the jet engine for some time.

However, such a large output engine was unnecessary except in airplanes.
This engine was too awkward to use in vehicles, so it never gained general
acceptance. Nevertheless, this engine was the realization of many people's
dreams.

Hino Motors and GM Oppose Each Other with Stars Afloat on Sea

First, I will recount the dream of Hino Motors (then Hino Heavy Industry
Co.), the plans of which had lain in a corner of the drawing room. Around
1942, the radial engine concept was planned under the responsibility of
engineer Kyoji Mutoh (later appointed as president of Hino Motor Sales
Co., Ltd.) in response to the Japanese Army's need. The military specified a
water-cooled, radial, seven-cylinder, 80-hp, diesel engine. A prime requirement was that the engine be lightweight enough to allow four soldiers to
disassemble and carry the engine. The final weight could be no more than
200 kg, including the reverse gear (used to reverse the screw rotation so as
to move a ship backward). To meet this weight goal, aluminum was used as
much as possible. As illustrated in Fig. 27-1, the propeller was driven by the
engine that was laid horizontally on the bottom of a landing craft. This
engine layout was an unusual idea. If the design were successful, this engine
could have held a prominent niche in the history of engines.

However, the United States was also working on a similar scheme. General
Motors was producing a lightweight and compact four-row radial, that is, 16
cylinders and 1200 hp. This engine was reportedly mounted in a submarine
chaser for hunting Japanese submarines (Photo 27-1). Thus, across the
Pacific Ocean, Hino Motors and General Motors faced each other with each
"star" (radial engine) afloat on the sea, though the scale differed between
them.

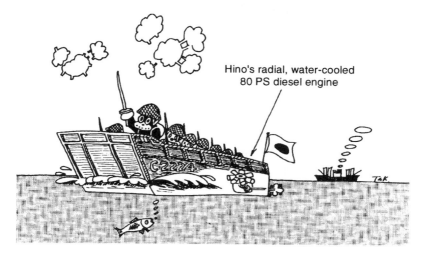

Fig. 27-1 Hino's water-cooled radial engine planned for landing craft.[10-2]

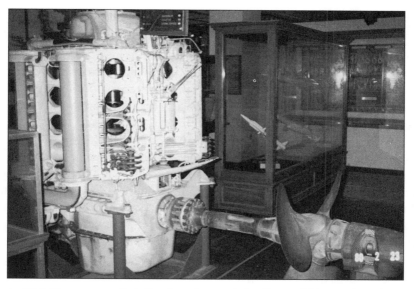

Photo 27-1 Four-row radial diesel engine made by General Motors for submarine chaser: Variable pitch and reversible propeller. 1200 PS/1800 rpm, 2200 kg (piston is removed and stacking of four-cylinders in four rows can be seen) (U.S. Marine Corps Museum).

Success of Gnome Engine

The radial engine was originally developed to serve as the powerplant for aircraft. Just as Bleriot's Anzani air-cooled engine had problems with over-heating in its first crossing of the Strait of Dover, the initial radial air-cooled engine also had inadequate cooling capability. To cope with this limitation, an engine intended to enhance the cooling performance by rotating the engine together with the propeller was developed. Conceived from this innovative idea was the 1909 Gnome engine (Photo 27-2), a collaborative effort of Laurent Seguin and his younger brother. However, the Seguin brothers initially made this engine for a Grand Prix racing car. Their design, called the rotary[1] engine, solved the overheating problem and spread rap-idly to become the most popular aircraft engine in World War I (refer to Appendix A27-1).

The success of the Gnome engine resulted in a number of similar engines; these spinoffs include the Bentley in England, the Siemens in Germany, and the Rhone in France, to name a few. In Japan as well, the forerunner of Hino Motors, Gasuden (Tokyo Gas & Electrical Industry Company, Ltd.) manu-factured the Le Rhone engine on license[27-1] (Appendix 27-2).

Rhone later merged with Gnome to establish Gnome-Rhone, going on to manufacture the Gnome-Rhone engine for several years. In this merger, both the company names and their engine names were joined. Moreover, it is interesting to note that the engine design also appears to have merged two different elements. Photo 27-3 shows the Gnome and Rhone engines and the 1920's Gnome-Rhone engine. As shown in the photos, the Gnome-Rhone engine appears to have been made by simply overlaying the design drawings of the two predecessor engines. Were only simple addi-tions made on the company name and design because both company's administrative executives did not agree to the loss of their own company name and their engineering staffs did not concede the change of their own designs? As a compromise, they just combined everything. If this is the case, then this merger might be said to be the corruption of engineering. However, when the post-merger engine is carefully examined, it seems that both companies were willing to give and take as necessary. For example, from the Gnome engine, the intake valve in the piston was removed, even though it had appeared to be a clever idea (see Appendix A27-1). Also the pushrod, which had not been incorporated in the Rhone engine, was added

---

1. In the general term, a rotary engine is one in which the piston rotor rotates. It is equipped with a rotor housing in lieu of cylinders. The rotary engine as used here by the author indicates the engine itself rotates about the stationary crankshaft, though the usual cylinders and reciprocal pistons are used.

Photo 27-2 Gnome 50 PS engine (1909): Engine and propeller are coupled into an integral unit, so that the propeller rotates together with the engine. Mounted on Henry Farman Model III biplane for its first flight, during which its excellence was recognized (Movieland of the Air Museum).

to the front face of the engine. Thus, technical progress appears to have been made. We should not hang onto our pride when unnecessary. Even when we have had to swallow our pride, we can see the legitimacy of good engineering in the resultant product and understand the fresh philosophy of concerned engineers.

Photo 27-3 Gnome-Rhone engine fabricated by joining the Gnome and the Rhone engines: [Top] Gnome 160 PS engine (1917); [Center] Rhone 120 PS engine (1917); [Bottom] Gnome-Rhone engine provided with the Gnome exhaust valve gear mechanism and the Rhone suction pipes (1920) (Musée de L'Air Paris).

Appendix A27-1 The Gnome Engine Was Formed from an Abundance of Ideas

In the Gnome engine, the pistons and cylinders rotate at a speed of about 1150 to 1250 rpm. As shown in Fig. A27-1, the crankshaft is fixed to the airplane structure and does not rotate. The rear shaft of the crankshaft is hollow, through which gasoline and air are supplied, but this engine does not have a carburetor. The gasoline, which was gravity-fed, flowed through the inside of the crankshaft, entered the crankcase, and entered the combustion chamber through the intake valve in the piston crown.

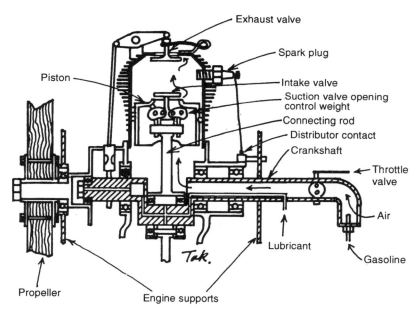

Fig. A27-1 Gnome engine (only one cylinder shown schematically): Four-stroke cycle, air-cooled, radial seven-cylinder rotary type. 110-mm bore, 120-mm stroke, 8L displacement, 50 PS/1200 rpm. Crankshaft (hatched area) fixed to machine body. Engine and propeller rotate as an integral unit.

The engine needed a carburetor badly, but either the carburetors were not yet available or were considered unreliable at that time. In any event, there was an air throttle valve (Fig. A27-1) and a fuel needle valve (not shown in Fig A27-1). To start the engine, both valves were set to a predetermined mark, which provided the correct air/fuel ratio and the amount of mixture needed (both approximate) for idle. In general, the only other power setting

used was full power. When ready for take-off, the pilot opened the air throttle wide open. Because the air/fuel ratio immediately went above the lean
mixture limit, the engine died. However, the large rotational inertia of the
engine kept it rotating while the pilot opened the fuel needle valve and
adjusted it to obtain the correct air/fuel ratio. Then, the engine remained at
full power until the mission was complete. For landing, the pilot needed to
control the power output. To obtain this control, an ignition cut-out button
was provided in the cockpit that would permit short bursts of power with
intermittent shut-off during those times that less than full continuous power
was required. Castor oil was conventional at that time for engine lubrication. However, castor oil will not dissolve in gasoline and therefore the two
cannot be mixed. Therefore, castor oil was supplied separately into the
crankshaft at a fixed rate from the oil pump.

The gasoline atomized in the crankcase mixes with air properly and enters
the combustion chamber through the intake valve located at the top of the
piston. After ignition and combustion, the exhaust gas was discharged
through the exhaust valve on the top of the cylinder. The intake valve automatically opens due to a negative pressure in the combustion chamber
when the piston moves toward the bottom of the cylinder. However, since
this valve has a tendency to remain open because of the centrifugal force
caused by engine rotation, a small weight is attached to the bottom of the
valve to counteract the centrifugal force. In some versions, a cam is provided at the upper end of the connecting rod in order to control the opening
timing of the intake air valve, though it is not shown in this figure. It is not
known if the weight and its mechanism were used together with the connecting rod cam.

Appendix A27-2 The Origin and Growth of Gasuden's Aeroengines, the Shimpu (KAMIKAZE) and the Tempu (AMAKAZE)

The first Japanese domestic aeroengine was produced by Gasuden (Tokyo
Gas & Electrical Industry Company, Ltd.) in 1928. The company record[27-2]
at that time is quoted below.

"Presently, a majority of the principal engines used for civilian and
national aircraft are manufactured in domestic private and government-
owned factories. However, in any case, the manufacturing license has
been acquired from a foreign organization. It is regretful that our inde-
pendence is yet to come in this field. Following the governmental policy

for encouraging domestic products, our company has aimed to relieve Japanese aircraft manufacturing industry from the above-mentioned disadvantage and began research and manufacture with domestic materials, based on our original design, this spring. Despite our expectation of hardship in this project, it advanced steadily, and the original work was completed at the end of business term. The completed aircraft engine was named 'Shimpu' [Author's Note: Shimpu means *in God's wind*, and is probably influenced by the name of great engine 'whirlwind' or 'Jupiter'] and application was submitted to the aviation bureau subordinate to the Ministry of Communications. In the presence of authorized inspectors, an operational inspection and a variety of strict tests were carried out continuously for 50 hours. During this long period, our product had no troubles and completely satisfied the standards stipulated in the aviation laws. Thus, we received a commendation from the witnessing inspectors and will surely be granted an airworthiness certificate by the appropriate authorities soon."

These words convey the enthusiasm of the Gasuden staff at that time. For the successful completion of this engine, Gasuden was commended by the Minister of Communications and was awarded a letter of commendation and a silver cup. Later, other companies such as Nakajima and Mitsubishi began the domestic production of aeroengine. After one year or in 1929 (or 1930?) the Nakajima famous Kotobuki engine received an official examination of endurance operation.[27-3]

Shimpu (Kamikaze in some English translations) initially had 130 hp, which was developed up to 160 hp in the Shimpu Type 11 (Type 95, which is the Japanese code number). The Shimpu engine was used in the primary trainer planes of the Japanese Army and Navy. These planes were nicknamed Red Dragonflies. On the other hand, Tempu, which means *in Heaven's wind* (Amakaze in some English translations) underwent development up to Tempu revision 5 (Army's code number Type 98) having 515 hp. This engine was used in medium and advanced trainer airplanes and Type 98 close support reconnaissance aircraft (aircraft for reconnaissance in direct cooperation with ground forces) (Photos A27-1 and 2). The Gasuden aeroengines and aircraft were initially designed and manufactured in the company's automobile division. Subsequently, Gasuden assumed responsibility for manufacturing the Koken long-range research aircraft designed by the Aeronautical Research Institute of Tokyo Imperial University. In May 1938, this aircraft established a world record for the length of its cruising range, demonstrating Japan's dominance in aeronautical engineering at that time (Photo A27-3). The aircraft division was then separated as an

*Photo A27-1 Japan's first mass-production aeroengine "Shimpu" (God's Wind):
115-mm bore, 120-mm stroke, 8.72L displacement, 130 PS/1800 rpm,
expanded to 240 PS.*

independent company named Hitachi Aircraft Company, Ltd. During World
War II, this company played an active role by developing several original
engines. One of these engines was the "Ha-51," a two-row, 2500-hp, 43.8L
displacement radial engine with 22 cylinders, made from a double row of
single row air-cooled radial engines of 11 cylinders.

In concept, this engine was similar to the Pratt & Whitney Model R4360
radial four-stroke engine with four rows of seven cylinders, the world's
largest air-cooled radial engine. It also had a similarity to the Junkers Jumo

Photo A27-2 Type 98 Ki-36 close support and reconnaissance aircraft [Type 99 (Ki-55) advanced trainer]: Equipped with the Gasuden engine (Ha-13A made by Hitachi Aircraft Company, Ltd., 515 PS/2000 rpm) (Royal Thai Air Force Museum).

Photo A27-3 Koken long-range research aircraft under assembly in the Gasuden Ohmori factory: Lean mixture combustion was applied to reduce fuel consumption. As a result, the exhaust gas temperature rose. The unique air cooling system was invented and adopted to cool the exhaust valve. The Roots blower required for air cooling was designed by Y. Azuma, Gasuden. After assembly, the aircraft could not be taken from the building because the wing was blocked by the door. Therefore, the building was cut. (This incident demonstrated that all involved staff members were overexcited by this project.)

Model 222E radial two-stroke engine with four rows of six cylinders, which was Germany's ultralarge output engine in the final stages of World War II (see Chapter 31). However, the one-row arrangement with the large number of 11 cylinders was not duplicated among the world's engines. For this arrangement, the relative open angle between the intake and exhaust valves was narrowed due to the limited space between cylinders with limited engine diameter for the aeroplane. This angle is of great importance to cooling between the intake and exhaust ports or valves (see Chapter 28). The angle was widened in the Pratt & Whitney engine to increase the power output. Yet, the reasoning behind the open angle in the Ha-51 engine is unknown. The Ha-51 had the following specifications; 130-mm bore, 150-mm stroke, with two-stage supercharger, and manifold fuel injection system. Its fuel injection pump was a swashplate-type made by Hitachi Ltd. (Photo A27-4).

Photo A27-4 One of unique works Ha-51, 130-mm bore, 150-mm stroke, 43.8L displacement, 2450 PS/3000 rpm, 22-cylinder engine: Photographed at the Gasuden Tachikawa factory. Company records indicate this engine was reassembled as ordered by the U.S. Armed Forces in 1952 (Courtesy of Mr. J. Ogawa, 1985).

Chapter 28

Dream in Star-Shaped, Radial Engine (II)

The failure of Samuel Langley, who neglected to consider human foibles. A decision made with reckless abandon, which yielded a period of remarkable ideas.

Century's Masterpiece Born from a Hungry Spirit

I had earlier attributed the idea of the radial rotary (turning) engine to the Seguin brothers. However, a passenger car with an air-cooled radial rotary (turning) engine had been placed on the market in the United States two years before the Seguin brothers fabricated their long-distance Grand Prix racing car, that is, in 1906. This car was called the "Adams Farwell." Only one Adams Farwell automobile remains, and that is in the Harrah Automobile Collection. It is a rear-engine car having an innovative design for its time (Fig. 28-1, Photo 28-1). According to its sales literature[(28-1)], the Adams Farwell engine incorporated a compact design, did not require a flywheel, and had an excellent cooling ability. Therefore, it is highly probable that this engine was a valuable source of information for the Seguin brothers, who completed their superb engine.

In the quest for knowledge, information is not received simply for the asking. Instead, information should always be sought and snapped up like a hungry eagle that never fails to spot the minute movements of its prey. The Seguin brothers hungered for an idea to improve their own Grand Prix car. Because of this need, they saw the opportunity to use innovative ideas successfully. Given the opportunities opened up by World War I, they became famous and were successful. The moral to the Seguin success is that

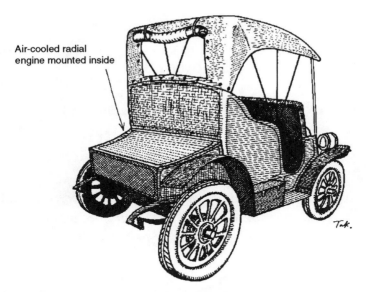

Air-cooled radial
engine mounted inside

Fig. 28-1 Adams Farwell automobile (1906) with air-cooled radial engine, five-cylinder, 40 to 45 PS, priced at $2500. Air-cooled radial engine mounted inside.

Photo 28-1 Engine of the Adams Farwell car: Innovative air-cooled, radial rotary-type engine with 127-mm bore, 127-mm stroke, 8.05L displacement, 40 to 45 PS. Vertical cooling fins accommodate the centrifugally forced airflow (Harrah Automobile Collection).

engineers must always keep a sharp eye out for the next plan and have the ambition to carry it through.

Tragedy of Langley's *Aerodome*

The origin of the radial engine is older yet. In 1894 Stephen M. Balzer designed and manufactured a car using a radial engine as the powerplant. The vehicle, currently exhibited at the Smithsonian Institution in Washington, DC, looks like two bicycles coupled together as shown in Photo 28-2. Inside the undercarriage is a three-cylinder radial rotary engine. This engine attracted the attention of Samuel Langley (then Secretary of the Smithsonian Institution). Langley later competed with the Wright brothers to accomplish the first successful airplane flight. Balzer received a contract from Langley to manufacture the engine of Langley's airplane (named the *Aerodome*). However, Balzer failed to complete the engine successfully because he had drastically underestimated the development time. Such a development effort would probably have taken at least two years. Balzer, because of his enthusiasm for the radial engine, reportedly agreed to complete the engine in a three-month timeframe. No development effort can be successfully completed only with enthusiasm.

Photo 28-2 Balzer's quadricycle made in 1894, perhaps the second car made in the United States. The Duryea automobile was manufactured in 1893. A full-fledged rotary engine is mounted under the floor (Smithsonian Museum).

After the Balzer attempt failed, both the rotary and nonrotating radial engines were tested for Langley's *Aerodome* by young Charles M. Manly of Cornell University. As a result of these comparative tests, the nonrotating radial engine was selected, according to Professor C.F. Taylor.[28-2] Manly incorporated the nonrotating radial engine into the *Aerodome* even though Langley's earlier contract with Balzer showed that Langley preferred the rotary engine. The nonrotating radial engine was used because tests had indicated that the rotary radial engine had a lower power output. This decreased output was apparently caused by the effects of centrifugal force on the intake valve. After switching to the nonrotating radial engine, the power output reportedly doubled.

Manly's engine was technically outstanding for his time. It used a 1.6-mm-thick cast iron cylinder liner (the Hino Motors 1.5-mm cast iron cylinder liner is currently one of the thinnest in the world), and a hollow connecting rod. These innovations allowed the engine to achieve a weight per unit of displacement volume of 5.4 kg/liter and a weight-to-horsepower ratio of 1.17 kg/PS. These levels are excellent even though these values represent dry weights and exclude accessories, oil, or fuel. The modern-day automotive gasoline engine has approximate values of 70 to 120 kg/liter and 1.2 to 2 kg/PS, both of which are higher than the Manly engine. It is said that this lightweight engine survived a 10-hour continuous test run; if so, it was a masterpiece at that stage of engine development (Photo 28-3).

To complete the story, nine days before the Wright brothers accomplished their first flight, the *Aerodome* failed in its second test flight and plunged into the Potomac River in Washington, DC. The pilot in this failed flight was Manly himself. Yet Manly had never before even attempted to fly an airplane! In fact, he had not even undergone ground school training with the plane. A historical photograph taken from a catapult on a ship shows the *Aerodome* just before it fell into the water. Manly must hold the record as the only engineer thrown into the ice-cold Potomac River twice.

Since these events, both Langley's *Aerodome* and Manly's engine have received a high technical ranking. However, I can say that the *Aerodome's* fall was not a simple technical failure but instead was a failure to consider the overall man-machine relationship. Even though preliminary tests may give the designers confidence in their work, any system that does not consider the man-machine relationship at its very beginning will fail, even in today's age of advanced automation. Basically, the machine must be considered as an extension of human abilities or as a surrogate of man. Therefore, man must provide some input into the man-machine relationship. This

Photo 28-3 The Manly five-cylinder radial engine mounted to the Langley Aerodome, which competed with the Wright brothers' plane in the first successful flight: 127-mm bore, 140-mm stroke, 8.87L displacement, 52 PS. The cylinder is air-cooled; only the cylinder head is water-cooled. The cylinder liner is made of 1.6-mm-thick cast iron, reinforced by 1.6-mm steel pipes. The connecting rod is hollow. Weight-to-horsepower is 1.17 kg/PS, and weight per unit of displacement volume is 5.4 kg/L (These values are achieved today only in engines for racing cars) (Smithsonian Museum).

relationship needs a preliminary lesson. The wing of Langley's *Aerodome*, which fell into the Potomac, is in the warehouse of the Smithsonian Institution (Photo 28-4). Current plans are to restore the *Aerodome*. I would prefer that the wing be left unrepaired so as to give a living demonstration of technology to engineers.

The Root of the "Star" or Radial Engine Was in Australia

Let us return to the story of the radial rotary engine. According to literature, Laurence Hargrave, an Australian, visualized the radial piston concept as a compressed air engine in 1887[28-3], one year after Benz manufactured the first automobile. At that time, Hargrave taught aeronautics in New South Wales in Australia. He succeeded in test-flying a model flapping-wing aircraft equipped with a radial rotary engine[28-4] (see Fig. 28-2). Later, Hargrave invented the box kite, which was adopted by the famous Santos Dumont. Dumont's "box-kite" aircraft made the first powered flight in

Photo 28-4 Wing of Langley's Aerodome *awaiting restoration in the warehouse of the Smithsonian Museum. However, I would prefer that the wing remain unrestored so as to provide instruction to engineers (Smithsonian Museum).*

Europe. Hargrave's initial airplane already had a "spinning star," which is a rotary radial engine. Hargrave reportedly designed more than 50 kinds of aircraft engines from 1885 to 1915. However, it is difficult to believe that he wanted to rotate the engine in his flapping-wing aircraft (Photo 28-5) to improve engine cooling. Wasn't it Balzer who rotated his engine for better cooling? Anyway, we must say it to be epochal that Gnome introduced the idea of a rotary mechanism for cooling, independently of Hargrave or Balzer. Regardless of who conceived the idea, the rotary engine reached its peak of production during World War I.

More Valve Consumed Than Fuel

During World War I, England's All British Engine Company (ABC) abandoned the rotary radial engine and adopted the plain radial (nonrotating) engine. In the final stages of the war, the ABC's Wasp engine was mounted on a fighter aircraft produced by the British Aerial Transport (BAT) Company. This aircraft could achieve very high speed. Obviously, the designers expected that the high flight speed would result in a sufficient airstream flowing over the engine to cool it without engine rotation.

Fig. 28-2 The inventor of the rotary engine also invented the box kite. The box kite evolved into the Santos-Dumont 14 bis and had the honor of making the first powered flight in Europe.

Photo 28-5 One of Hargrave's aircraft engines: He reportedly designed more than 50 kinds of engines between 1884 and 1915, some of which were used in Europe (Power House Museum).

However, this self-cooling concept did not work. The Wasp engine was another example of inadequate cylinder head cooling. Unfortunately, the engine garnered a bad reputation, as did its larger brother, the Dragonfly engine, manufactured at the same time. The Wasp engine designers did not sufficiently understand the technical aspects of the engine cooling problem. Only after the engineers thoroughly understood the principles of engine cooling should ABC have abandoned the proven rotary radial engine. The engineers' poor understanding of the technical principles of cooling is demonstrated when the only measure taken to improve the Wasp's cooling capabilities from the Gnome engine was to copperplate the cooling fins. There was almost no change in the cylinder structure from the earlier Gnome engine.[28-5] (See Appendix A28-1.)

Change should not be made just for change's sake. Change should be made only after fully examining all possible contingencies. Insufficient time to carry out these careful experiments is no excuse. Even in the face of a rapidly escalating war, engineers must make extraordinary efforts to complete a detailed test program.

An even worse case was the Dragonfly engine, which was designed by simply scaling-up the poorly cooled Wasp engine. In this larger engine, thermal deformation of the cylinder head area caused the valves to burn one after another. The valve wear rate (in units of kilograms per operational hour) was reported to be greater than the fuel consumption rate of the engine. Yet, fueled by this frantic determination, the nonrotating radial concept continued to be used in the Cosmos Jupiter engine (forerunner of the Bristol Jupiter, on which Japanese aircraft engines such as Nakajima's Kotobuki were later modeled) as well as other radial engines.

However, with the changeover from the rotary radial to the nonrotating radial, some of the disadvantages inherent in rotating the engine disappeared immediately. For example, centrifugal forces pushed the oil on the cylinder walls into the combustion chamber. As a result, the oil consumption was very high, reaching as much as 30% of the fuel consumption. The unburned castor oil was discharged into the slipstream, together with the exhaust gas, to quickly blacken the pilot's face.[28-6] The airplane mounting this engine was equipped with an elegant cowling. However, the cowling was not a cover to reduce air resistance, but rather to prevent the pilot from breathing the castor oil.[28-7] (See Photo 28-6.)

The nonrotating radial ABC engine consumed 20 g of oil per horsepower-hour, while the rotary radial Gnome engine used 90 g per horsepower-hour, more than four times as much. See Fig. 7-2 in Chapter 7.

Photo 28-6 Engine cowl (cover) attached to avoid the pilot's breathing of castor oil: Bottom view of REP Model K plane (Musée de L'Air Paris).

Another major disadvantage of the rotary radial had to do with turning the airplane in flight. The airplane mounting the rotary radial engine is like an airplane with a large spinning top mounted on its nose. When one attempts to turn a spinning top in any direction, a force is produced at right angles to that direction. This force is called the *gyro effect*. Therefore, when the airplane turns in any direction, its nose is also turned at right angles to that direction due to the gyro effect (Fig. 28-3). This unwanted feature causes poor maneuverability of the airplane. The great sacrifice made to increase cooling may have been felt again upon abandoning the rotary engine.

However, we must acknowledge that the idea of using the rotary engine in airplanes was an excellent one. The fact that this engine was used in at least one generation of aircraft engines signals the victory of engineering. Also, the decision of ABC to abandon the dominant rotary radial engine in favor of the nonrotating radial was the correct one in view of its understanding of the technological trends. Still, engineering efforts that fail to give the finishing touch to the program are unfortunate.

Appendix A28 Cooling Problem in the ABC Engine

The iron cylinder head of the ABC Wasp engine was plated with copper to improve the cooling performance of the cooling fins. Copper does have a

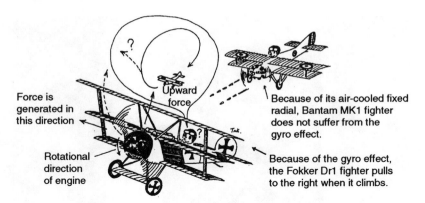

Fig. 28-3 Duel of Fokker versus Bantam. When a gyro (engine) is rotated upward,
the axis of rotation is deflected at right angles to the force. This phenomenon is known
as the "gyro effect."

larger thermal conductivity than iron. However, is cooling facilitated by
copper plating? As illustrated in Fig. A28-1, the wall thickness of the iron
cylinder head is x, gas temperature is T_1, and the coolant temperature is T_4.
The quantity of heat transferred through the iron cylinder head to the coolant in unit time is given by the following equation:

$$Q = KA(T_1 - T_4)\left(\frac{Kcal}{h}\right) \tag{1}$$

where K = overall heat transfer coefficient (Kcal/m^{2}h°C)

$$K = \frac{1}{\left(\dfrac{1}{K_1} + \dfrac{x}{C_{FE}} + \dfrac{1}{K_2}\right)} \tag{2}$$

where

A = Surface area of wall (m^2)
K_1 = Heat transfer coefficient on the coolant side of the wall
         (Kcal/m^{2}h°C)
K_2 = Heat transfer coefficient on the combustion gas side of the
         wall (Kcal/m^{2}h°C)
C_{CU} = Thermal conductivity of copper (332 Kcal/mh°C)
C_{FE} = Thermal conductivity of iron (58 Kcal/mh°C)

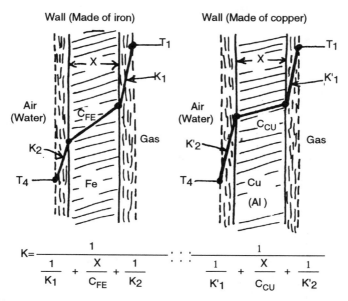

Fig. A28-1 Temperatures across head wall, and overall heat transfer coefficient.

The values of K_1 and K_2 depend on many factors (such as the velocity of gas flow across the surface), but they usually vary between 10 and 50 Kcal/m^2h°C when the medium is air. When the surface of the iron cylinder head is plated with copper, the K value is obtained by setting the value of x/c equal to:

$$\frac{x}{c} = \frac{x_{FE}}{C_{FE}} + \frac{t}{C_{CU}} \tag{3}$$

Now, in Eq. (2), let the value of K_1 and K_2 be equal to 50 Kcal/m^2h°C, x equal to 2 cm, and the plating thickness equal to 0.2 cm (as an example). The value of the plating thickness t per C_{CU} is about 6×10^{-6}, which is negligibly small compared to X_{FE}/C_{FE}, which is 1.1×10^{-4}. This small value means that the effect of the plating on heat transfer is negligible, and copper plating is an ineffective cooling improvement. Moreover, both those values added together are small compared to $1/K_1 + 1/K_2$, so the heat flow through the cylinder head is minimally affected by the thermal conductivity of the cylinder wall, much less by a thin plating of copper. The human is an animal with many illusions. Therefore, we must always confirm the logical and scientific truths.

Fig. A28-2 compares the head of the Cosmos Engineering Jupiter engine, which appeared slightly later than the ABC engine, with the Gibson head, which subsequently became popular among air-cooled engines. The Jupiter engine had some success owing to the use of an aluminum head, but excessive cylinder head deformation prevented a satisfactory service life. As time passed, the Jupiter head evolved into the Gibson head. The Gibson head is a result of detailed experiments on the Renault air-cooled V8 engine (Photo A28-1) made by England's A.H. Gibson and S.D. Heron. The clearance between valves was increased to allow better cooling of the critical zone between the valves. This cylinder design made high power output possible and provided the basis for the development of subsequent high-output air-cooled radial engines.

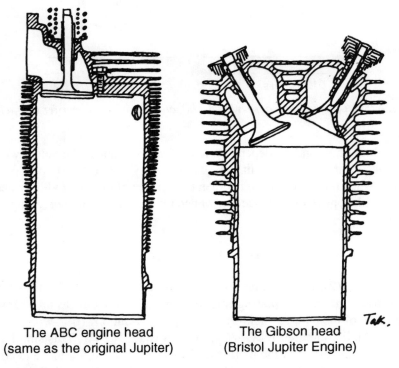

The ABC engine head
(same as the original Jupiter)

The Gibson head
(Bristol Jupiter Engine)

Fig. A28-2 The head of the ABC engine (the same as the original Cosmos Jupiter) and the Gibson-type head. The Cosmos Jupiter engine later became the Bristol Jupiter engine, and its head was replaced with the Gibson type, which is unique in that the valves are inclined to flow the air.

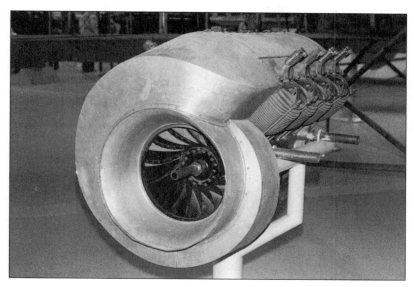

Photo A28-1 Renault air-cooled V8 engine, with which Gibson and Heron repeated detailed experiment (50 hp, 1908): Push-type cooling design with radial fan (Type 100 diesel engine employed suction-type fan, see Fig. 23-4) (Musée de L'Air Paris).

Chapter 29

A Group of Fallen "Stars" (Radial Engine)

A new product does not always contain new technology. Is it possible to be a product even if its technical viewpoint is out of sight?

�֎

Brief Appearance and Extinction Like a Meteor

In Balzer's time, neither the automobile nor its engine was yet formulated. Therefore, the radial engine mounted on an automobile should be accepted as a design concept. Rather, adoption of the rotary engine may be admired as an innovative design.

How should the Adams Farwell car be evaluated? The emergence of this car (Fig. 29-1) must have provided a valuable source of information for the Gnome engine. However, the shape and structure of the automobile were still being established at the time of Adams Farwell, so his design concept cannot be accepted unconditionally. It is true that weight was reduced with the elimination of the flywheel. However, did these advantages of the Farwell car surpass its drawbacks when comparing its complicated fuel and ignition systems, and the overall space, with those of other common designs? An engineer may emphatically answer "No!"; yet, some products may require a newness and a sense of novelty, which dazzles users, that extends beyond the domain of pure technology. The public soon awakens from its bemusement. If, after awakening, no fruit is still in the buyer's hand, the merchandise will soon disappear from the market. In other words, if the buyer doesn't receive value for his money, the product will vanish from the marketplace. Then, from this viewpoint, we trace the history of some radial engines, which appeared and then disappeared.

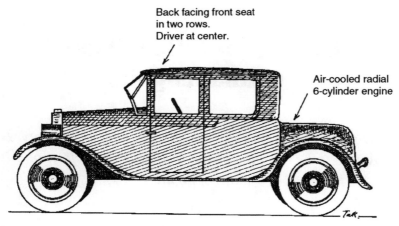

Back facing front seat
in two rows.
Driver at center.

Air-cooled radial
6-cylinder engine

Fig. 29-1 The 1925 Julian automobile: The brake was adjustable from the driver's seat. The long slogan "Snappiest, most beautiful, and easiest riding car in America" was used.

People Tracing "Stars" (Radial Engine)

It was 1925, or 20 years after the Adams Farwell car, when Julian Brown, reportedly an automobile designer, manufacturer, and inventor, successfully designed a new automobile. He was also a wealthy owner of a restaurant and club. His car, illustrated in Fig. 29-1, was made of aluminum and had a seating capacity of five passengers. The driver sat in the center seat. Across from the driver, two passengers sat facing the rear, while in the back seat two persons sat facing the front. This car was equipped with a radial twin-row six-cylinder, 60-hp engine as shown in Photo 29-1. The car, which got 8.5 km/L of fuel, was the sort that a rich playboy, who dreamed of a leisurely drive with two beautiful women in the seats opposite him, would like. However, Brown ended up making only his one car. Although the car appeared to have been a rather good one technically, it was probably too expensive to be competitive.

We move on to Europe in 1919. The Frenchman Marcel Leyat designed and made an air screw (air propelled) car according to his own theory and drove it through the Paris streets (Photo 29-2). Since cars such as the Renault and Peugeot still had exposed driver seats, the same as old horse-drawn carriages, dashing Marcel's car was certainly a demonstration of his

Photo 29-1 Julian engine: Air-cooled, radial, twin-row, six cylinders, 60 PS. Though this engine was based on the aircraft engine, the nonrotating type rather than the rotary type was adopted. Rather good design sense can be felt on the cooling fan, etc. (Harrah Automobile Collection).

Photo 29-2 The 1920 Marcel Leyat: Driven by propeller, this car ran through the Paris streets amid the more conventional automobiles (Musée de L'Automobile Le Mans).

engineering skills. With the spoke wheel reshaped with cloth, this car traveled at 70-80 km/h with a fuel consumption reportedly of 17-20 km/L.[29-1] Since the car had only a two-person capacity, it was rather economical to operate.

It was reported that Leyat built several different versions of this basic propeller car design. His initial engine was a horizontally opposed two-cylinder type as shown in Photo 29-2. Later, he mounted other engines such as the Anzani radial three-cylinder engine in his car. Then, around 1930, he reportedly exhausted his funds and requested financial support from the famous violinist M. Zino Francescatti and others.[29-1] Indeed, this distinctive type of car may possibly have been well-suited for Francescatti, who enthusiastically played the "Devil's tremolo," composed by Paganini.

On the 1919 Paris streets, the Leyat car would have surely attracted people's attention. Later, however, the formerly exposed driver seats in other cars were being enclosed in the vehicle, and the owner driving his own car was becoming popular. Thus, with these developments his propeller car lost any advantage it may have had. Although there is no way of knowing his thoughts after 1919, I wonder if he himself thought his car was an experiment of technical interest.

About 10 years after the Leyat vehicle was conceived, the Italian Contessa Lisetta Trossi entered her Monaco-Trossi in the 1935 Italian Grand Prix held at Monza. This car mounted a two-stroke, eight-cylinder, four-liter radial engine similar to an airplane engine (Photo 29-3). This engine had a rating of 6000 rpm with 250-hp output. Most racing vehicles during this time had their engines mounted at the front of the vehicle. Thus, the design of this car may have been appropriate. However, little could be found in the literature about the vehicle, perhaps because the Monaco-Trossi had some lack of consideration as a car. Even from an aerodynamic viewpoint, its design was somewhat inadequate; for example, a spinner cap shielding the center part of the engine would have been desirable.

These designers were not the only people interested in "Stars" (radial engine). For example, Gabriel Voisin designed several airplanes and automobiles during World War I, and he considered several different positions to mount the engine. Around 1938, Voisin designed the concept shown in Fig. 29-2. This automobile, however, was not realized. A prototype car XPF1000 (Fig. 29-3), released in 1960 by the famous body designer Pininfarina, had the same layout as that of the 1938 Voisin design. Pininfarina reportedly created this model to make an aerodynamically ideal vehicle. The prototype achieved a 20% reduction in fuel consumption. The exquisite

Photo 29-3 The 1935 Monaco-Trossi: Engine-exposed front face looks intrepid (close-up at the bottom). Radial eight cylinders, 4L displacement, 250 PS/6000 rpm (Museo dell' Automible Carlo Biscaretti do Ruffia).

body of the XPF1000 bears a close resemblance to the Japanese Type 100 command reconnaissance plane designed by Mr. T. Kubo. I wonder if

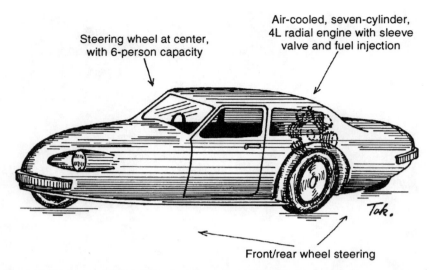

Steering wheel at center, with 6-person capacity

Air-cooled, seven-cylinder, 4L radial engine with sleeve valve and fuel injection

Front/rear wheel steering

Fig. 29-2 Voisin "Coccinelle" rhombus car (1935): The last dream in vintage-car era (1920s to 1930s). (Dream from his Voisin reconnaissance plane? See Fig. 30-2.)

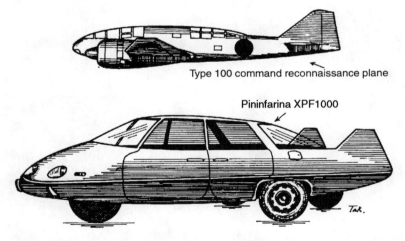

Type 100 command reconnaissance plane

Pininfarina XPF1000

Fig. 29-3 Pininfarina XPF1000 (1960): Its style was claimed to be aerodynamically ideal. The image is quite similar to the Type 100 command reconnaissance plane (1943).

Pininfarina came up with the idea for his car after he had seen a captured Type 100 plane that had been stored in England.

I was greatly disappointed when this aerodynamically conceived model was later converted into a commonplace, four-wheel, rear-engine vehicle (Fiat 600D Aerodynamic Sedannet Model Y in 1962) that soon disappeared from the marketplace. It is my belief that the single-wheel, rear drive of the rhombus arrangement contributed greatly to the 20% reduction in fuel consumption (of course, only at a rather low speed?). Then, when the design returned to the conventional four-wheel style to correct some problems inherent in a single-wheel drive, the excellence of that model was lost. Although Pininfarina's objective may have been fulfilled, today's engineering procedures require a more comprehensive analysis of the advantages and disadvantages of a design even before the prototype would be built.

Product Value Increased by Technology Fulfilling the Users' Needs

What were those radial engines that flashed across the sky and then disappeared like meteors? Were they on the right technological path or were they mere technical trials or experiments? Did they merely want to display their dazzling or fantastic characteristic as merchandise?

Every product should be designed and engineered to meet the users' needs. Consumers may sometimes purchase products that deviate from the right path technically; however, if this deviation is excessive, then these products will soon disappear. Thus, when an engineer designs a new product, it is important that the amount of deviation from the commonly accepted trend be determined so that the product's lifetime can be projected. It is necessary always to be aware of the right path so as to prepare for the next product cycle.

Chapter 30

Six-Monkey Village or
Salmson Still Carrying Its Point

*The first and last water-cooled radial aeroengine. Salmson's
achievement has been transferred by his junior.*

✂

The First and Last Water-Cooled Radial Engine

The "six-monkey village" in the title of this chapter is a phonetic equivalent
in Japanese used by the men of old as a nickname for the Salmson engine
(superb reconnaissance plane). The phonetic equivalent is written as "six-
monkey village": monkey (phonetic equivalent for "Sal" in Japanese); six
(for "mu"); village (for "son"). In 1919, this airplane was first imported into
Japan. In 1920, domestic production began in the Tokyo arsenal. Its engine
was manufactured in Tokyo Gasuden (presently Hino Motors) located close
to the Tokyo arsenal. This plane (Fig. 30-1) proved to be a favorite and was
frequently used for important missions until the Manchurian Incident. The
engine in this plane was a water-cooled radial, probably used at this time
only in airplanes. As explained previously, the radial engine greatly
increased the exposure of the cylinder to air, which substantially aided in
cooling the engine. Because of this increased cooling, the radial engine was
light and easy to maintain, resulting in enhanced reliability. Further, there
was no danger of coolant leaking as a result of enemy aircraft fire. Because
of these features, this engine was used in many important missions. However, a limiting characteristic is that the frontal area is too large to allow
adequate streamlining of the plane's nose. Thus, all the apparent advantages
of air cooling would be lost when water cooling was employed for the radial

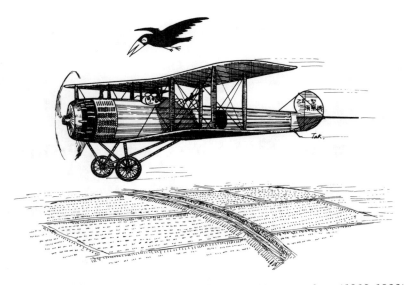

Fig. 30-1 Salmson 2A2 (type 2, form 1) reconnaissance plane (1919-1933).

engine. Why then was such a system conceived and even successfully flown in numerous missions?

The first water-cooled radial type designed by Emile Salmson had seven cylinders. This engine was completed in 1911 and was mounted on a Breguet biplane. Since Gnome's rotary engine was completed in 1919, both rotary air-cooled radial and nonrotating water-cooled radial engines were completed at approximately the same time. This dual milestone is not unlikely because the low speed of airplanes at that time resulted in insufficient air cooling with the nonrotating engine, thus giving rise to the rotary engine. In the same vein, it can be thought that water cooling was invented because air cooling proved to be insufficient. It is natural that improved cooling would increase the output per cylinder.

According to some records, World War I fighter pilots preferred to fly planes equipped with radial engines rather than the in-line or the V-type engines because of the radial's increased reliability. It was reported that the in-line or the V-type engines often caused failure of the crankcase (i.e., the mainframe of the engine). One possible reason for this increased failure in the in-line engine (and the V-type as well) is that the crankshaft is longer, and more bearings are required to support the crankshaft between cylinders. However, the machining accuracy of these components was not always sufficient. Another cause of failure of the crankcase was the longer crankshaft combined with the torsional vibration produced by the propeller. This torsional vibration was a difficult problem that evaded understanding until later.

In addition, in-line engines are not fully balanced, and forces due to unbalance, i.e., internal moment, are generated (Appendix A30-1). This concept was not fully understood during World War I. Therefore, aircraft were designed with no consideration of this problem. Thus, there were sufficient reasons to warrant using the water-cooled radial engine.

Note that the radial engine had a far shorter crankshaft, requiring only two bearings to support it. Even with air speeds too slow to cool the nonrotating radial engines, the disadvantage of having a wide frontal area must have seemed minor compared to the reliability problems experienced by the in-line and V-type engines. Because of these features, among others, the radial engine may have been loved by many pilots (Fig. 30-2).

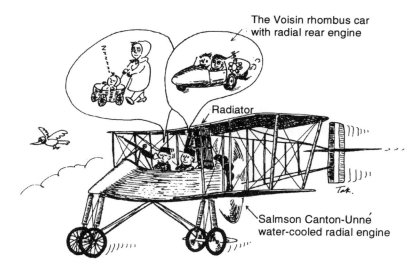

Fig. 30-2 Voisin LA5B2 reconnaissance bomber (1915): Looks like a baby carriage with a rear engine. This riding comfort led to the later concept of the Voisin rear engine car.

Canton-Unné Engine

Encouraged by the success of the seven-cylinder engine, Salmson designed a nine-cylinder engine. This nine-cylinder engine was quite popular among the Japanese and was nicknamed "six-monkey village." This engine was exported not only to Japan, but also to the United States and to England. During this time, it was used in an exceptionally large number of planes. The success of this engine was supported by another technological break-through, the crankshaft-connecting rod mechanism called the Canton-Unné system.

In the radial engine configuration, the connecting rods of all cylinders meet at the center to rotate the crankshaft. Normally, the connecting rods would collide and interfere with each other, making this engine unworkable. To resolve this problem, the crankshaft is usually turned by using separate pins shifted from each other by a small degree. This system inevitably causes the top dead center (that point at which the piston comes at the topmost end of the cylinder) to be slightly shifted among the cylinders with respect to the angle between them. Therefore, the stroke does not match among the cylinders either (see Fig. A30-4).

To design the first radial seven-cylinder engine, Salmson hired two talented Swiss engineers, Georges Henri Marius Canton and Pierre Georges Unné. After working on this angular deviation, which was peculiar to the radial engine, for a period of time, they eliminated the problem with an ingenious mechanism (see Appendix A30-2).

Both Salmson's seven-cylinder and subsequent nine-cylinder engines incorporated their newly invented mechanism, so both engines are called Salmson's "Canton-Unné" engine (Photo 30-1).

This engine was mounted in France's first commercial passenger plane *Farman Goliath* in 1919 and serviced flights from Paris to London or Casablanca. This plane achieved a record altitude of 5100 m with 25 passengers aboard, thus proving its excellence (Photo 30-2). However, this was the last of the water-cooled radial engine like the rotary radial engine. After this engine, Salmson made only the usual air-cooled radial aeroengine. Afterward, his company manufactured only automobiles (Photo 30-3).

Salmson's Successor

Just after World War I, Salmson's company (Société des Moteurs Salmson), as well as other airplane manufacturers, decided to manufacture automobiles. However, Salmson died in 1917. Fortunately, his pioneering spirit had been inherited by his close associate Emile Petit and his junior staff members.

The new company left a large imprint on the history of automobiles. For example, in 1922 this company was the first to mass-produce cars with the

Photo 30-1 Salmson "Canton-Unné" type M9 engine: 130 hp for Voisin and Salmson reconnaissance planes. Domestically manufactured by Tokyo Gasuden (presently Hino Motors). Output later enhanced to 280 HP (Musée de L'Air Paris).

twin overhead cam (TOHC), which provided improved high-speed performance. The TOHC engine, also called DOHC, is one equipped with two camshafts for air intake and exhaust at the top of the cylinder head. In 1927, they produced an engine with the first dyna-starter (generator and starter coupled to each other). Especially significant is the TOHC mechanism called the inverted bucket type (with the cam contact area shaped like a bucket placed upside down) still used for high-performance sports cars today. The TOHC was used by W.O. Bentley (see Chapter 20), which has since been succeeded by the postwar *Lagonda*.

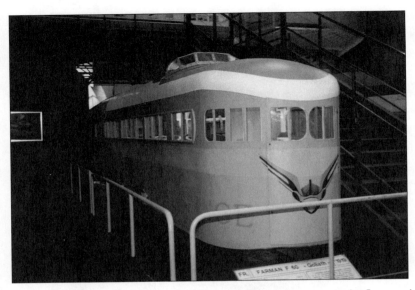

Photo 30-2 Fuselage of the Farman Goliath *resembling an express train: Large wings were attached to the top and bottom of this fuselage. Using two Salmson engines, this gigantic airplane flew a route linking Paris, London, Brussels, and Casablanca. In Japan, this plane was used as a Tei (D) type bomber (Musée de L'Air Paris).*

Photo 30-3 The Salmson 1926 model Grand Sport VAL (Musée National de L'Automobile de Mu-Lhouse, Schlumpf Collection).

Salmson's Progressive Idea Admired by Benz

In June 1954, when the aftereffects of World War II were substantially over, the Benz racing car raced for the first time in the France Grand Prix. The car had an innovative in-line, eight-cylinder, 2.5L, 300-hp engine. This car (Photo 30-4) won the 1954 Grand Prix and every race it entered thereafter. The Benz vehicle won 15 successive Grand Prix races before it retired from racing.

Photo 30-4 Benz's racing car winning in the 1954 France Grand Prix: The engine of this Benz formula car, which won first place in all subsequent races, was, so to speak, an imitation of the Salmson engine.

The engine of this car receives its output from the center of its eight cylinders, that is, the joining point of the two four-cylinder blocks. The blocks were designed to equally divide the force applied to the crankshaft, thereby reducing the weight. Also, the engine employs roller bearings for the crankshaft, direct gasoline injection, and the desmodromic system, which opens and closes the valve without using a spring. I remember that all our engine design staff, including myself, were so amazed at such an extremely innovative design that we were silent for awhile after being told of the structural characteristics of this engine. However, the Salmson in-line, eight-cylinder racing engine produced 27 years earlier (in 1927) had much the same design as the Benz racing car engine, except for gasoline injection (see Appendix A30-3).

There is no doubt that Benz engineers studied Emile Petit's design and imitated it. According to the literature[30-1], Salmson's eight-cylinder engine was also imitated in the 1931 Alfa Romeo model. Alfa Romeo's Vittorio Jano incorporated the Salmson concept into his design when he fabricated the sports car Monza and then the famous racing car P3. The Salmson engine was never again manufactured after the May 1930 Grand Prix car. However, this engine was responsible for a number of technological innovations, beginning with the water-cooled radial engine as an independent field differing from the marketability of merchandise.

Appendix A30-1 Internal Moment of Engine

When a heavy person stands on a log bridge, the logs deflect more, which increases the risk of breakage. This increased risk is because the bending moment, M, applied to the bridge becomes larger, and the stress applied to the bridge is proportional to the moment under the same cross-sectional area, as shown in Fig. A30-1. Now let's replace the log bridge with a crankshaft. In addition to the inertial force caused by the piston and connecting rod, etc., the crankshaft absorbs a large force due to the explosive pressure, which acts as a moment. On the other hand, the crankcase, which forms the main frame of the engine, receives a moment along with the rotation of the engine. This moment is called *internal moment*. Fig. A30-2 shows the engines of one cylinder and of in-line six cylinders. In the one-cylinder engine, the explosion pressure is restrained between the piston and cylinder head. This pressure and the inertial force due to the piston and connecting rod are both applied to the crankshaft, causing a bending moment. However, no moment is applied to the crankcase (at each bearing part).

On the other hand, the crankshaft of the six-cylinder engine receives the same moment as in the one-cylinder engine (strictly speaking, its value differs some because the crankshaft is coupled with the next one), but a different moment occurs on the crankcase. That is, the gas pressure (explosion pressure) of each cylinder is counterbalanced inside the cylinder. Only the inertia force of the piston and connecting rod is applied as a centrifugal force whose phase is different among the cylinders as shown in the sketch at the left of Fig. A30-2. Therefore, those centrifugal forces act on the crankcase as a moment in the in-line engine. This moment is termed *internal moment*.

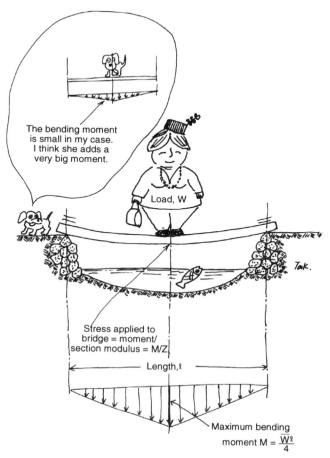

The bending moment is small in my case. I think she adds a very big moment.

Load, W

Tank.

Stress applied to bridge = moment/ section modulus = M/Z

Length, ℓ

Maximum bending moment $M = \dfrac{W\ell}{4}$

Fig. A30-1 Bending moment proportional to load W at the same bridge length.

In the radial engine (single row), cylinders are placed in a radial pattern on the same plane. Therefore, the internal moment is not applied to the crankcase as in the one-cylinder engine. Therefore, stress does not occur. In contrast, in the in-line or V-type engine, it is a matter of course that the internal moment is significantly affected by the value or presence of the balance weight attached to the crankshaft. Let me give as an example the in-line, six-cylinder engine. Even without a balance weight, the front and rear sides are symmetrical, and equal firing intervals are maintained with respect to engine rotation. Therefore, balance is kept externally, and the rotation appears to be smooth. In actuality, however, the internal moment varies largely with the presence or absence of the balance weight.

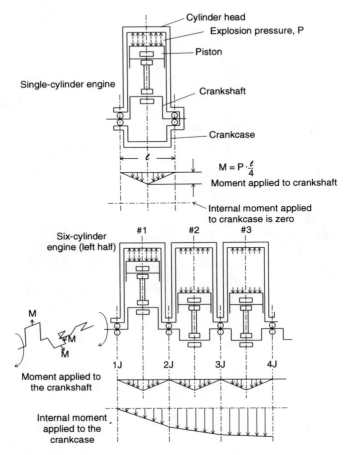

Fig. A30-2 Internal moment of engine.

Fig. A30-3 illustrates the calculation of the internal moment in an in-line, six-cylinder engine. Since the inertial weight of the crankshaft for each cylinder revolves along with engine rotation, the vertical moment varies in response. For example, this figure shows the vertical moment when the fourth bearing (4J) is at maximum, and the horizontal moment corresponding to the former. In this example, 4J reaches the maximum position when the piston of the first cylinder (#1) is at 30° before top dead center (BTDC).

This example is dependent on the use of the balance weight. When the balance weight is not attached, the moment value becomes approximately 2.5 times larger. In a V-type, eight-cylinder engine, the internal moment without the balance weight is five times larger than with the balance weight.

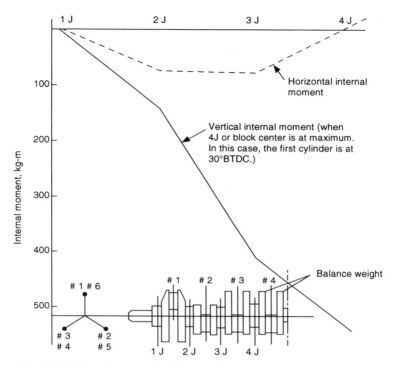

Fig. A30-3 Actual example of internal moment (Hino HO7C engine).

During the World War I era, the internal moment was not recognized, and the engine was not provided with the balance weight. Therefore, the in-line and the V-type engines often resulted in problems such as cracks or failure of the crankcase. As a result, pilots did not rate these engines highly. After advances in tribology enabled the oil film thickness in the bearing area to be calculated, it was noted that the value of this internal moment has a large influence over the oil film thickness. In recent years, the balance weight of the crankshaft has been designed in various configurations to keep the oil film thickness below the limit value.

Needless to say, the internal moment should be taken into account when the strength of the cylinder block is being determined. In addition, it has become evident that shear force has a close relationship with local stress.[30-2] These factors have been examined in detail in the design of the cylinder block.

Appendix A30-2 Canton-Unné System

The connecting rods of all cylinders cannot be coupled with a single crankpin in a conventional radial engine. Therefore, the master rod is provided with knuckle pins, to which "slave" rods are connected, as shown in Fig. 30-1. As a result, the length differs by ρ from the master rod, and the phase angle with respect to the center of the crankshaft is different from that of the master rod. Therefore, both the stroke and the TDC position are different among cylinders.

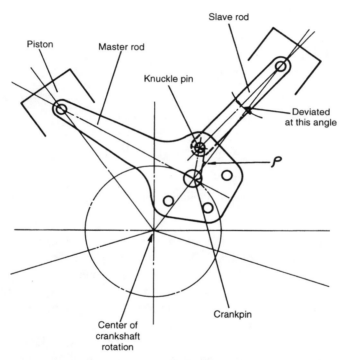

Fig. A30-4 Master rod and link rod of radial engine.

To solve this problem, Canton and Unné devised the ingenious system illustrated in Fig. A30-5.[(30-3)] That is, the slave rods are not connected to the master rod. Instead, the slave rods are coupled with the knuckle pins on disc F, which is rotated around the fixed gear K via gears M and L. Gears L, M, and K are mated by link N. With this arrangement, disc F rotates once around its axis as it rotates once around the crankshaft axis; the radius from the center of the crankshaft rotation to each knuckle pin stays constant. This

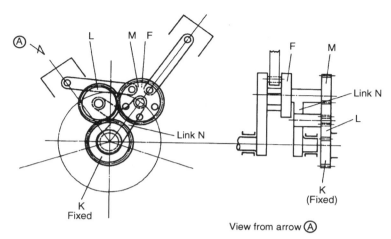

Fig. A30-5 Canton-Unné system.

configuration eliminates the differences in phase angle and stroke among cylinders.

In the early development of the radial engine, this measure was not incorporated, retaining the unbalanced status. The Canton-Unné system was used only for two generations of Salmson engines. It was then replaced by another, simpler solution to the problem. The length of the link rod among cylinders was changed, and the cams of the sparking magnets were set at unequal angles. This method replaced the Canton-Unné system because it was simpler and less expensive to produce. We often find a simple, unsophisticated design that produces a better product than a more complicated arrangement.

Appendix A30-3 Similarities Between the Benz Formula Engine and the Salmson Engine

Fig. A30-6 illustrates the Salmson in-line, eight-cylinder racing engine manufactured in 1927, and Fig. A30-7 illustrates the Benz in-line, eight-cylinder race engine made in 1955. I will explain their similarities in respect to the desmodromic system used in both engines.

In the usual valve gear system, the valve is opened and closed because the valve spring permits the valve to trace the cam profile. However, in the desmodromic system, a special-profile cam and follower forcibly actuates the valve without the use of a spring, as shown in Photo A30-1.

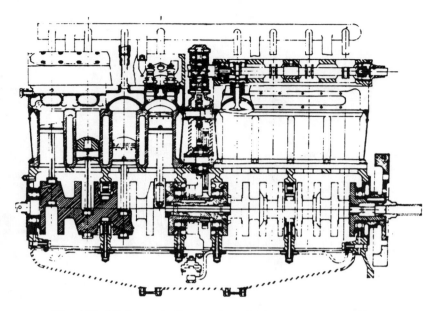

Fig. A30-6 Salmson in-line, eight-cylinder race engine (1927).

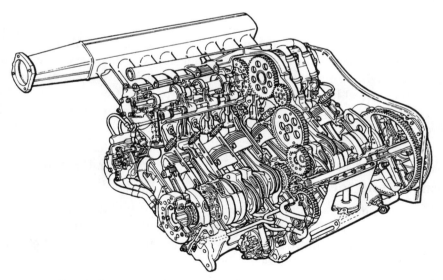

Fig. A30-7 Benz in-line, eight-cylinder engine (1954 to 1955).

In the spring-actuated system, the rotational speed of the engine is restricted due to the vibration in the spring, which is caused by inertia force of the system. Therefore the opening height or lift of the valve is restricted, which

Photo A30-1 Desmodromic system (valve gear)
(Briggs Cunningham Automobile Museum).

determines the performance. To avoid this restriction, the valve spring must be stiffened even more. As a result, the contact pressure with the follower becomes excessive and durability is degraded. To prevent this degradation, the cam, follower, valve spring, etc., must all be enlarged. A vicious cycle results, preventing the design from being finalized.

If the valve can be opened and closed forcibly by a geometrical mechanism without having to use a valve spring, the above problem will be eliminated, and a larger lift is available than could be obtained by the usual system. The larger lift results in higher engine speed with no restrictions, as shown in Fig. A30-8. I understand why the Benz engineering staff closely evaluated and eventually adopted the concept of the old Salmson engine.

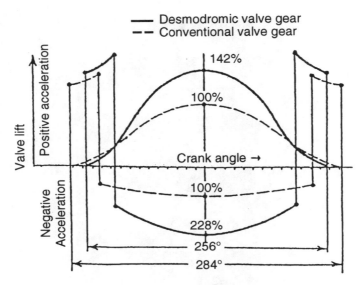

Fig. A30-8 Valve lift widely enhanced by desmodromic system.

A disadvantage of the desmodromic system, however, is that it requires immediate fine adjustment for a slight wear of valve seats. Otherwise, the seating, particularly of the exhaust valve, etc., will burn. To resolve this problem, Salmson combined the valve spring with the desmodromic system to create the semidesmodromic system. In contrast, Benz avoided the semi-desmodromic system and utilized a complete desmodromic system by incorporating an innovative fine-adjustment mechanism.

Both the Salmson and Benz engines consist of two four-cylinder blocks. This configuration is also a major Salmson technical point incorporated by Benz into its engine. By dividing into two blocks, Salmson solved the problem of the rigidity of the cylinder block. Most cars at that time mounted each engine directly on the frame without placing rubber mounts between the engine and the car frame. As a result, the cylinder block was often broken due to the torsion of the frame in such a long engine as the eight-cylinder type. However, the two-block design permitted the engine to flex enough to avoid breakage. In consequence, the crankshaft and camshaft were also given greater rigidity and torsion resistance. Benz carried this concept even further by removing the crankshaft's main output from the center. It is understandable that Benz conceived of the technical modifications by adequate thought, thus avoiding an exact copy of the Salmson engine. Good imitation must always be accomplished in this manner.

By the way, the desmodromic system that we have discussed was used only for the Scarab formula car in addition to the Benz formula car. This lack of use can be attributed to the following reasons: (1) At a valve lift approximating one-third of valve diameter, the valve opening area becomes nearly the same as the valve head area; beyond this point, the effect of a wider opening is not so noticeable. (2) The valve spring and other components were composed of improved material. (3) The desmodromic system required a high structural accuracy and a complicated fine-adjustment mechanism for a slight wear of valve seats. (4) The desmodromic system was expensive. There were other reasons; however, the desmodromic system still has its supporters and has actually been used in motorcycles. Note that the desmodromic system was invented by Ernst Henry, rather than Salmson. The first system was used in the Grand Prix car made by Peugeot in 1912, and the previously mentioned inverted bucket-type TOHC was first designed by Henry in 1919 (Ballot for the Indianapolis 500).

Note that the word "desmodromic" indicates his unique valve system. This word was taken from the Greek *desmos* meaning "bringing into close contact" and *dromos* meaning "running." I wonder if the Peugeot salesman coined the word in admiration of the car.

Chapter 31

Do "Stars" (Radial Engines) Twinkle Again?

Three big "stars" returned to six-monkey village (phonetic equivalent of "Salmson" in Japanese) or water-cooled radial engines. Will the internal friction-free characteristic be re-evaluated due to energy conservation?

�֍

The Fate of Radial Engines Like a Comet

The building housing the Conservatoir National de Arts et Matiers in Paris once served as a church (Photo 31-1). Therefore, the interior is rather dark and humid. While at this museum, I found a four-row radial model engine (Photo 31-2) stored in a cabinet in a corner of the museum. An introductory note accompanying the model indicates it was made by Fernand Forest in 1888. Forest is the first person who mechanically drove the intake and exhaust valves with today's configuration. As I explained previously, the early cars usually had a single cylinder as demonstrated in the Benz cars. The number of cylinders were then increased over time. So, I was surprised to see this old model of a multicylinder engine. It is a four-row, radial 32-cylinder engine. The air-cooled radial engine originally began with three cylinders, and then it came to have more cylinders and a larger output.

The ultimate product of this engine is the four-row, radial 28-cylinder, 3000- to 3500-hp engine completed by Pratt & Whitney in 1946. This engine has been cut in cross sections and carefully preserved at Lackland Air Force Base, Texas, and other locations (Photo 31-3).

Photo 31-1 Front of the Conservatoir National de Arts et Matiers in Paris: Building once served as a church.

When observing the Pratt & Whitney engine, I felt as if the Forest model, built 58 years earlier, had been the wooden mockup for this engine. In 1885 Benz and Daimler completed their one-cylinder gasoline engine. Only three years later, Forest's imagination may have predicted the ultimate progress of that engine. His foresightedness is beyond words.

Trial Manufacture of a Liquid-Cooled Radial Engine in the United States and Germany

The longer we look at the Pratt & Whitney four-row, radial, air-cooled, 28-cylinder engine, the more complicated and ingenious it appears. The cooling air guide plate, placed as if it were threaded through the ingenious

Photo 31-2 Fernand Forest built this model of a four-row radial engine as early as 1888: Hinting the appearance of a 3500-hp engine in 1946 (Conservatoir National de Arts et Matiers in Paris).

Photo 31-3 Ultimate "star," Pratt & Whitney R4360, air-cooled, four-row, radial, 28-cylinder engine: 71.5L displacement, 3500 hp. Intercooler at bottom center, oil cooler at left, and turbocompressor at right (Kalamazoo Aviation History Museum).

structure, is a piece of art. To obtain this particular layout, the placement would have had to have been repeated countless times (Photo 31-4).

Photo 31-4 Pratt & Whitney R4360, air-cooled, four-row, radial, 28-cylinder engine: Baffle plate of 3500-hp engine, its complicated profile is as exquisite as art (Lackland Air Force Base).

If air cooling presents such difficult cooling problems, it would seem natural to use water cooling as was done in the Salmson water-cooled engine instead of using the difficult air-cooled engine. In fact, the trial manufacture of this engine was undertaken in both Germany and the United States in the final stage of World War II.

Photo 31-5 shows the Junkers Jumo Model 222E, liquid-cooled, six-cylinder four rows (24 cylinders) engine that finally achieved 3000 hp. Though the trial manufacture began in 1941, mass production was only realized in 1945, with the engine being mounted on the Junkers JU288 plane (Photo 31-6).

In Germany, another gigantic engine program was in progress. It was a water-cooled, four-row radial, 28-cylinder engine capable of achieving 4000 hp. This engine was intended to drive a contra-propeller, which means that two propellers are turned in opposite directions on the same axis with two double-row radial engines at the front and rear. This drive method is

Photo 31-5 Junkers Jumo Model 222E engine: Liquid-cooled, radial 24 cylinders, 2500 PS/3000 rpm, 60° intervals, six cylinders × 4, 49.8L displacement, 2-stage/ 2-speed supercharger, 140-mm bore, 135-mm stroke, 1370-kg weight (Deutsches Museum, München).

Photo 31-6 Junkers JU288 interceptor fighter using the Junkers Jumo 222 engine (Deutsches Museum, München).

also ingenious. Gears divide the motive power of the rear engine among five shafts. These shafts are threaded through the small gap between the cylinders of the forward engine to the front, where the power is connected to the propeller shaft by the gear drive again. The engine was BMW Model 803, and it was scheduled to be mounted on a gigantic bomber *Focke Wulf* FW Model 238 with a flight range of 16,000 km. However, the war ended before its bench test was completed (Photo 31-7).

Photo 31-7 BMW Model 803 engine: Liquid-cooled, radial 28 cylinders (total of radial 14 cylinders in two rows), 4000 PS/2950 rpm, 156-mm bore, 156-mm stroke, 85.5L displacement, 4130-kg weight, 1600-mm diameter (Deutches Museum, SchleiBheim).

On the other hand, Photo 31-8 shows the American counterpart, the prototype Lycoming XR-7755 Type 3 engine, which appears to have 36 cylinders because of its nine cylinders in four rows. This very big 127L engine incorporated an ambitious design of variable valve timing and variable ignition timing and was intended to be mounted on long-range aircraft. Though it had 5000 hp at 2600 rpm, the war was over before its flight test.

Unlike these approaches, Japan had undertaken a large engine program dependent on air cooling. This engine was planned for the Nakajima Aircraft Work *Fugaku*, a massive six-engine bomber intended to attack the United States mainland in a nonstop flight from Japan. Its design began in

*Photo 31-8 Lycoming XR-7755 Type 3 engine: 5000 PS/2600 rpm
(Smithsonian Museum).*

1943, and the machining of materials was reportedly underway in 1944. But Saipan's surrender led to the interruption of this project, which was never resumed. The planned engine has air-cooled, four-row radial, 36 cylinders, 94.6L displacement, 5000 hp/2800 rpm specifications (Fig. 31-1).[27-3]

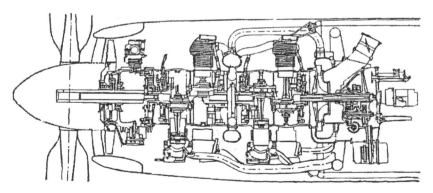

Fig. 31-1 Nakajima "HA54" engine: Air-cooled, radial 36 cylinders, 5000 PS/2500 rpm, 96.4L displacement, three-speed supercharger, 146-mm bore, 160-mm stroke, weight 2450 kg.

Roots of French and American "Stars"

The radial engine has its roots in the 1887 Hargrave rotary engine as noted previously. In Europe, a nonrotating radial engine was made in the same year (1888) that Forest designed his model. The device was a steam engine called the Adianomique engine, shown in Photo 31-9. The Adianomique has been preserved, together with its principle model (shown in Photo 31-10), in the Musée de L'Air Paris.

Photo 31-9 Charles Renard's Adianomique radial steam engine (1888) (Musée de L'Air Paris).

The designer was said to be Charles Renard, a French army engineering officer who had graduated from Ecole Polytechnique, Carnot's alma mater. From the principle diagram, I imagine the engine works in the following

Photo 31-10 Principle model of Adianomique engine (Centenaire de la Recherche Aeronautique a chalais-Meudon, 1977).

manner. The steam was introduced into one cylinder and then moved sequentially to the subsequent cylinders while expanding. The steam is discharged sequentially. This scheme may have been designated as "Adianomique." It is a radial eight-cylinder engine.

Actually, a still older example is a steam pump shown in Photo 31-11. It was made by George H. Corliss in 1875 and used in Providence, Rhode Island, in the northeastern United States. From the photograph, I suppose that three connecting rods comprise one unit. The central cylinder of each unit serves as a water pump, and the left and right cylinders function as steam cylinders. According to the museum explanation, this radial engine can supply pulsation-free water while completing one revolution every few minutes.

This American root does indeed resemble a radial engine, while the French root has the shape of confetti or star. Actual history does not indicate that the French use their sense of romanticism when naming an engine.

Photo 31-11 The American root has a radial shape as seen here. It does not have the shape of a star: Corliss' steam pump in 1875. Used as a water pump in Providence, Rhode Island (Smithsonian Museum).

Do the "Stars" Go Out? Future of New American and German "Stars"

We have found the beginning or the root of the "stars" (radial engines). What future is in store for the "stars"? The 28-cylinder, 3500-hp engine considered to be the ultimate "star" type was used in some ultralarge airplanes after World War II, but its use in such an application did not last long (Photo 31-12). The radial engine is now mounted only in a sightseeing plane in service over Vancouver, Canada. It does not appear that the "star" (radial engine) will have another day in the sun.

In 1980, however, the U.S. National Aeronautics and Space Administration's Lewis Research Center released radial three- and six-cylinder aero diesel engines jointly developed with Teledyne Continental Motors Ltd.[31-1] It seemed that the radial engine may be reborn as an energy-conserving engine for small airplanes (Fig. 31-2), but this is uncertain.

Meanwhile, a new radial engine or "star" was born in Germany. The new star is the Zoche aero diesel, manufactured by Michael and George Zoche

Photo 31-12 Gigantic Convair Model XC-99 using six ultimate "stars" or 28-cylinder, 3500-hp engines: The size of this plane may be estimated from the cars under the wing. The inside of the vertical tail fin looks like a castle tower (author at center) (San Antonio Air Museum).

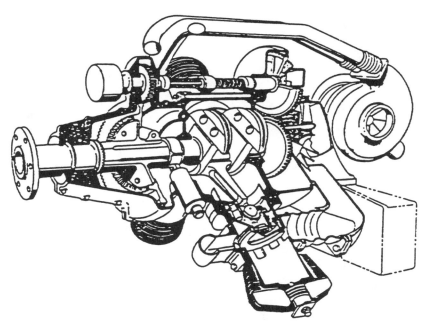

*Fig. 31-2 Sketch of Teledyne Continental air-cooled radial diesel engine: 400 PS/ 3500 rpm (*Automotive Engineering, *February 1980).*

as a trial. They installed the Junkers Jumo aeroengine, the first and last successful aero diesel engine, in their combination laboratory and living room, worked out a number of epochal innovations for overcoming the restrictions of using the diesel engine in airplanes, and achieved 0.5 kg/PS (weight per horsepower). Their engine comes in two configurations, the two-stroke cycle, radial four-cylinder, 150-hp model and the two-stroke cycle, double-row, eight-cylinder, 300-hp model (see Appendix A31). These engines are currently undergoing bench testing. I wish them success in their efforts (Photo 31-13).

Photo 31-13 Zoche ZO engine: two-stroke cycle, four-cylinder, 150 PS/2500 rpm (eight cylinders for 300 PS type), 95-mm bore, 94-mm stroke, 2.7L displacement (5.4L for 300 PS type), 89 kg weight, Schnürle scavenging.

A radial engine has two advantages, though they are not overwhelming. One advantage is a high mechanical efficiency in that the loss of power due to mechanical friction is less than that of an in-line engine. The reason for this decrease in power loss is that the crankshaft can be shortened, requiring only two bearings to support the crankshaft. Thus, the load due to inertia is reduced to zero as explained previously (see Appendix A30-1). However, the Pratt & Whitney four-row radial engine has five bearings. Usually, the four-cylinder in-line engine for small passenger cars has five bearings, while the six-cylinder engine has seven bearings. As noted before, even the smallest improvement results in saving energy. From this viewpoint, the radial five-cylinder, two-bearing engine has some attractions.

The other advantage of the radial engine is a basically higher reliability than the normal in-line engine. As discussed earlier (Chapter 30), this difference in reliability is attributable to the longer crankshaft of the in-line engine. A longer bent crankshaft mechanism results in various vibrations on the engine and makes its support difficult. One of the factors is the previously mentioned internal moment. Even today, this internal problem cannot be resolved easily, and it still significantly affects reliability. The radial engine is a peaceful structure free from such an internal discord.

Energy saving means that an engine is reliable for a long time with a minimum fuel consumption. The star shape or radial pattern basically meets this energy-saving principle. This was the true reason for the NASA-Lewis/ Teledyne and the Zoche's revival of the radial engine. Will the radial engine survive as a "pretty planet" rather than a huge fixed "star"? I expect some new "stars" to appear that will make it clear why many other "stars" have fallen from the sky of the engine world.

Appendix A31 Zoche Aero Diesel Engine

As discussed in an earlier chapter, the aero diesel engine has a severe disadvantage in that black smoke emission increases as air becomes thinner at higher altitudes; in addition, the aero diesel engine is heavy (see Chapter 33).

To cope with this problem, Zoche employed a turbocharged two-stroke cycle engine as a basic system. The problem of black smoke can be solved by turbocharging because when air density becomes low, the load applied to the compressor of turbocharger is decreased and rotation is increased in compensation. The Zoche series-connected a turbocharger to the mechanically driven centrifugal scavenging blower (the same compressor as the one used for turbocharger).

Also, Zoche, Sr. and Jr., eliminated the master rod (see Appendix A30-2), which had been thought to be indispensable for a radial engine, fully utilizing the advantage of the principle of a two-stroke cycle, i.e., one of the measures for reducing the weight. In the intake/exhaust stroke of a four-stroke cycle, the connecting rod bearing receives the inertia force or load on the side opposite the explosion pressure as well. By contrast, in the two-stroke cycle, the load is received only in the direction of the explosion. Also utilizing this characteristic, the Zoche eliminated even the bearing cap and received four connecting rods with a single crankpin. In addition, the cylinders and the crankcase were made of aluminum, and the inner (refer to Chapter 30) wall of each cylinder was coated with a compound material (Ni-SiC) tradenamed *Nikasil* (Mahle Company), all of which served to reduce the weight of the engine.

Because of its large compression ratio, a diesel engine requires a large starter and battery. For a smaller structure, Zoche developed a small air pump and a free piston compressor (pressurization to 10 atm) to compose a pneumatic start system. Compressed air is delivered into the inlet of the scavenging pump for its start. However, if the fuel injection nozzle is inserted into the cylinder with the usual design, the diameter of the entire engine becomes large, so the frontal area increases when the engine is mounted on an airplane.

Therefore, the prototype engine in the present stage is mounted on its side. I think that future improvement of this fuel injection nozzle is the key to the success of their engine. Since fuel injection pressure is reportedly 1200 atm (about 120 MPa), excellent combustion can be expected after the layout has become successfully completed.

Chapter 32

Glory and Tragedy of Packard (I)

Background of tragedy, invention and technical progress of diesel engine. Introduction and application of existing technology to be considered and the decision to be made on it.

Impact of *Life* Magazine

In the previous chapter, I noted that the suddenly revived radial engine was diesel. Before dreaming of this engine's potential impact, it is necessary to be aware of a radial diesel engine that led a spectacular and short life, together with the designer. The engine that we are discussing is the Packard aero diesel engine. Its manufacturer, the Packard Motor Car Company, had produced a number of splendid cars and engines. It was eventually ruined and disappeared from this world. I wonder if the death of the Packard aero diesel engine was an evil omen of this company's collapse.

In the winter of 1945, just after the end of World War II, I spent a night on a mountain in the heart of the Shinshu (Nagano) district, Japan. The night was very cold because the house was buried in snow, and we had no heater due to the wartime shortage of these commodities. I staved off the cold by putting on as many blankets (discards of the defeated Japanese military) and futons (Japanese bedding) as I could. However, I still could not sleep because of the shock and excitement that I experienced upon reading the American magazine *Life* for the first time that night. A person who had been returned to Japan from the United States by a repatriation ship during the war had brought a few back-issues of *Life* and had stayed temporarily at the home I happened to visit. The American lifestyle that I glimpsed in the *Life* magazine was as follows.

People in shirt sleeves were chatting merrily with a winter scene showing through the window, and their gorgeous dishes astounded the Japanese, who had to spend much of their time each day in finding food. The Japanese had only a wood-burning cooking stove and a charcoal cooker, while the American kitchen had an electric stove capable of cooking with multiple pots and pans. In wartime Japan, electricity consisted of a lamp that had been severely restricted by the wartime blackout regulations. (Afterward, I bought some nichrome wire and a switch and made an oven manually for my mother. I remember she was very pleased to have it.) The thing that impressed me most about the pictures in the magazine was the various cars, particularly the most beautiful model, the Packard (Fig. 32-1).

Fig. 32-1 The 1942 model Packard Clipper: The image of this beautiful car kept me awake for a long time. This car was produced until the time of the Midway sea battle.

Achievement of Successive World Records by Packard

The Packard Company, which was dominating the U.S. luxury car market, had suddenly announced its plan to produce the aero diesel engine in 1928. The reason for this sudden announcement is not known with certainty. However, it is possible that, stimulated by the success of Charles A.

Lindbergh in crossing the Atlantic Ocean, Packard president Alvan Macauley or its chief designer Lionel M. Woolson may have wanted to manufacture an engine with a better fuel consumption than Lindbergh's engine, namely, the Wright "Whirlwind" aeroengine.

In August, three months after Lindbergh's successful May 21, 1927, flight that crossed the Atlantic, the Packard Company completed a license agreement with Hermann I.A. Dorner, a solid-fuel injection diesel engine researcher then living in Hanover, Germany. Thus, the Packard diesel engine was to be based on the Dorner unit injector (detailed later) fuel injection system.

The new engine strived for the same output and weight characteristics as the Wright "Whirlwind." After only one year, or on September 19, 1928, Packard succeeded in the first flight with this engine mounted on a Stinson-Detroiter plane (Photos 32-1 and 32-2). Then, in May 1929, the plane crossed the American continent in 6.5 hours, demonstrating that the fuel cost for this flight was only $4.68, about one-fifth of the fuel cost for a gasoline engine. The next year, 1930, the Packard Company began its commercial-based production. On May 25, 1931, the *Bellanca* monoplane mounting the Packard diesel engine took off from Jacksonville, Florida, to challenge the endurance flight record. This plane flew for three days and established a new world endurance flight record of 84 hours and 33 minutes. Further, in 1932, this engine was mounted in the Goodyear airship, which made a world altitude record with the use of a diesel engine. These successes attracted worldwide attention.

For example, the engine was manufactured by Walter in Czechoslovakia as the Walter Packard diesel engine. On March 31, 1932, U.S. President Herbert Hoover awarded the Robert J. Collier Trophy to the Packard Motor Car Company as the outstanding performer in the aeronautical field. The award ceremony was held at the White House with high officials from U.S. Department of Commerce and other agencies in attendance. Among the attendees was Amelia Earhart, a woman pilot who later disappeared mysteriously above the Pacific while piloting the Lockheed Electra for the round-the-world flight. During the award ceremony, President Hoover highly praised the Packard engine, stating that it was an unprecedented pioneering job (Photo 32-3).

Everyone believed that this engineering project was a brilliant success. The following year, 1933, however, this diesel engine project was abandoned, which resulted in closing the new factory costing $650,000 (a tremendous amount of money at that time) and terminating 600 newly employed

Photo 32-1 The Wright "Whirlwind" engine mounted to the Spirit of St. Louis, *which was the first airplane to cross the Atlantic Ocean [top], and Packard diesel engine manufactured in rivalry to the Whirlwind [bottom]: Spiral pipe is an oil cooler (Ford Museum).*

Photo 32-2 Stinson-Detroiter: Mounting the Packard diesel engine and verifying that fuel consumption was only one-fifth in the flight crossing the American continent (the airplane shown in this photo has the rival Wright "Whirlwind" aero engine) (Ford Museum).

workers.[32-1] Why? Before determining the cause, it is necessary to know the status of diesel engine technology at that time.

Fierce Competition in Improvement

Almost all of today's large trucks and buses use a diesel engine as their power source. The first successful application of a diesel engine was in the Benz 50-hp, five-ton vehicle. The vehicle was completed in February, 1924, only three years before Lindbergh crossed the Atlantic Ocean. Then in August, 1924, six months after the Benz vehicle, Maschinenfabrik Augsburg (MAN) introduced its 40-hp, four-ton vehicle.

About 27 years had passed after Rudolf Diesel in 1897 invented a diesel engine and succeeded in its operation until these successful applications. This large gap of time existed because a small fuel injection device suitable for automobiles had not been designed.

As commonly known, a diesel engine operates on the following principle. Air is ingested into the cylinder, and the piston then compresses the air, increasing its temperature. When the compressed air reaches a sufficiently high temperature, a light oil is injected into the cylinder. This injection is

Photo 32-3 Collier Trophy awarding ceremony[30-1]: President H. Hoover (at right end) highly praised this engine, saying it was an "unprecedented pioneering job." Seen behind the engine was Ms. Amelia Earhart who was lost in the South Pacific. Tragedy was unveiled (Smithsonian Annals of Flight).

followed by spontaneous ignition and explosion. Therefore, to be injected, the fuel must be atomized into the smallest droplets possible. Dr. Diesel succeeded in obtaining adequate atomization by blowing fuel along with the highly compressed air (Photo 32-4). This idea can be said to be the key to the success of the diesel engine. Unfortunately, this methodology requires a separate air compressor in addition to the engine. The resultant engine size was too large to be used for automobiles. As a result, the diesel engine had been used only for stationary powerplants or marine propulsion.

MAN and other companies had attempted to mount the diesel engine on vehicles since the year following Diesel's invention of the engine, but they had all failed. Photo 32-5 shows a prototype engine made by Safir Company in 1908, an example of the failed engines. The Swiss company attempted to remodel a gasoline engine into a diesel engine under a license agreement

Photo 32-4 Rudolf Diesel's engine for research (1893): Mounting an air compressor and cylinder for fuel injection to this gear, diesel engine was completed in 1897. It had 20 PS/172 rpm. This photo shows the engine made in 1893. A large cylinder for compressed air was added to the 1897 engine, which successfully worked. Standing by the engine was the author (KHD Museum).

with the Saurer company. The air compressor was skillfully placed at the front of the engine as shown in this photo, but this engine was not completed because the fuel could not be atomized into sufficiently small droplets at low speeds.

Vehicles always accelerate from a low speed to a higher one. To enable a diesel engine to be compact enough to be fitted on a vehicle and to atomize the fuel sufficiently at low speeds, it is necessary to achieve high-pressure solid injection without using compressed air. It was an unusual circumstance when both Benz and MAN completed the solid-injection diesel engine in the same year (Photo 32-6). Note that the solid injection system itself was completed first by Vickers in England in the year 1910.

Photo 32-5 Compact prototype diesel engine manufactured by Safir Company: Manufactured for vehicles in 1908, the engine failed because of inadequate atomization of its fuel into droplets (Deutsches Museum, München).

Benz and MAN's Idea

Benz's idea had its origin in P. L'Orange's 1908 concept. L'Orange used the compression stroke of the piston to accumulate highly pressurized air in a reservoir connected to the engine cylinder by a passageway. The idea behind this concept was that the high-velocity flow of air in the passageway would atomize the fuel into fine droplets. While improving the L'Orange scheme, Benz invented the precombustion chamber system, which is still used in the Mercedes-Benz automobile diesel engines. Fig. 32-2 compares the L'Orange idea with today's precombustion chamber system and other diesel combustion systems.

MAN, on the other hand, imparted a swirling motion to the intake air to distribute the fuel droplets as evenly as possible in the combustion chamber. Two fuel injection nozzles were used. The swirling motion was produced by placing a guide (called the "shroud") on the head of the intake valve, as shown in Fig. 32-3. For information, the idea of using air swirl originated with Gibbon in 1895.

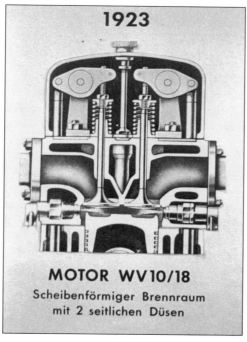

1923

MOTOR WV10/18

Scheibenförmiger Brennraum
mit 2 seitlichen Düsen

Photo 32-6 First diesel truck (1924): The MAN four-ton truck and its combustion chamber. Six months earlier in the same year, Benz completed a truck based on the prechamber system (MAN Museum).

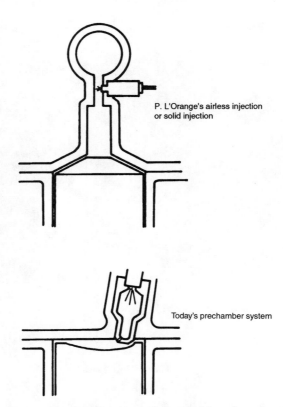

P. L'Orange's airless injection or solid injection

Today's prechamber system

Fig. 32-2 (a) P. L'Orange's solid injection idea in 1908 and combustion chamber of its prechamber system: Benz's first automobile diesel engine used this prechamber system.

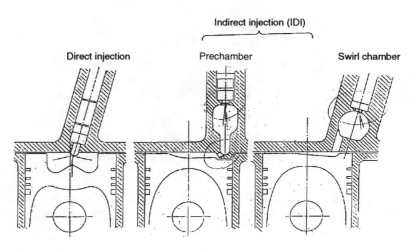

Indirect injection (IDI)

Direct injection   Prechamber   Swirl chamber

Fig. 32-2 (b) Today's diesel combustion systems.

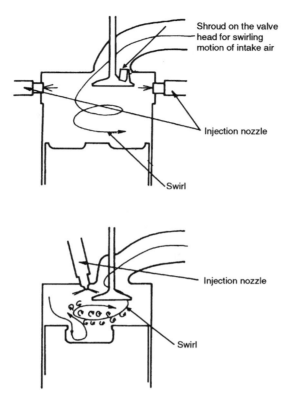

Fig. 32-3 Combustion chamber of the first MAN automobile diesel engine in 1924 (top) and combustion chamber of today's direct injection system.

The Dorner engine, which had been adopted by the Packard Company, had the same design philosophy as the MAN system, but it had only one fuel injection nozzle. The intake air was swirled by a helically shaped intake air port, a method similar to the one now used, as shown in the lower sketch of Figure 32-3. Dorner's vision deserves close attention. The information-gathering ability, the engineering judgment, and the decisiveness of the Packard engineering team that took up Dorner's engine were superb.

However, technology is sometimes ironic. Packard did make a mistake in choosing this method of fuel injection; unfortunately, adequate technical knowledge of the principles of fuel injection did not exist at that time. The direct injection system was still immature. As a result, the combustion system on the MAN diesel engine (the first diesel used in a truck) was soon changed to an "air cell," another type of indirect injection combustion system (refer to Appendix A33-1).

Shortcomings of Diesel Engine

After Packard decided to use Dorner's technology of direct fuel injection system, Packard's chief designer Woolson promptly began to reduce the engine weight (refer to the next chapter).

Usually, diesel engines have a weight per horsepower about 1.5 to 3 times larger than gasoline engines. The reason for this increased weight is that a diesel engine relies on self-ignition, which depends on high-temperature compressed air induced by a high compression ratio. As a result, its combustion pressure is much higher than a gasoline engine. To withstand the high pressure, a robust structure is required. The combustion pressure of a naturally aspirated diesel engine is about 1.5 times higher than that of a naturally aspirated gasoline engine.

When the swept volume is the same, the diesel engine produces only about two-thirds the horsepower of the gasoline engine. Why is the power output smaller, even though the combustion pressure is higher?

First, since combustion is an oxidation reaction, there is a specific weight of air that will completely oxidize one gram of fuel without leaving excess oxygen. This weight of air is called the *stoichiometric air/fuel ratio*. The gasoline engine operates with an air/fuel mixture very near the stoichiometric air/fuel ratio. It is necessary to have this ratio because an air/fuel ratio much greater than stoichiometric is difficult to ignite with a spark plug, and one much smaller than stoichiometric (fuel-rich) is very inefficient. The stoichiometric mixture is supplied to the gasoline engine by a carburetor or by fuel injectors in the manifold, and this mixture of air and fuel is well mixed and nearly homogeneous.

In the diesel engine, the fuel is injected into the combustion chamber near the end of the compression stroke and ignites spontaneously. As mixing between fuel and air occurs, burning continues. This process is very heterogeneous. Soot is formed during combustion because some of this fuel burns with insufficient oxygen and the combustion of this fuel is not completed. As more fuel is injected, more and more soot is produced. Therefore, the air/fuel ratio of the diesel engine must always be higher than stoichiometric to prevent excessive amounts of soot. This requirement means that less fuel is present in the diesel engine cylinder than in the cylinder of the gasoline engine, and diesel engine power is therefore reduced. Current diesel engines can use only about 70-80% (in case of the naturally aspirated engine) of the fuel used by a gasoline with the same swept volume.

In diesel engines, the utilization factor varies with the combustion system. For example, the diesel engine provided with a precombustion chamber system (IDI system) has a utilization value of about 80%; the naturally aspirated direct injection system has a value about 70-80%; and the turbocharged direct injection system used for most large trucks has values of approximately 50-70%. In other words, the direct injection system is still less developed than the precombustion chamber system even today.

Another reason that the output of a diesel engine is less than that of the gasoline engine is that gasoline engines can operate at a high rate of speed because the combustion rate increases with the engine speed. Diesel, on the other hand, has a reduced combustion efficiency at high speeds because of the longer ignition delay and longer injection duration (in crank angle), and also because of the slow mixing. In diesel engines, the government-mandated smoke limits are very hard to meet at high speeds. Since the diesel engine has a high compression ratio, the energy required to revolve the engine itself, namely friction horsepower, is larger than that of the gasoline engine. The friction loss is large in proportion to the engine's rotational speed. Therefore, when speed is increased to boost the output, the friction loss raises enough to offset the output component of the engine. The maximum speed that a gasoline engine can reach is about 10,000 revolutions per minute (for a race engine or other high-performance vehicle); a diesel engine can reach only about 5000 rpm.

Advantages of Diesel Engine

As the reader already knows from earlier parts of this book, a diesel engine has a number of disadvantages in comparison with a gasoline engine. Then why is a diesel engine used? The answer is that a diesel engine has good enough fuel consumption to offset these disadvantages. When comparing fuel consumption per horsepower/hour at the maximum output between the best diesel and the best gasoline engine, the diesel engine uses only about 70% of the fuel that the gasoline engine uses. Partial load condition (in which the accelerator is kept halfway depressed) is the condition in which an automobile usually travels and includes acceleration and deceleration. Under partial load, the fuel consumption of a diesel engine can be as little as 60% of the fuel required by the gasoline engine. These percentages are based on Japanese traffic conditions. In the United States, the gasoline vehicle gets a little better mileage.

The reason that a diesel engine has such good fuel consumption is its high compression ratio required for self-ignition. The higher the compression ratio, the better the thermal efficiency (refer to Appendix A4). The gasoline engine cannot utilize this high compression ratio because of the resulting knocking phenomenon.

As long as fuel economy is measured using fuel volume, diesel fuel has another advantage. Diesel fuel has a specific gravity about 10% larger than that of gasoline, that is, one liter of diesel fuel is 10% heavier than a liter of gasoline. The amount of energy in a specified weight of diesel fuel is almost the same as that of gasoline, so the amount of energy in a liter of diesel fuel is 10% greater than gasoline. When fuel economy is measured by volume (i.e., in kilometers/liter), diesel fuel would produce 10% greater fuel economy than gasoline, even if the engines were otherwise identical.

Another important reason for higher efficiency in diesel engines is that, while diesel uses an air/fuel mixture with around 40% excess air, the gasoline engine runs with a stoichiometric mixture; the leaner mixture results in higher efficiency because with a lean mixture the combustion temperatures are lower with sufficient oxygen. Lower combustion temperature reduces heat losses.

A better fuel consumption signifies that the energy possessed by fuel is used efficiently, and a lower combustion temperature due to a higher air/fuel ratio reduces the heat quantity released to the coolant. This reduced heat means that the radiator can be downsized, and the cooling fan in an air-cooled engine can be made smaller. The radiator size, for instance, can be reduced by more than 35%.

Another advantage of a diesel engine is that it has a higher durability, or a longer service life, as a result of the robust and heavy structure required to sustain the high combustion pressures. As mentioned previously, the peak cylinder pressure (combustion pressure) of the diesel engine is more than 1.5 times that of the gasoline engine. If the same stress is put on a structure but at a higher pressure, then that structure must be thicker. As an analogy, let us consider a circular bar with diameter D loaded as shown in Fig. 30-1. The stress is proportional to $1/D^3$, while the deflection is proportional to $1/D^4$. Namely, to keep the stress the same, the increase in the diameter must have a greater rigidity that is proportional to the increase of the diameter. Using this analogy, one can easily understand that if an engine (diesel) is designed for higher cylinder pressure, its deflection is smaller than the engine (gasoline) designed for a lower cylinder pressure if the stress is designed as the same as the diesel. A higher rigidity gives a better durability. Otherwise, a diesel engine requires a more precise machining (closer tolerances) to keep the finely tuned combustion, and the component for heavy-duty vehicles designed for longer life target. The precise structure inevitably gives a better durability. Because of this long life and excellent fuel consumption, diesel engines are now being used extensively in commercial vehicles.

When this diesel engine is mounted on an airplane, the maximum range will be increased 40% or more according to a simple calculation. Even if fuel cost is the same, the operating cost will be at least 30% lower. However, the several disadvantages mentioned earlier must be overcome by some means. Then, how did Woolson attempt to resolve those problems, particularly the weight problem that is most significant for use in an airplane? And why did he fail in his attempt? The answers are given in Chapter 33.

Glory and Tragedy of Packard (II)

Engine failed due to bad odor. An honor student who forgot basics. However, many ideas should be evaluated.

✄

America Trailing Behind Europe

First, I want to comment on the Wright "Whirlwind" aeroengine that Packard admired. The United States had pioneered aerospace technology, which had originated from the Wright brothers, Manly, and Balzer. However, at the end of World War I, the U.S. lagged behind Europe in technology. Some surplus aeroengines that were unused in the war were brought to the United States after the end of the war. Among these surplus engines was a three-cylinder radial engine.

Charles L. Lawrence manufactured and sold 28-hp horizontally opposed, two-cylinder engines in which two pistons move in the same direction rather than in the opposite directions. Lawrence produced a three-cylinder radial engine by emulating the surplus European-made engine. In 1921, he remodeled this three-cylinder radial engine into a nine-cylinder, 180-hp engine. This engine tweaked the interest of the U.S. Navy. Eugene V. Wilson, the U.S. Navy's power division manager, wanted a 200-hp class radial engine. He felt that the engine could be realized by enhancing the power of the Lawrence engine. However, Lawrence lacked the funds to develop the engine.

On the other hand, Wright Company, which was manufacturing the Hispano Suiza engines through a licensing agreement, did not have experience in producing an air-cooled engine. The Wright Company was founded by the Wright brothers and underwent several name changes including

Wright-Dayton and then Wright-Martin. In 1929, the company was merged with the Curtiss Company to establish the Curtiss-Wright Corporation.

However, after World War II, the original Wright Company had dropped from the aircraft industry (refer to Chapter 12). Wilson advised Wright's president, F.B. Rentschler, to negotiate an agreement with Lawrence, which was done.

The Wright Company had hired several talented engineers, including A.V.D Wilgoos and G.J. Mead, in preparation for developing a new engine. In addition, the famous Samuel D. Heron of Farnborough, England, joined the company and was placed in charge of the cylinder development. Heron increased the distance between the intake and exhaust valves at the cylinder head until the distance was wider than in the Jupiter engine so as to provide adequate cooling performance and high reliability (refer to Appendix A28).

Then, this engine (named the Whirlwind) caught Lindbergh's eye and led to his success in crossing the Atlantic Ocean. Lindbergh himself changed the design of the engine's system for lubricating the rocker-arm bearing. Normally, the rocker-arm bearings are greased periodically for general service. However, for long-range service—such as the New York to Paris flight—a magazine-type attachment is substituted for the pressure-gun fitting, so that the grease in the magazine is fed to the bearing slowly but continuously throughout the flight.[33-1] Success cannot be achieved by rushing everything to completion. This truth may be recognized from Lindbergh's meticulous care and plan for his flight.

Packard's Challenge for Lightweight Diesel Engine

Lindbergh's success greatly increased the reputation of the Wright engine. The U.S. Navy promptly decided to use this engine for its fighter aircraft and was also considering replacing the Packard engine in the Navy's patrol boat with the Wright Whirlwind engine. Packard's concern can be imagined. To reestablish the company's reputation and to market an engine notably superior to the highly thought-of Whirlwind, the Packard Company began to design a diesel engine that would outperform the Whirlwind.

Packard's chief designer Woolson designed a magnesium crankcase to reduce weight, and he fastened the crankcase and cylinder with two hoops instead of the heavier bolts (Photo 33-1).

Since the combustion pressure of the diesel engine is about 1.5 times higher than the gasoline engine, it is natural that the crankshaft would be heavier. To

Photo 33-1 Contrivance for weight reduction: Cylinder was fastened to the crankcase with two hoops. This device provided a lighter weight than bolts. The apparent pipe at the bottom of this photo is actually a hoop. A turnbuckle is provided at the center. A single valve is used for both the intake air and exhaust valves. The tube attached to the cylinder is a port commonly used for intake air and exhaust, also designed for lighter weight (Smithsonian Museum).

reduce this extra weight, Packard used a small-diameter crankshaft comparable to that of a gasoline engine. This smaller crankshaft was used because the counterweights were pivoted on crank cheeks, and a powerful compression spring absorbed the maximum impulses by permitting the counterweight to lag slightly. Also, the propeller was protected from excessive acceleration forces by mounting a rubber vibration damper (Photo 33-2). Further, a single valve was used for both the intake air and exhaust gas instead of two valves as in the case of conventional design, thus eliminating the weight of one valve. As a result, Packard gave birth to an aero diesel engine whose weight and output were equal to those of the Wright Whirlwind gasoline engine, but the fuel consumption rate was at least 30% better.

Fatal Blow Due to a Wife's Complaint

The newly designed Packard diesel engine succeeded in its test flight, broke world records one after another, and received an award from U.S. President Hoover. However, this engine had an unexpected problem. The engine had a

*Photo 33-2 Rubber vibration damper at the root of the propeller hub
(propeller removed in this photo).*

strong exhaust odor. Even today, exhaust odor is annoying in a diesel engine
with a direct injection system. Methods to minimize this odor are important
technical concerns, particularly during the winter and during engine starting.

Each airplane equipped with the Packard engine flew with black exhaust
smoke trailing behind it (sometimes the plane would stream out white
smoke by blowing out the glowplug as a starting aid). It was reported that
when passengers disembarked from the plane, their clothes and their lug-
gage smelled so strongly of the exhaust smoke that they could not rejoin the
public for a while. In addition, the engine vibration was still heavy. Passengers came to dislike the Packard engine plane. The steps taken to restrict the
black smoke, which is necessary for any diesel engine, were inadequate.
Even today, the horsepower (torque) of a diesel engine is restricted by the
smoke level. I am not aware of the exact level of diesel technology for
reducing the smoke level in Packard's times. Also note that the smoke
exhaust is substantially increased at high altitudes due to the decrease of air
density. To minimize the visibility of the soot-stained fuselage, the commercial airplanes mounting the Packard engine were painted black (Photo 33-3).

The pilots, as well as the passengers, came to dislike the Packard engine
plane. After a pilot flew for an hour or so without being protected by a

Photo 33-3 Stinson plane mounting Packard diesel engine: The Stinson plane was painted black to make the soot staining due to exhaust gas from the Packard engine inconspicuous (Ford Museum).

windshield glass, his face was as black as though he had just finished an Indy 500 race. C.D. Chamberlin, who first piloted the Packard engine-mounted Stinson plane, said: "Whenever I came home after piloting a Packard engine plane, my wife told me that you must have flown with that oil burner again. You smell terrible." As we know, a wife's opinion often exerts a decisive influence over anything. This poor opinion is the beginning of the Packard diesel engine's downfall.

Disasters Made Further Attack

On April 23, 1930, the *Herald Tribune* relayed the news from Attica, New York: "Today, an airplane mistook a snow-covered hill for an airfield because of a blizzard and crashed into the hill. Three persons died. One of the casualties was Mr. Woolson of the Packard Company. He was an engineer who adopted a diesel engine for airplanes." The next year, 1931, another tragedy occurred. On June 27, Parker D. Cramer left Detroit with the Packard diesel engine-equipped *Bellanca* seaplane in an attempt to take the great-circle route to Copenhagen via the North Pole. When the plane began taxiing to take off in a small port of the Shetlands, the final stop point, a person on the quay hurriedly signaled by swinging a yellow sheet.

He had received storm warnings in the Copenhagen region. However, the crew of the airplane thought the message was only "Good luck! Bye." They took off from the water, circled the small town once, and then flew away. A radio station in Sweden heard a calling voice, "Hello, hello, hello ...," but the airplane never reappeared. After a few weeks, the crew's articles wrapped in oilpaper were found on the sea. Their letter said that the plane had successfully landed on the ocean. According to Robert B. Meyer, it can only be surmised that engine failure, probably due to a clogged oil filter, caused the plane to go down.[32-1] The oil used in a gasoline engine is apt to become thinner if it is used for a long time. By contrast, the oil for a diesel engine becomes thicker due to soot if the combustion is poor. Therefore, the oil filter clogs earlier.

Unfortunately, the world was in an economic depression. The price of the Packard diesel engine was 35% higher than the Wright Whirlwind engine. The Packard engine was disliked by both pilots and passengers. In addition, the plane accident claimed the life of the project leader and most ardent supporter. Thus, Cramer's forced landing on rough seas beyond any hope of rescue sounded the death knell for the diesel engine project. The project was abandoned, and the factory was closed.

Essence of Failure

Packard's technical failure was analyzed by Robert B. Meyer.[32-1] Based on his analysis, I would like to list the important factors according to my own opinion (refer to Appendix A33-1).

(1) *Premature initiation of production for a new technology*—As we noted earlier, the diesel engine itself was still in its infancy. The direct injection system particularly required more research and evaluation before its production. It is well known today that a diesel engine emits a higher-density exhaust smoke at lower air densities (higher altitudes). A supercharger is indispensable when such an engine is used for airplanes. The more successful aero diesel engine Junkers had a supercharging system. Woolson himself was applying for a patent on the same invention. Thus, Packard's attempt to fly with a diesel engine was at least three years too early.

(2) *Inadequate technology for the fuel injection system*—The fuel injection pressure was recorded as 70 atm. This value is extraordinarily low from today's viewpoint. The technology on not only the fuel injection system

but also diesel combustion itself was yet to be established. The completion of the direct injection technique in three years or so could not have been expected. Packard's greatest error may be its selection of Dorner as the partner in a technical tie-up, since his product had not been proven to be saleable. For an earlier completion of a product, the partner should have been selected from among those who had established technology. Even if such a partner had been selected, another three years might have been required to complete the project.

(3) *Engine output too low*—While the Packard diesel had the same power rating as the Whirlwind engine for continuous operation, another important power rating for aircraft engines is the "Take-Off Power" rating. The engine must be run at this higher power level for only a few minutes before decreasing power. About the time of the introduction of the Packard diesel engine, oil refiners were able to increase the octane number of gasoline. Thus, gasoline engines such as the Whirlwind were able to increase their Take-Off Power rating without combustion knock. In other words, the Packard diesel's competition became immediately stronger. This experience shows that product developers should attempt to foresee the possible technological advances in competing products.

(4) *Price too high*—The Whirlwind engine cost $3000, while the Packard engine was sold at $4025. Even this price difference of $1025 might have been allowed if the diesel engine had not caused such strong vibration, heavy smoke, and odor remaining on clothes. The Packard car (Photo 33-4) was selling for as high as $3250 at that time even though the Ford Model A automobile was selling for only $511 (Photo 33-5). A product can be sold for any price if the buyers recognize the value in the merchandise as being worth the money.

Packard's Concern

The background of Packard's development of this engine has already been discussed. An excellent engine called the Whirlwind appeared as a rival, posing a serious threat to the dominance of the Packard aeroengines. Packard was eager to regain its old dominance in one fell swoop. This desire has also been detailed before. Why was Packard so concerned? In 1916, the Packard Company was the first in the world to mass-produce cars with the V12 engine. This eminence was due to the leadership of Packard's vice president, Jesse C. Vincent. Spurred by this success, Packard manufactured a 250-hp aero engine in 1917. The famous Liberty aeroengine, whose development was planned and led by the U.S. government, was said to be a

Photo 33-4 The 1929 Packard "045" dual-windshield Phaeton Dietrich body cost $3250 (Pate Museum of Transportation).

Photo 33-5 The 1930 Ford Model A Phaeton cost $440 (The 1928 model cost $511) (Ford Museum).

scaled-up version of that Packard aeroengine. Packard received a large amount of defense contract money from the government.

The Liberty engine gained a certain level of success technically. Packard intended to increase the horsepower of that engine by expanding the scale and with other modifications. This company increased the capacity of the 27L Liberty engine to 41 liters and made other modifications to enhance its output. However, its poor reliability caused this engine to be unsuccessful.[28-5] It is possible that this failure made Packard nervous and could have resulted in too much money being poured into its aero diesel engine, resulting in a heavy loss. Were the technical problems thoroughly examined by returning to the basic points before expanding the Liberty engine? Note that Packard's V12 engine was never used for airplanes. Instead, it was used in torpedo boats, where it gained recognition and success.

Subsequently, Packard Company gave birth to some excellent cars. During World War II, this company produced the Rolls-Royce aeroengines as well, making great contributions to the air force of the Allied Powers. Packard Company, which could rightfully boast of its technological advance, collapsed soon after World War II. Why? Let us trace the process.

Appendix A33-1 Combustion in Packard Diesel Engine

MAN, which began with the direct injection system in 1924, widely modified that injection system and the shape of combustion chamber in 1927. After six years with the direct injection system, MAN switched to the air cell type as mentioned previously. In the case of the Packard, the principle of swirling the intake air was also adopted by Dorner. However, it can be said that the technique of obtaining a more rapid mixing of air and fuel droplets by combining a higher injection pressure with air swirl and combustion chamber design was not yet fully developed in the Packard Company. It was reported that Packard's fuel injection pressure was 70 atm, while the present direct injection system usually has 700 atm or more. Since the specification of Packard's injection nozzle is unknown, the accurate size of the fuel droplet cannot be calculated. However, in today's engine, the mean fuel droplet diameter is approximately 10 μm with a multihole nozzle; thus, it becomes 30 μm, substantially larger, at the 70 atm used in the Packard diesel. Although a swirl was given to the intake air, I believe that the technique existing at that time could not provide the proper swirl.

Thus, the fuel was burned without being adequately mixed. In such a case, however, the emission of black smoke can be somewhat reduced and fuel consumption can be maintained at a satisfactory level by advancing the fuel injection timing. The fuel injection timing refers to the point in time at which the fuel injection begins before the piston reaches the upper end of the cylinder (called the top dead center or TDC). This timing is essential because fuel will not burn immediately after it is injected into the cylinder. That is, a certain amount of time is required for the fuel droplets to be mixed with the heated air and for preflame chemical reactions to occur (this time is called ignition delay). To effectively transfer the cylinder pressure, which follows the combustion progress, to the piston, fuel is injected into the cylinder just before TDC. The time before reaching TDC is expressed in a rotational angle of the crankshaft, that is, before top dead center (BTDC) __$^\circ$ (degrees).

When advancing the fuel injection timing, or increasing the time period between injection and arrival at TDC, ignition takes a longer time since the temperature of the air in the cylinder is still low. Therefore, fuel mixes better with the air. However, because the amount of fuel injected during the ignition delay becomes larger, combustion occurs suddenly. At higher temperatures and pressures, the entire combustion process is facilitated, and the exhaust smoke level decreases (Fig. A33-1). However, if the injection timing is advanced too much, the combustion process will not proceed smoothly due to rough combustion in the initial stage. Smoke emission will increase.

However, a combustion dependent on an advanced fuel injection timing entails a high combustion pressure and a high rate of pressure rise. Since the maximum pressure of the Packard diesel reportedly was 105 atm, it can easily be imagined that the fuel injection timing was advanced as far as possible. The rate of pressure rise per crank angle may have been much larger than 10 kg/cm^2/deg. A modern diesel engine usually has 85 atm (in case of natural aspiration) of maximum pressure and 4 kg/cm^2/deg of rate of pressure rise. The Packard diesel engine probably generated excessive noise and vibration due to the high rate of pressure rise. In 1931, Packard reduced its compression ratio from 16 to 14 to improve these combustion characteristics. The reduced compression ratio increased the ignition delay, the rate of pressure rise, and sometimes even the maximum cylinder pressure. The smoke level was decreased; however, the odor of the exhaust gas became even stronger than before. Packard may have found a better set of combustion properties by reducing the compression ratio.

One result of these new combustion properties is that the engine had a very bad odor. With a low fuel injection pressure, large fuel droplets adhere to

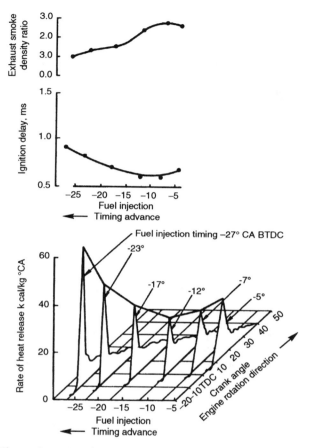

Fig. A33-1 When advancing the fuel injection timing, the ignition delay increases and the exhaust smoke decreases. Heat release, or the quantity of heat generated per unit time, also becomes larger. Combustion can be thought to be noisy due to the high rate of pressure rise (Hino test engine, 2400 rpm).

the wall of the combustion chamber before they evaporate. The droplets are then exhausted as unburned hydrocarbons and aldehydes due to intermediate chemical reaction, thus resulting in an odor. This odor decreases as the engine power is increased. The odor must have been terrible during idling and taxiing on runways, particularly in cool weather.

Appendix A33-2 How the Packard Diesel Affixed the Cylinder

Packard fastened the cylinder with two hoops as shown in Photo 33-1. Fig. A33-2 shows the design drawing of the entire engine. In the longitudinal section at the left, two circular-section hoops are discernible at the lower end of the cylinder. These hoops were used because they were lighter weight than the bolts used in general design. For fastening with bolts, rather large bosses are necessary to permit cutting the threaded holes of the bolts. These bosses substantially increase the weight as shown in the conventional design in Fig. A33-3.

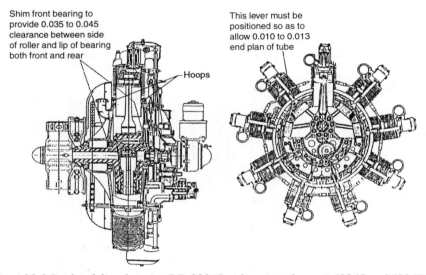

Shim front bearing to
provide 0.035 to 0.045
clearance between side
of roller and lip of bearing
both front and rear

Hoops

This lever must be
positioned so as to
allow 0.010 to 0.013
end plan of tube

Fig. A33-2 Packard diesel engine DR-980 (Smithsonian photos A 48845 and 48847): Fuel is injected with a plunger for each cylinder (unit injector).

Was the hoop fastening really a good idea? Each cylinder bolt must fasten the cylinder to the crankcase while withstanding the cylinder pressure, as shown in Fig. A33-3. Therefore, a large tightening force (load) is applied to the bolt so that the cylinder will not separate from the crankcase (float) upon combustion (about three times the allowance factor, which means tightening force by the maximum press force is needed under normal load condition).

Fig. A33-4 shows a joint diagram used to design the clamping force. The diagram shows the relationship of the tightening force to the deformation. As the bolt is tightened further, it elongates, and the boss shrinks to keep an

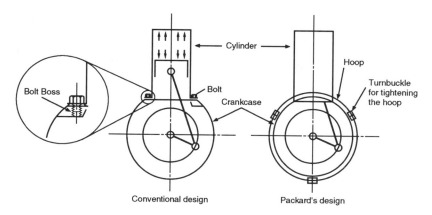

Fig. A33-3 Design of cylinder-fastening bolt.

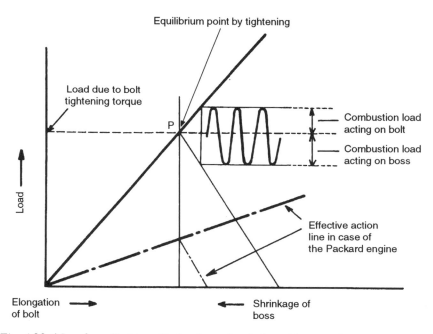

Fig. A33-4 Load applied to cylinder-fastening bolt and boss and their deformation.

equilibrium as equilibrium point P in the figure. Point P is designed to keep some allowance factor. This load is called the initial clamping force. When a combustion load is applied under this condition, the load is shared between the bolt and the boss. As a result, the bolt elongates and the boss (on the bolt side) tends to release its shrinkage. Therefore, the fastened part will separate (float) if the initial clamping force is weak. Packard's hoops were fastened in the circumferential direction instead of the axial direction of the cylinder axis. If the tightening torque (force) is the same, then the elongation of the hoop is much bigger due to its longer hoop length, the same as the circumferential length of the crankcase shorter than the fastening bolt length of conventional design. In other words, in the same elongation of the bolt or hoop, the fastening force to the axial direction by hoop is less than a conventional bolt.

Even though Packard would have applied a much higher tightening torque for the initial clamping force to the hoop, the diameter seems to have been too small to apply enough tightening torque. Hence, the cylinder is apt to float, with a resulting risk of oil and gas leakage. Did these problems occur with the engine?

Chapter 34

Glory and Tragedy of Packard (III)

The highest quality may not always be the most suitable.
Miserable end due to an error in determining the proper quality.

❦

Playing Active Role in World War II

Although the Packard Company had a big setback as a result of its diesel engine, it grew steadily until World War II. The efforts of this company in the war were highly valued. For instance, Heron stated: "Packard's achievement is a great contribution hardly conceivable in that hard situation."

I begin the story with the Patrol-Torpedo (PT) boat, which was powered by the Packard engine. In 1938, Hubert Scott-Pain's British Power Boat Company, England, introduced its private venture PV70 boat. Although the Scott-Paine company had built a series of motor torpedo boat (BTB) for the Royal Navy, this boat was a radical departure from its contemporaries in both configuration and concept. The ELCO Naval Division factory in the United States produced a boat that was directly traced to this imported PV70. The plans were not obtained by blueprints, but by measuring every part of the boat as a working model. Following minor modifications, the new boat was accepted by the U.S. Navy as the Patrol-Torpedo boat, and assembly began just before World War II.

Shortly before World War II, a beautiful photograph of this boat cruising at a high speed was introduced to Japan. Yet it appears that the Japanese Navy paid no particular attention to this boat. After the war began, however, its activity was amazing. Its first achievement was in taking a leading role in General MacArthur's escape from Corregidor. Thanks to the success in this escape, MacArthur was later appointed as the supreme commander of the

South Pacific theater, and the Allied Forces successfully reoccupied the Philippines and then occupied mainland Japan. Yet, MacArthur's escape was more than a simple escape. He carefully observed the PT boat's mobility during his escape, perceived its effectiveness, and requested the War Department in Washington to field many of the boats to support a strategy of hopping from island to island in the Pacific. Thus, the Packard engine came to be fully utilized (Photos 34-1 and 34-2). As a result, the Japanese Marines, nicknamed "The Tokyo Express" because they were pumping supplies to the Guadalcanal island, were badly beaten by the PT boats. During the war, a PT boat with Lieutenant John F. Kennedy in it encountered the Japanese destroyer *Amagiri* and was badly damaged when it hit the *Amagiri*'s hull. When Kennedy later became President of the United States, he received a congratulatory card with messages from the surviving crew of the *Amagiri*. Touched by this thoughtful message, the president displayed the card in his private room. It is a very poignant story.

Photo 34-1 Packard engine installed on a PT boat: Annoying the Japanese Imperial Navy in the Solomon Sea.

Several opinions always result when any significant historical event is being discussed. A reader offers the following comments, which may be useful for the reader in forming his or her own opinion.

It is certainly true that the PT boat carried MacArthur from the Philippines. However, thereafter the PT boat was a total failure. It sunk no Japanese shipping whatsoever and in each encounter with the Japanese

Photo 34-2 Packard 4M2500-type engine for PT boat: 1200 PS (instantaneous output 1500 PS), with reversing gear, 1340-kg weight (PT boat museum).

Navy, the PT boats were sunk or damaged. For this reason, Kennedy's boat was at sea at night, because in the daytime, the life of the PT boat was short.

The idea that the PT boat was a success was due only to U.S. propaganda during the war as well as a successful movie.

By the way, the crew of the *Amagiri* did not see Kennedy's boat. Some thought they saw a boat, some not. Most thought they had collided with floating debris.

Then, the B29 bombers, which raided mainland Japan from a remote base in Saipan, were assisted by P51 fighters, which mounted the Packard-made Merlin engine. The Merlin engine had its origin in the design of Rolls-Royce. After obtaining its license from Rolls-Royce, Packard modified the original design. The Packard Merlin engine U.S. patent was then adopted by Rolls-Royce. This incorporation of the Merlin design was due to Packard's technological accumulation and reputation.

For the reader's information, the torpedo boat was not completely ignored in Japan. In 1940 when the Pacific War began, a torpedo boat was purchased as a sample from Italy. Japan began to seriously study this boat only after it received the hard blows from the PT boats in the Solomon Sea. Thus,

Japan initiated an urgent effort to develop a similar boat, including the engine. No engine could be developed from scratch in such a short time period. So, the Mitsubishi Kinsei air-cooled radial aeroengine was used, and a few units were available for action in the final stages of the war. Needless to say, the problem of cooling the engine on a boat could not be solved as easily as it was in the air-cooled aeroengine. Consequently, this development project ended, leaving a meaningless fuss and an engineering officer's suicide.[34-1] Upon purchasing the torpedo boat from Italy, it was reported that the supplier asked the buyer, "Why don't you purchase several of these boats? Do you know we have had an order for many of these boats from England?" (Perhaps because of inadequate domestic supply?) If the source of this information had been determined, the effectiveness of the torpedo boat might have been more evident. If the Japanese Navy had acquired at least 20 of these boats, then perhaps Japan could have controlled the enemy's wild attacks in the Solomon Sea.

If the background and trend had been analyzed carefully, the Italian recommendation would have resulted in an order for 20 boats. However, the exact transmission of site information, proper background analysis, and cultivation of sharp sensitivity were important roles for the development division to play, which is the same as it is today.

Packard's Advanced Technology Fast

In the 1970s, all engine manufacturers faced a number of tough problems due to government regulations on exhaust emissions. One of these problems was the *cavitation pitting* of the cylinder liner. This term refers to the small pits that the coolant forms on the outer surface of a cylinder. In severe cases the pitting erodes completely through the cylinder wall and the cooling water enters the cylinder. Needless to say, the engine is abruptly put out of commission (Appendix A34). This phenomenon is comparable to a cancer that consumes the internal organs of man. Hino Motors was also troubled by this pitting problem. This cancer occurs unexpectedly when the combustion temperature is lowered by retarding the fuel injection timing so as to reduce NO_x in the exhaust emissions.

Yet, the Packard Company already performed a clinical experiment on this cancer in 1956. Ironically, Packard's results were presented at the technical meeting of the Society of Automotive Engineers (SAE) in June of the same year that Packard cars were removed from the market. This important paper revealed the exact cause of the cavitation. Unfortunately, this was the last technological demonstration of Packard, which had boasted a long tradition of technological pioneering.[34-2] The Packard research was very helpful to Hino Motors as well as other diesel engine manufacturers in developing methods for preventing cavitation pitting.

This effort was proof of the high technological level maintained by Packard. In its main automobile business, Packard always led other manufacturers technologically. In the 1930s, this company introduced cars with automatic transmissions (AT) for the first time. In the 1940s, the company adopted hydraulically powered windows. In the 1950s, Packard dominated the market by the most advanced technologies such as a parabola-shaped combustion chamber and torsion bar suspension. In 1942, U.S. President Roosevelt presented the stamping die of the 1942 model Packard car, famous for its elegant style, to U.S.S.R. Prime Minister Joseph Stalin as a symbol of their nations' friendship. This die later gave birth to the ZIS automobile (Photo 34-3).

Photo 34-3 Packard's illegitimate child ZIS (1946): Its mask is nothing but Packard's (Moscow Science Museum).

Bad Luck Was the Cause

The prosperous Packard Company faded from the world after its 1956 model Clipper, even though it had put into practice a slogan of always giving priority to quality and was recognized for the high quality of its products by the market, users, and technological authorities. In fact, according to the results of the 1955 *Popular Mechanics* survey, the highest evaluation point "Excellent" was given to as many as 97% of all Packard products. If all this is true, then why did this excellent company so suddenly disappear?

Even though Packard had some decidedly unlucky experiences as a company, several factors should be examined as part of its downfall. In 1955 the production plan was for 100,000 units to be built, but only 55,517 units were produced. Further, in the following year, the number of 1955 model cars still in the dealers' showrooms was so large that they had to be greatly discounted to move them. In addition, in 1955, the Utica plant was equipped with the newest and most modern manufacturing equipment, and the remodeling was heavily advertised in the related industrial and academic circles. The investment proved to be excessive. Were there any forewarnings of the problems before the company reached such a dilemma?

A company always has some unlucky experiences. But this bad luck usually has some beginnings in the company actions as well. A simple self-affirmation as being "unlucky" is the beginning of one's downfall. Instead, we should ask why were we "unlucky"? Why did we lag behind the trend? Do we have a proper business plan as a company? Timely questions or self-examinations such as these may protect a company from failure.

Packard's downfall began with the end of World War II. Packard knew it had a problem when its market share of cars in the United States fell from 12 to 4%. During the war, the company had poured all of its energy and efforts into munitions production. Further, during the postwar demand recovery period, the suppliers allocated material based on the prewar demand during the years 1939, 1940, and 1941. Compounding its problems, Packard's main sheet steel supplier, which formerly supplied Packard with 60% of its sheet steel requirements, had sold its plant. This problem was the first of Packard's continuing post-war material shortages.

Excessive Quality and Inadequate Quality Control

The distinction between airplane production and automobile production (which may be said to be the same as the distinction between the defense and civilian industries) is one point to be considered. Post-war Packard was unable to make this distinction. Between the two industries, there are large technological differences in not only the design, but also in production engineering, that is, the finish accuracy. During the war, the Ford Motor Company attempted to manufacture the Pratt & Whitney aeroengine but failed initially. After receiving full-fledged support from the Pratt & Whitney Company, Ford began to produce a satisfactory product.[34-3] In contrast, Packard Company was able to manufacture the Rolls-Royce Merlin engine without outside support. Unfortunately, this superb engineering talent had an effect opposite of what was intended. I wonder if Packard's planned production efforts had always suffered because the Packard vehicle had so many areas with higher quality than was really needed for a car.

The highest level of quality may not always be the most appropriate quality. It is necessary to incorporate the "proper quality" in any market that is undergoing change. The market does not reward excess quality. It only says, "Excellent." Although it may be necessary to stay one step ahead of the competition, there is no need to be ten steps ahead. Packard lost the proper balance between design engineering and production engineering/feedback of marketing information and between its marketing plan and marketing techniques.

In 1956, Packard recalled 5400 cars twice due to a defective rear axle. Further, because the rubber pad in the seat was considered too stiff, it was replaced on all cars without charge. This latter recall was a result of Packard's failure to provide proper guidance on quality control for an affiliated company. The company lost control of its actions. The compact and elegant style that had so impressed a young man (me) in an underdeveloped country (Japan) had turned into an alcoholic and profligate son (Photo 34-4). Its brilliant history suddenly came to an end. The Packard Company could not reverse its downward slide. Finally, the shell of the once proud company was acquired by an industrial engine manufacturer, D.W. Onan & Sons Inc., in 1961.

Appendix A34 Cavitation Pitting of Cylinder Liner Wall

Cavitation pitting on the outside cylinder liner wall is a result of liner vibration. When the cylinder liner moves suddenly to the inside due to vibration, the pressure in the area just evacuated by the liner outer surface rapidly drops below the vapor pressure of the coolant. Bubbles are formed in this area (see Fig. A34-1). Then, when the cylinder liner returns to its outside position, the pressure rapidly rises locally and the bubbles rupture. The reasons that the breaking of the bubbles creates a shock load great enough to form pits, through the cavitation phenomena, are very complex. The likely cause is the result of one or two theories, that is, the shock wave theory and the water hammer theory.[34-4] The water hammer theory would be easier to

Photo 34-4 The 1954 Packard Panther-Daytona: This vehicle is a descendant of that well-defined Packard car. An alcoholic, profligate son may be imagined. When the business of a company declines, its design will degenerate because evaluation lacks spirit (NT. Dawes, The Packard, 1942-1962).

understand if one envisages the breakage pattern as having the shape of a spear head as shown in the figure and the spear head attacking the external cylinder wall. Photo A34-1 shows the bubbles formed on the outer surface of the cylinder liner. The bubbles break due to vibration.

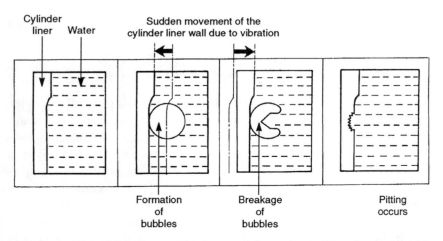

Fig. A34-1 Cavitation pitting: Vibration causes formation and breakage of bubbles. The schematic is based on the water hammer theory.

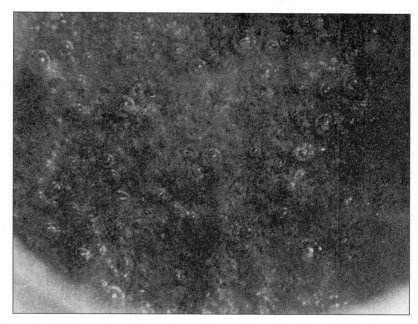

Photo A34-1 Formation of bubbles on the outside wall of the cylinder liner (Hino test engine, 1800 rpm, 2/4 load).

The process of bubble formation and breakage as a result of the cylinder liner vibration is shown in Fig. A34-2. A large number of bubbles accumulate on a limited area on the cylinder liner wall. These bubbles are counted by high-speed camera from the observation window on the cylinder block. The number of bubbles is shown to correlate with the variation of amplitude of the liner wall. With the increase in amplitude, that is, as the wall moves to the outside, the number of bubbles decreases; as the wall moves to the inside, the number increases. Bubble formation and breakage occur along with the vibration.[34-5]

The vibration occurs because of the instantaneous swing of the piston head (piston's transverse and rotational movement) as shown in Fig. A34-3. In the Hino Motors engines, the combustion pressure increases at the moment of the piston head swing due to the control of exhaust gas, which changes the vibration of the cylinder liner. With the retardation of injection timing, the combustion pressure diagram is shifted. The figure illustrates the instantaneous swing of the piston head in comparison with the offset pin piston (piston in which piston pin is provided off-center as shown in the figure).

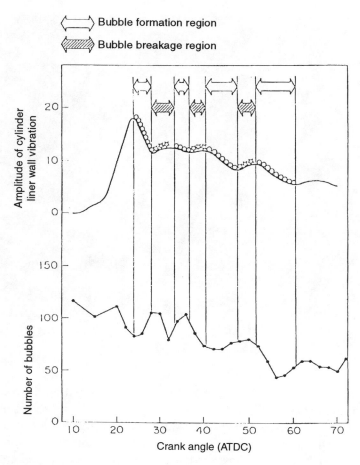

Fig. A34-2 Bubbles on external wall continuously form and break due to the vibration of the cylinder liner. During the bubble breakage, cavitation pitting occurs.

As an interesting comment, the sale of a submarine propeller processing machine by Toshiba Machining Company to the Soviet Union in 1987 was deemed to be a violation of the Coordinating Committee for Export to Communist Areas (COCOM) rule. The sale was considered a violation because the sound from a propeller made from this machine could no longer be detected with SONAR (Sound Navigation And Ranging). The SONAR could not hear the breaking sound of the cavitation bubbles because the propeller could be manufactured in such a shape as not to cause cavitation.

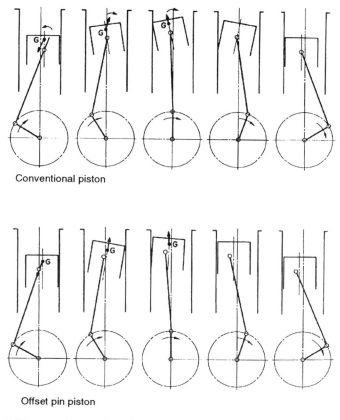

Conventional piston

Offset pin piston

Fig. A34-3 Piston swings its head every stroke: The shock caused by the piston head hitting the liner results in cavitation. Piston head-swinging behavior and effect of offset pin piston.

The sound caused by breakage of bubbles can be detected by the acoustic emission method. Fig. A34-4 shows an example of detecting the cavitation inside an engine as a sound though it does not correspond to a submarine propeller.

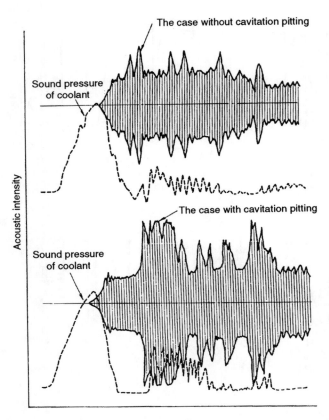

Fig. A34-4 Sound at occurrence of cavitation pitting as detected by the AE method (Hino test engine).

Chapter 35

Voyager and KOKENKI

Both challenged for lean burn. Although a twin-engine plane, the concept is actually that of a single engine. Both avoided an adventurous development of a new diesel engine.

✄

Voyager Was Conceived on a Paper Napkin

In Chapter 31, I touched on a faint sign of the radial engine's revival. This radial engine was the Teledyne Continental's aero diesel engine. In the autumn of 1986, the *Voyager* thrilled the world with its successful round-the-world flight without landing or refueling. It was reported that the *Voyager's* engine was a Teledyne Continental engine, so I thought the engine might be diesel. However, it was actually a gasoline engine. Even though the engine was not a "star" or radial engine, I will comment on the dream of *Voyager* as powered by the Teledyne Continental special engine after I tell the story of the flight.

The *Voyager* airframe was designed by the Rutan brothers, Dick and Burt. While explaining the concept to his older brother Dick in a coffee shop, Burt Rutan sketched the initial design of the aircraft on a paper napkin. The completed craft weighed about 820 kg (including the equipment) and carried a fuel load of about 5700 liters (about 4200 kg), with which the entire round-the-world flight of 46,000 km was covered. Dick piloted the *Voyager* in its flight, accompanied by his girlfriend Jeana Yeager, who cut her blond hair short to reduce weight.

On the other hand, the *KOKENKI*, namely, the KOKEN long-range research aircraft (refer to Appendix A27-2), had the following specifications according to Hino Motors documentation: Empty weight of about 4200 kg and a fuel load of 7500 liters (about 5500 kg), with which the *KOKENKI* flew 11,651 km, setting the 1938 world distance record. The *Voyager* was loaded with fuel weighing five times its own weight, while the *KOKENKI* was loaded with fuel about 1.3 times its weight. The difference between them can be attributed to 50 years of progress in structural materials (primarily, the honeycomb structure and a sandwich structure of graphite fiber and plastic sheet). Also important was an advance in design engineering, caused by the computer's ability to perform a more accurate stress analysis, thereby reducing the required safety margins. However, these advances were not the sole causes of such a great achievement. In addition, there were modifications on the engine that reduced fuel consumption and a twin-engine design that skillfully combined the advanced aircraft materials with innovative aircraft design.

The Essence of Engineering Management

For the *KOKENKI*, a unique air-cooled exhaust valve was invented to prevent the exhaust valve from being burned by an irregular combustion due to the lean burn (lean burn indicates that a relatively small amount of fuel is being burned with a large amount of air) required to reduce fuel consumption (refer to Appendix A35). Because of this valve, a fuel consumption of 180 g/PS-h was achieved. Since the usual fuel consumption at that time was 220 to 230 g/PS-h, approximately a 20% decrease in fuel consumption resulted. Initially, a diesel engine was planned to be used in the *KOKENKI*. In fact, the research expenses were said to have been approved because the program title involved research on a long-range airplane with a diesel engine.[35-1]

However, Professor Kiyoshi Tomizuka (later professor emeritus of Tokyo University) was apprehensive about the practical use of the diesel engine, which was still at a technically low level at that time. As a result, Kiyoshi emphatically rejected the use of a diesel engine and insisted instead on a modified Kawasaki BMW-9C engine, with which the team had experience. He also recommended that the research team investigate the lean-burn system further before it was used in the new aircraft. Considering the history of the previously discussed Packard diesel engine, we can understand that his opinion was indeed the correct one. I respect Professor Kiyoshi Tomizuka's determination and efforts that resulted in his sacrificing the honor of completing the first aero diesel engine. He had to oppose the majority opinion that favored using the diesel engine in the long-range flight.

It is evident that priority should be given to long-range continuous flight. To achieve this long-range flight, the use of a well-known and established engine is more appropriate even though it does not appear to be fashionable. People may accuse you of working only with an old-fashioned and commonplace engine. Yet, managing this procedure of modification correctly is the essence of engineering (Photo 35-1).

Photo 35-1 Fly! KOKENKI *(1938, KOKEN long-range aircraft): This aircraft set a world record by abandoning a temptation to use an aero diesel engine and improving the rugged Kawasaki-BMW (licensed) engine. Also the decision by the pilot, Lieutenant Commander Fujita, and others to resist a temptation to make "one more round" resulted in the flight's success (courtesy of Asahi Shimbun).*

On the other hand, it is interesting to note that the circumstances surrounding the *Voyager* bore some resemblance to the *KOKENKI*. As previously noted, Teledyne Continental had released a prototype diesel engine the year before the Rutan brothers conceived of the *Voyager*. They undoubtedly must have thought about the use of a diesel engine at least once. However, their decision was the same as for the *KOKENKI*. The Rutan brothers sidestepped a new and unproven design in favor of the Teledyne Continental Model IOL-200 engine, which had been modified from the tried and true Model O-240 already on the market.

As a result, the Continental unmodified O-240 engine was used as the front engine. At the rear of the plane was installed a second and innovative new engine. This engine was a second O-240 engine modified for improved fuel consumption by applied lean burn (Fig. 35-1 and Photo 35-2). These engines were planned to be used in the following way. During the early stage of flight when the fuel is abundant and heavy, the *Voyager* is raised up to about 5000 m by using both engines; the front engine is then shut off. In consequence, the aircraft gradually decreases in altitude because of insufficient power. After the aircraft has fallen to about 3000 m, the front engine is restarted to return the aircraft to its former altitude. This procedure is repeated as necessary during the flight. By the final stage of flight, the craft is much lighter because much of its fuel has been consumed, requiring only the rear engine to power the aircraft. Their plan is described in a little more detail in the following paragraphs.

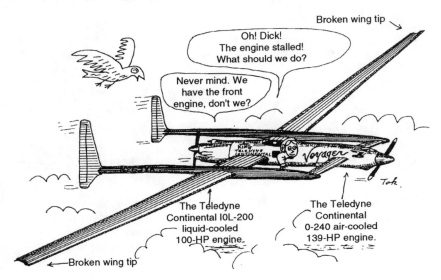

Fig. 35-1 Fly! Voyager *(1986): Though twin-engined in a tandem layout, the plane mainly used its rear engine. The front engine was a "part-time" worker that worked while the plane was still heavy due to a full fuel load.*

For setting the main wings at the best lift/drag ratio, or obtaining the most efficient lift against air resistance, the angle of attack (wing's angle with respect to advancing direction) was selected as 1 degree. This small angle requires an airplane to fly at a high speed when the tank is filled with fuel and has heavier weight. During this time, the plane speed is increased to about 200 km/h or more by both front and rear engines.

Photo 35-2 Voyager *damaged its wing tip by scraping the ground when it took off with its full load of fuel. "Should we return? Or should we go?" Rutan vacillated; however, his confidence in the machine as a result of his having participated in the design resulted in a "Go," and the attempt was gloriously successful (Smithsonian Museum).*

After the plane is lightened as the weight of the fuel decreases, the flight is continued at 80 km/h using the rear engine alone.[35-2]

Well-Conceived Design

For the primary rear engine, the method of cooling was changed from air to liquid to improve combustion by cooling the combustion chamber area more evenly. Also oil cooling was adopted for the piston. This design enabled the compression ratio of the engine to be increased from 7 in the original engine to 11. Because of the increased compression ratio and the lean-burn system, the engine improved its fuel consumption as much as 20% and could challenge the world's record (see Fig. 35-2). Mr. Ron Wilkinson was in charge of this design.[35-3]

The twin-engine design exhibited its major advantage during a serious crisis in the flight. When the *Voyager* turned as it came close to the finish line, the main rear engine stalled and could not be restarted. The starter had been removed to minimize the plane weight. The cruising altitude gradually decreased to 1700 m. At this point, the pilot, Rutan, prepared to restart the rear engine by accelerating the plane as fast as possible. The slipstream caused the rear propeller to windmill, the rear engine restarted, and the

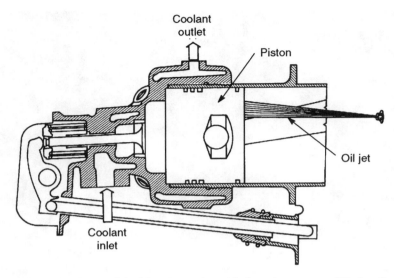

Fig. 35-2 Main engine of the Voyager: *Air-cooled engine was modified to liquid-cooled type, and the compression ratio was enhanced from 7 to 11 by cooling the piston with oil, thereby reducing fuel consumption.*[35-3]

Voyager finished its flight. It was later determined that the rear engine had stalled because of the dust that had accumulated in the fuel line during the journey.

The configuration of the *Voyager* may appear strange. However, let's look at the shape carefully. Its wings are extremely long for reducing induced drag (resistance due to an eddy occurring at the end of the wing). To support these long wings, there are two fuselages that also serve as fuel tanks. In addition, the canard is used to shorten the fuselage length, thereby reducing the weight and surface resistance (friction drag). So, we can understand that this design was conceived through a strenuous and careful process, that is, think, think, think, and think again!

Every designer must think his design through thoroughly, that is, think, think, think, and think again! This careful thought is his destiny. A good design cannot be completed in a sloppy and amateurish way. However, joy at the completion of a successful project and the endurance of his destiny is the privilege given to each designer. It is no exaggeration to say that this joy blesses human life. Both the *Voyager* and the earlier *KOKENKI* are the crystals that gave joy to all mankind as well as the engineers who fulfilled their destiny.

Admirable Decision to Land Far Before Fuel Shortage

After the *KOKENKI* successfully broke the world record, it approached the Kisarazu Airport, still having enough fuel for an additional three rounds. The flight route was a four-sided course. The *KOKENKI* landed successfully amid thunderous applause of the spectators. Afterward, the engine was examined, and it was discovered that the Roots blower used to air-cool the exhaust valve (an air blower, see Photo A35-1) was heavily damaged. Since the degree of damage is unknown, an easy conjecture should be resisted. However, it can be imagined that if the damage of blower vanes had been more extensive, the worn-out metal fragments would have entered the exhaust valve and severely damaged the engine.

The damage to the Roots blower could not have been detected in the cockpit. Did the experienced pilot Lieutenant Commander Yuzo Fujita (later Commander) intuitively know of the damage? Did the excellent engineer Chikakichi Sekine on board or co-pilot Petty Officer 2nd Class Fukujiro Takahashi (later Chief Warrant Officer) or anyone else perhaps detect a faint sign of anomaly sensitively? Or was a change already evident in the exhaust temperature, etc.? I cannot know which of these is the true reason that caused the *KOKENKI* to land with fuel remaining for additional distance.

Yet, this decision to land was obviously the proper one because the continuous three-day flight of the *KOKENKI* gave Japan its only FAI-recognized aeronautical world record. Just before the completion of any challenging attempt or momentous development, the tension that had been built up is apt to collapse. However, it is essential in any attempt to possess enough willpower to maintain the meticulous and detailed care until the end, however terribly tired he or she may be.

Appendix A35 *KOKENKI's* Lean Burn

Today, the greatest concern of gasoline engine manufacturers is how to reduce fuel consumption and CO_2 emissions without increasing the harmful exhaust gas components. When reducing the quantity of fuel for the same intake air volume, that is, forming a lean mixture, both fuel consumption and NO_x decrease as shown in Fig. A35-1. However, the lean burn has the following drawback. Because combustion becomes rough (the cylinder pressure varies over a wide range from cycle to cycle), the change in engine output torque increases until the car cannot travel smoothly. One of the two solutions for this rough driving is to complete the combustion cycle smoothly in a short time by properly forming a turbulence of intake air in the cylinder such as previously discussed in the HMMS. The second solution is to maintain the air and fuel ratio as lean as possible by utilizing a mixture sensor and to distribute the gas blend evenly among all the cylinders. Each of today's car manufacturers is making a serious approach that is unique to each company. The practical limit of the air/fuel ratio that can be used today is about 22. Note that in the case of lean combustion, the combustion fluctuation increases and both combustion temperature and rate of combustion decrease. Generally, the exhaust temperature drops as shown in Fig. A35-2.

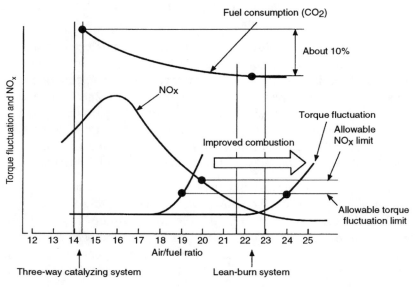

Fig. A35-1 Lean-burn system.

Combustion fluctuation was considered a matter of course in the *KOKENKI* aircraft. The uncontrolled fluctuation greatly troubled the researchers. The practical air/fuel ratio at that time was approximately 19. Then why was an air-cooled exhaust valve (see Fig. A35-3) required even though the exhaust temperature decreased? To obtain an answer, we need to know the actual condition of the aeroengine at that time. During the time of the *KOKENKI*, the practical air/fuel ratio of aeroengines was about 8 to 10 during take-off and climbing and 12 to 13 at cruising. These values indicate a fuel-rich state because the mixing ratio was just enough to permit a reaction between the air and fuel. This minimum ratio is the stoichiometric mixture ratio of about 14.8. This fuel-rich mixture was intentional because the designers wanted to

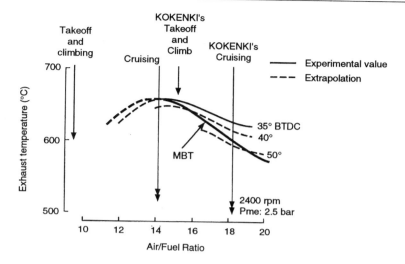

Fig. A35-2 KOKENKI's *exhaust temperatures at take-off and climbing were supposed to be much higher than usual. Base data are of a single-cylinder engine (under full load) from Ricardo research laboratory. Air/fuel ratio values are plotted for reference. They are not the actual data. During cruising, exhaust temperature is much lower because of a partial load.*

utilize the cooling effect of the excess fuel. Without this cooling capability, there was extreme concern of piston knocking and damage to the exhaust valve and other parts of the engine caused by local overheating of the combustion chamber wall, etc.

In the case of the *KOKENKI*, the air/fuel ratio in full-power operation at take-off and climbing was about 13.5, indicating a slight fuel-rich status. The time period of take-off and climbing with the full fuel load is a relatively long period, and it must be endured safely. An air/fuel ratio of 13.5 indicates a rather lean fuel content in comparison with that of general airplane at maximum output. Therefore, it can easily be understood that exhaust temperature at take-off and climbing becomes high, and the valves need to be cooled, as shown in Fig. A35-2.

According to the record at that time, the air-cooled exhaust valve suppressed the combustion fluctuation, permitting the practical air/fuel ratio to be reduced from 16 to approximately 19.[30-3] Through detailed experimentation, the quantity of air required for valve cooling was determined to be 3.7 g/sec per valve.

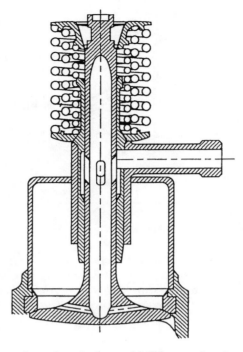

Fig. A35-3 Air cooling valve unique in the world: Why wasn't a simple sodium-cooled valve adopted?

Incidentally, the Roots blower (shown in Photo A35-1) for the air-cooled exhaust valve was the one under study in Gasuden for its TEMPUU engine. Photo A35-2 shows the TEMPUU engine under study, and Photo A35-3 shows a *KOKENKI* engine with the Roots blower installed. The study on supercharging an aeroengine with the Roots blower was almost a global attempt during that time. Unaided challenge by Gasuden for this subject deserves respect.

Photo A35-1 Disassembled Roots blower (Auto + Technik museum): Seen at right are two rotors that function as a kind of air pump with cycloid profile. At left is its housing, where air enters from the top and is discharged toward the opposite side compressed by the rotor's revolution. This blower was first used by Paul Daimler for an aeroengine in 1917 to 1918. "Roots" was taken from the name of its brother co-inventors, F.M. and P.H. Roots.

Photo A35-2 TEMPUU Type R, mounting Roots blower: Two units were mounted at the rear end of the engine. Only one blower on the near side can be seen in this photo. 460 PS/2,190 rpm (Courtesy of Professor Seiichi Awano).

Photo A35-3 Kawasaki-modified BMW-9 for KOKENKI, *700 PS, mounting the Roots blower for air-cooled exhaust valve: The Roots blower was mounted at the rear end of the engine. The two black holes are intake air ports (Courtesy of Professor Seiichi Awano).*

Chapter 36

The Mystique of the Daimler-Benz DB601 Engine (I)

Roller bearing and Dyna Panhard. Before evaluation, a unique design must be distinguished from the mainstream of engineering.

Fateful Confrontation

In January 1931, the German Transport Ministry ordered Daimler-Benz AG to develop a V12-cylinder, water-cooled, 800- to 900-hp aero engine. Germany's secret rearmament, which was prohibited by the Versailles Treaty, began with this order for an aeroengine placed by not the Air Ministry but the Transport Ministry. This action served as "the announcement of the conception" (Annunciation) of the Daimler-Benz DB600 series, which played such an amazing role during World War II mounted in the main German planes.

This engine is an inverted V12 gasoline liquid-cooled engine. The carbureted version was completed in 1935. Subsequently, the carburetor was supplanted by gasoline being injected directly into each engine cylinder.

In conjunction with the 1937 rearmament declaration of Germany, the engine was installed in the Messerschmitt Me109 fighter and had a spectacular unveiling at an international aviation show held in Switzerland (Fig. 36-1). When World War II broke out, the engine was manufactured by Italy's Fiat, Japan's Kawasaki Aircraft Co., Ltd., and Aichi Aircraft Co., Ltd., through licensing. This V12 engine was mounted in the main airplanes of the Axis Powers and confronted the Rolls-Royce engine of the Allied Powers, a formidable rival since World War I. The Daimler-Benz engine was mounted in

Italy's Macchi fighter, Japan's Hien (Ki-61) fighter, as well as others, and in Germany's main airplanes such as the Messerschmitt fighter.

Fig. 36-1 Me109 V13 fighter leading others in the Alps circulation race: In the 1937 international show held in Switzerland, several types of Me109 were entered, including those mounting the Benz engine and Junkers Jumo. The planes were victorious in the round-the-Alps race, the Alps circulation race, and the climbing/ descending races. Other countries withdrew their entries from the races in anticipation of defeat. It was the public debut of the DB600 engine (the pilot was Mr. Franke).

Opposing the Axis Powers aircraft was the Rolls-Royce Merlin engine, which was mounted in the English Spitfire fighters and, through licensing by Packard, in the American P51 fighters, which fought fierce battles at war fronts (Photo 36-1). These battles were fateful confrontations between the Rolls-Royce engine, which was developed from a copy of the World War I Benz engine, and the Daimler-Benz engine that was revived (refer to Chapter 21). In Japan, however, the licensed version of the Benz engine caused

Photo 36-1 [Top] The Hien with a Daimler-Benz engine that was licensed for manufacture by Kawasaki Aircraft Company, Ltd. [Bottom] P51 with a Rolls-Royce engine that was licensed for manufacturing by Packard (Musée de L'Air Paris).

extensive and repeated problems, primarily related to excessive crankshaft wear. The engine with enhanced power of 1450 hp was particularly troublesome, and its production eventually became impossible.

Beauty with Her Head Changed

In the spring of 1945, I was still a junior high school student, and I was dispatched to a factory as a member of the students' labor service during the war. There, I heard a bleak rumor that the engine factories in Kawasaki were raided by B29 bombers and the airplanes without "heads" (engines) were left in the factories (Fig. 36-2). After the war, I knew, however, that it was not raids by B29 bombers that delayed production of the aircraft but rather manufacturing obstacles primarily caused by the crankshaft and bearings.

Fig. 36-2 A dark rumor circulated at the site of student mobilization for labor at munitions factory.

It is said that Zhao Feiyan (she is called "Cho Hien" in Japan) was one of the most beautiful women in Chinese history, who could rival Yang Guifei. She is said to have had a well-proportioned figure with a petite head. Though I do not know who named the stylish fighter with a liquid-cooled engine "Hien," I wonder if he had a vision of that ancient beauty when he gave the engine the name. However, the small and beautiful head of the beauty was replaced ruthlessly with a rugged air-cooled engine. This modification was in preparation for the imminent outbreak of the war and the resultant fierce battles. Although somewhat slower at maximum speed, the

Type 5 (Ki-100) fighter created from this modification was an excellent plane with enhanced climbing power and strong air battle performance.

The public debut of the DB600 occurred in 1937, when several types of Me109 aircraft entered the Switzerland international airshow. These German aircraft included those Messerschmitt Me109 craft mounting the Benz engine and Junkers Jumo. Fig. 36-1 illustrates a Me109 V13 fighter leading others in the Alps circulation race. Piloted by Mr. Franke, this aircraft won so decisively in the round-the-Alps race, the Alps circulation race, and the climbing/descending races that other countries withdrew their entries from the races in anticipation of defeat.

The Story of Engine Bearing

Why did the crankshaft and bearing in the engine cause so much trouble during production (damaged during break-in)? I had this question, but I was unable to get an answer for a long time. Then I happened to come across Professor K. Tomizuka's thesis that the roller bearing should not be used in the connecting rod of a crankshaft. The professor used the All British Engine Company's (ABC) radial air-cooled engine (refer to Chapter 26) and the Daimler-Benz DB600 engine as actual examples, and pointed out that the failure of these engines was attributable to an improper use of roller bearings for crankshaft.[36-1]

During this time, I had a special interest in the roller bearing as a result of the fresh design concept of the French-designed Dyna Panhard (Photos 36-2 and 36-3) and the innovative use of the roller bearings in its engine. I had learned of the Dyna Panhard while the engine of the Contessa 900 (one of the Hino passenger cars) was being designed. The Panhard had an engine of only 850 cm^3 displacement, 60 hp (1964 model), an overall length of about 4.6 m, and a weight of only 850 kg. At the time, the TOYOPET had an engine of 1500 cm^3 displacement, 62 hp, an overall length of about 4 m, and a car weight of 1000 kg. This comparison shows how advanced the structure of the Dyna Panhard was. In fact, after 1953, the Panhard car won several Le Mans 24-hour races in its class. One of the secrets in obtaining 60 hp from an engine as small as 850 cm^3 was the unique design of its roller bearing. Fig. 36-3 illustrates the roller bearings in the big end of the connecting rod. To minimize friction between adjacent rollers as they rotate, smaller rollers were positioned between the adjacent rollers[36-2] (refer to Appendix A36).

Photo 36-2 Back figure of advanced research car of Dyna Panhard: "Dynavia" Panhard (design began in 1944 and was completed in 1948). This car was being developed during World War II, and became, in 1953, the famous Dyna Panhard (horizontal two cylinders, air-cooled 30 hp) (Conservatoir National de Arts et Matiers, Paris).

Photo 36-3 Dyna Panhard: Its unique lightweight body and streamlined style are classics and are still not outdated. The author found one Panhard exhibited at a 1993 classic car show.

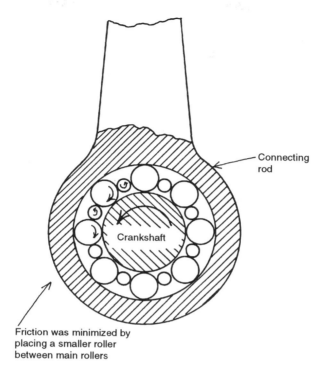

Connecting rod

Crankshaft

Friction was minimized by placing a smaller roller between main rollers

Fig. 36-3 Crankshaft bearing of the Dyna Panhard engine (roller area alone expanded for easier understanding).

Engineering and Company Compose an Integral Body

In Japan during the 1950s, it was decided to purchase and analyze several kinds of automobiles as a reference for studying the advanced automotive technology in foreign countries. The Japan Society of Automotive Engineers (JSAE) established a powerplant research committee in which opinions related to the engine were gathered and discussed. While attending one of the committee meetings, I promptly recommended that a Dyna Panhard be purchased. I explained the reasons for my recommendation and obtained most of the committee members' approvals. However, my proposal to purchase the Dyna Panhard car was denied by the JSAE upper-level organization. I later learned that Mr. Hanji Umehara had voiced the strongest opposition to my proposal.

Engineering is an integral part of any company. The characteristics and history of a company determine the level of engineering needed by that company. For instance, a company that has grown up with emphasis being placed on sales and service has different needs than the company with a history of poor service and quality; as a result, the features of their product are and should be different. Also, the mainstream of engineering must definitely be guided by the average value. In other words, we must always cultivate the ability to judge if an outstanding product is progressive or eccentric.

I was later told that Mr. Umehara had said, "Such an eccentric car should not be purchased." A long time has passed, and I have come to respect his deep insight into engineering. Subsequently, the Dyna Panhard Company disappeared, together with my favorite car, as it was absorbed into Citroën. Few people now know the name of this company.

My question then is, "What was the design of DB601's crankshaft bearing? Was it an eccentric design? Or a defective design?" My story continues to the next chapter.

Appendix A36 Dyna Panhard Engine

In the world's first speed race from Paris to Bordeaux to Paris in 1895, the Peugeot car, with the Daimler engine, claimed the victory. Actually, the Panhard & Levassor car had crossed the finish line 10 minutes earlier. However, the car had been disqualified because it had only two seats while four seats were required to compete. Since the race, however, Panhard Company had a number of successes and went on to dominate the European car market. After both Panhard and Levassor died, their company continued to produce only premium vehicles and gradually lagged behind companies that manufactured more popular cars.

At the end of World War II, this company attempted to regain its old dominance in a single stroke by putting the Dyna car on the market. The new vehicle was designed by J.A. Grégoire, who adopted the front-engine/front-drive (F-F) and developed an air-cooled, horizontally opposed 600 cm^3, 28-hp engine. This new model became the Dyna Panhard via the Dynavia's trial as mentioned previously. The Dyna Panhard engine had 850 cm^3 displacement with 42 hp, but this power was eventually increased to 60 hp. The Dyna Panhard was a very ambitious undertaking with an aluminum body and unique engine. In addition to the previously mentioned connecting rod bearing, the tappet was made of aluminum. Moreover, the engine adopted an automatic hydraulic valve gap adjuster, used a single torsion bar as a valve spring for both the intake and exhaust valves, and utilized a needle bearing at the rotating end of the torsion bar. The engine was filled with innovative ideas (Fig. A36-1). You can be sure that an engineer who saw this engine for the first time would have been awestruck by the design.

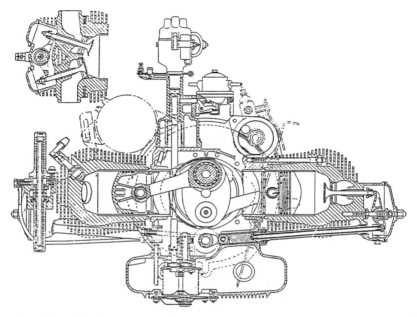

Fig. A36-1 The Dyna Panhard engine: 85-mm bore, 75-mm stroke, 851-cm³ displacement, 42 PS/5000 rpm (1958), power later expanded to 60 PS.

However, a good impression does not always ensure a successful product. The Dyna Panhard was later absorbed into Citroën, and its unique engine soon disappeared.

Chapter 37

The Mystique of Daimler-Benz DB601 Engine (II)

Although machining accuracy is a necessity for product function, this machining accuracy alone is inadequate.

A Basic Point Is Sometimes a Blind Spot

In 1967 for the first time in Japan, two Japanese car makers began the full-scale production of the direct fuel injection diesel engine. Hino Motors was one of the manufacturers, and Isuzu Motors was the other. Hino intended to increase the engine output to permit easier and faster driving on the ever-expanding highway system, and Isuzu targeted fuel conservation-conscious customers. Although both companies fulfilled their roles as pioneers, their engines were not accepted by the public. Neither engine lasted long (refer to Appendix A37).

The Hino engine had some problems with its direct fuel injection engine type EA100 because of its insufficient experience in this type of engine. One of those problems was the premature wear experienced by the cam follower. The cam follower is a part of the mechanism for opening and closing the valves. The valves, of course, admit air into the engine and discharge exhaust gas from the cylinder after combustion. This engine used the type of roller bearing known as the roller tappet system (Fig. 37-1). The pin of this bearing wore out in only tens of hours. Needless to say, all possible factors were analyzed and tested through failure analysis.

The appropriateness of the material was most in doubt. Various different materials and types of heat treatments were attempted, and the shapes and

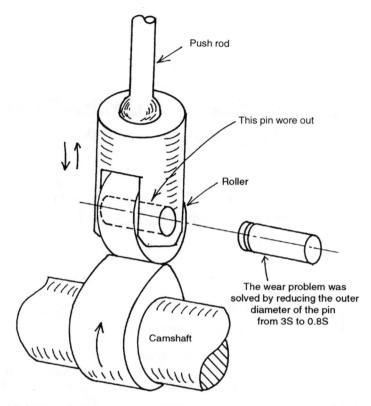

Fig. 37-1 Excessive wear of roller tappet caused by poor machining accuracy.

sizes of the groove for supplying the lubricating oil were varied. None of these attempts could resolve the problem. Other possibilities included incorrect handling in assembly or inadequate quality control.

The trial-and-error method of resolving the problem continued for a few months. Then the problem was suddenly solved easily and at a stroke. The key to the problem lay in the accuracy of the outer diameter of the pin corresponding to the axis of the cam follower.

In normal life, self-evident facts are often overlooked. However, in the world of engineering, people must make it a practice to always think from the most basic point. The initial surface roughness of the pin was about 0.003 mm in average amplitude. When the pin was polished to about 0.0008 mm or better in average roughness, the continuing premature wear stopped at once.

I remember my deep impression at reading the book written by Professor Masao Naruse near the end of World War II.[37-1] He pointed out that the accuracy of Japanese-made gears and ball-bearings was much lower than that of European products. As illustrated in Fig. 37-2, the surface roughness of the Japanese-made ball-bearing at that time was one digit higher than that of the European product (made by SKF), according to his description. It occurred to me that the failure to produce the Daimler-Benz 601 engine in Japan during World War II might have been a result of the poor surface finish of the domestic bearings and crankshaft. However, this possibility was only my thought.

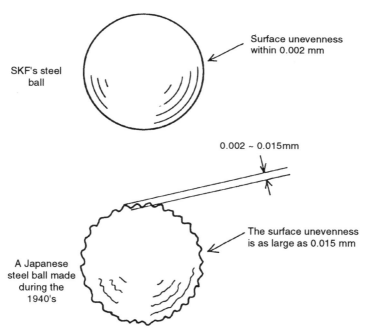

Fig. 37-2 Comparison of steel ball accuracy between Japanese and foreign ball-bearings made around 1940 (contents of Cradle of Scientific Technology, *authored by Masao Naruse, are illustrated for easier understanding).*

Testimony Obtained in Europe

In 1969 when the problem of the EA100 engine was finally resolved, I traveled to Europe to study the direct fuel injection engine. Taking the opportunity offered by this trip, I asked two persons my old question. One of them was Mr. Roggendorf, who had been involved in the development of all

DB600 series engines from the initial DB600 to the final DB610 at Daimler-Benz (refer to Chapter 17).

He told me, "Surely, the roller bearing caused some problems in the initial period. However, after renewing the hardness control, no problem arose." According to his explanation, the only problem that surfaced after the increase in power output in the DB603 (swept volume-up version of the DB601 engine) was the deformation of the cylinder liner, which meant that the piston was apt to seize. I knew that the powered-up DB603 version had other problems in Germany, but Japan had difficulties even with its predecessor, the DB601.

However, Mr. Roggendorf added, "The exact cause cannot be known. At that time, we used a number of war prisoners from enemy countries for engine manufacture. So, troubles often occurred because of the sand or other foreign material that was poured into the engine. The diameter of the 150-mm cylinder was widened due to an increase in output. As a result, the thickness of the cylinder liner was reduced to 2.7 mm. This thickness was only marginal when used in a high output mode with a supercharging pressure of 1.42 kg/cm^2," he continued.

Later I had the opportunity to ask Dr. A. Scheiterlein of the Austrian AVL research laboratory the same question. The doctor said, "I don't think that the crankshaft wear was caused by using the roller bearing. First of all, it was irrational to increase the ratio of horsepower to swept volume from 28 PS/L to 57 PS/L. A general degradation of reliability may have been unavoidable." See Photo 37-1.

Neither person would say that the roller bearing itself caused the trouble.

Is There Evidence That the Roller Bearings Were Ill-Suited for Use?

On the other hand, one piece of information that supports the "roller bearing unfit (ill-suited for use)" theory was the engineering change from the roller bearing to plain (shell) bearing (a bearing without using roller or ball). This change was found in an Engineering Order delivered from Germany once during the war, when the engineers were troubled by crankshaft and bearing damages. I could not find the reason for this design change in Germany, but I had thought that the change order was a result of the following event.

Three times, August 17 and October 14, 1943, and February 24, 1944, the ball-bearing factory (Vereinigte Kugellagerfabrik, VKF) in Schweinfurt,

Photo 37-1 Visiting Dr. Scheiterlein in Austrian AVL research laboratory: I happened to see Professor Uyehara of Wisconsin University there. From right, Professor and Mrs. Uyehara, Dr. Scheiterlein, and author. The doctor said that the problems of the DB600 series engine might not be attributable to the roller bearing in particular.

Germany, was bombarded by the U.S. Air Force.[37-2] I wondered if the Germans suddenly fell short of the roller bearings due to the bombing, and therefore changed the design that used the shell bearings. Later, I learned that this suspicion was not the case. I received a letter from Mr. H. Hoffmann explaining that the true cause was the inadequate capacity of the Benz bearing cage production facilities to permit expanded production (refer to Appendix A38-3).

As an aside, Germany's main fighter, the *Focke Wulf* FW190, was converted from its air-cooled radial engine to the DB603 engine of our interest to improve its performance, and it continued to engage in aerial battles. The conversion was made concurrently to the liquid-cooled inverted V Junkers Jumo engine as well as the Benz engine. The DB601 engine, whose production was impossible in Japan because of crankshaft problems, was given greater power, and it became mass-produced as the DB603 engine in Germany (Figs. 37-3 and 37-4). Thus, a total of 72,000 units of the DB600 series engines were manufactured before the end of the war. Beside the

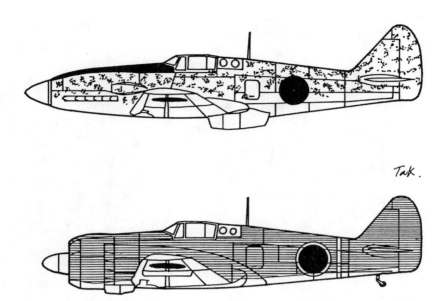

Fig. 37-3 Liquid-cooled inverted V converted into air-cooled radial: (Top) Ki-61II modified, Ha-140 liquid-cooled inverted V, 1450 PS (licensed version of DB601), 610 km/h; (Bottom) Ki-100I, Ha-112II air-cooled radial, 1500 PS, 580 km/h, converted to air-cooled engine due to delay of liquid-cooled engine production.

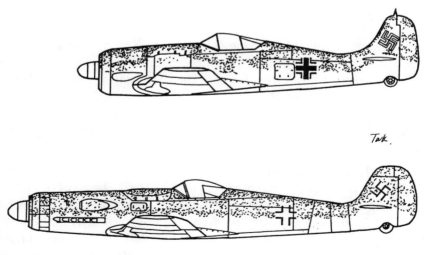

Fig. 37-4 Air-cooled radial converted into liquid-cooled inverted V in Germany: (Top) BMW801D-2 air-cooled radial, 1700 PS, 620 km/h; (Bottom) DB603E liquid-cooled V, 1800 PS at MW50 boosted, 2300 PS, 741 km/h.

fighter aircraft, these engines were adopted for all other airplanes and worked for the Third Reich, even as the German government tottered on the verge of collapse.

As a result, I came to doubt even more strongly that the application of roller bearing to the crankshaft was the true cause of poor reliability.

Appendix A37 Hino EA100 Engine

The Hino EA100 is the direct fuel injection engine that, concurrently with the Isuzu D920, was mass-produced for the first time in Japan. The EA100 incorporated an ambitious design including a short stroke, the four-valve with roller tappet, and twin starters. However, the basic specifications required for the extremely short stroke (140-mm bore, 110-mm stroke) were unreasonable, so combustion had a high rate of pressure rise. After being manufactured for a short time, this engine gave way to a new engine (Hino EF100) that had a 130-mm bore and a 130-mm stroke (Fig. A37-1).

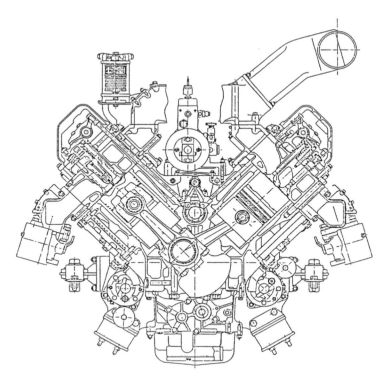

Fig. A37-1 Hino EA100 engine (1967): 280 PS/2600 rpm, 140-mm bore, 110-mm stroke, 13.5L displacement.

Chapter 38

The Mystique of the Daimler-Benz
DB601 Engine (III)

*Although engineering may call for a breakthrough, a haphazard
jump is undesirable. Determine whether your engineering is a
mere extension or innovation.*

Hitler's Anger

The rotary radial engines became popular during World War I. The engines
made by Gnome and Rhone both used a roller bearing. However, it can be
thought that reliability did not matter much at this time because the load of
such an engine may have been small and the load conditions in such a radial
layout may have been good as mentioned in Chapter 27.

In automobiles, the roller bearing came to be used for heavy-duty race
engines. In 1922, Fiat's Vittorio Jano applied a roller bearing instead of a
lead-tin alloy bearing (the white metal), whose allowable load had already
been reached. Jano used it in the Fiat Type 804 engine, which had some
influence over the subsequent designers. Many racing engines at that time
were influenced by the great success of the Fiat engine in using a roller
bearing, and excellent engines such as the Sunbeam, Alfa Romeo, Salmson,
and the Delage were originated using the Fiat engine's design philosophy
(refer to Appendix A38-1).

After Hitler came into power in January 1933, he watched the German
Grand Prix held in that year. Although he posed proudly in a boxseat for
honored guests, the Grand Prix resulted in a miserable defeat of the German
cars. The Bugatti T54 won first place, followed by Alfa Romeo. Among the

German cars, the Mercedes finished a distant sixth place.[38-1] Hitler's anger at Germany's poor showing can easily be imagined. Immediately, Hitler authorized a financial grant of about 450,000 marks (in 1933 value) to the German Grand Prix team. Immediately, Mercedes and Auto Union began to compete for the manufacture of a better racing car (Fig. 38-1). The Type W25 engine first developed by Mercedes adopted a roller bearing for the crankshaft, following the Fiat's achievement. This engine was used in the Nürburgring race held in May 1934 and contributed to the German victory (Photo 38-1).

Fig. 38-1 Bugatti 54 won an overwhelming victory in the 1933 German Grand Prix. Hitler was enraged at the poor German showing, and he ordered the German Grand Prix team to produce a new car capable of winning the prestigious race. Hitler allocated 450,000 marks to the production of a winning vehicle (shown here is the Bugatti 55, using the chassis of the Bugatti 54).

Since the design of the DB601 engine was initiated in 1931, it would be unnatural for this engine to ignore the contributions of the roller bearing to the engines led by the Fiat race engines since 1922. I think that the roller bearing had been completely accepted by the Daimler-Benz design staff at that time, as well as for the Mercedes Type W25 engine.

Photo 38-1 Mercedes W25 and its engine (Benz Museum): 354 PS, 78-mm bore, 88-mm stroke, 3.36L displacement. The duct from the Roots blower to two pressure-type carburetors is covered completely with fins. Later expanded to 5.66L displacement, 646 PS (engine shown here had 4.3L displacement and 462 PS) (Benz Museum).

Tracing Troubles in Japan

If the use of roller bearings was not the cause of the problems with the DB601 engine made in Japan (called Ha-40 and Ha-140 at Kawasaki Aircraft Company, Ltd., and the Atsuta 11 and Atsuta 21 at Aichi Aircraft Company, Ltd.), what was? As previously noted, I speculated that the trouble was caused by the poor accuracy of the bearing. In December 1978, I was able to speak to Mr. Junzo Uozumi (later chairman of Aisan Kogyo). During the war, he was in charge of the Atsuta engine in Aichi Aircraft.

According to Mr. Uozumi, the accuracy of the roller bearing was considered important and only rollers with a circularity deviation (accuracy of the outer diameter) within 0.002 to 0.003 mm were used in the engines. He recalled that, since the crankshaft had an insufficient hardness after carburizing, the project could not progress. Meanwhile, the design was changed to a plain (shell) bearing. Due to the difficulty in responding to this design change, the conversion was finally made to an air-cooled radial engine. However, I had some difficulty in understanding Mr. Uozumi's conversation and never fully understood his comments.

After a few years, Professors Tatsuo Takatsuki and Norimune Soda delivered lectures at an April 1981 conference on internal-combustion engines organized by Professor Kiyoshi Tomizuka. Both speakers commented on the DB601 engine. In particular, Professor Soda had access to a Kawasaki Aircraft report at that time and introduced the contents to the attendees of the conference. I borrowed the precious report and read it carefully (Photo 38-2). The entire aspect of the DB601 trouble becomes fairly clear when adding guesswork to the information collected from both professors' lectures, the contents of that report, conversations with Mr. Roggendorf, Chairman Uozumi, and Professor Tomizuka, and my own experience. Although the details are discussed in Appendix A38-3, the problem can be summed up as follows.

Major Causes of Trouble

The major problem with the DB601 engine was excessive wear of the circumferential surface of the crankshaft pin during service (Photo 38-3).

The primary cause of the excessive wear was the inadequate hardness of the crankshaft due to poor heat treatment of the outer surface. If a kitchen knife, or any knife for that matter, is made just of forged steel, then its edge will dull quickly and it will not cut well. Therefore, steel must be hardened by heating and then cooling rapidly (this treatment is called *quenching*). A

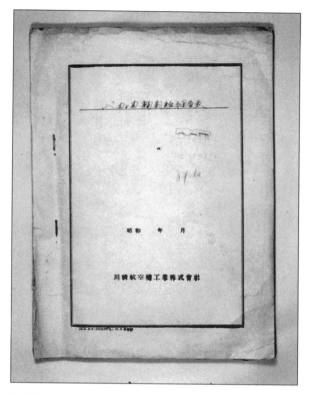

Photo 38-2 Report on investigation of excessive wear from crankshaft of Ha-40 engine (Japanese name of the DB601 engine) (Photo courtesy of Professor Norimune Soda).

good kitchen knife cuts well because of its excellent quenching. Although the same treatment is required for hardening a crankshaft, a somewhat more sophisticated method is employed. This method is called *carburizing and quenching* in which the carbon content of the shaft surface is increased so that the surface has a particularly high hardness. In the case of the DB601, the carburizing and quenching technique was insufficient. A secondary cause seems to have been an inappropriate shape of the roller. In order to distribute the weight evenly, the roller must have a slightly tapered end instead of a simple cylindrical shape. Otherwise, wear might occur. However, if the roller end is excessively tapered, skewing will occur, that is, the roller will walk (move) with a limp while rolling. In this condition, excess wear will occur with a peculiar pattern[38-2] as shown in Fig. 38-2. Fig. 38-3 shows the roller used for an automobile driveshaft as an example. Since the

Photo 38-3 Example of excessive wear on crankshaft of Ha-40 engine.

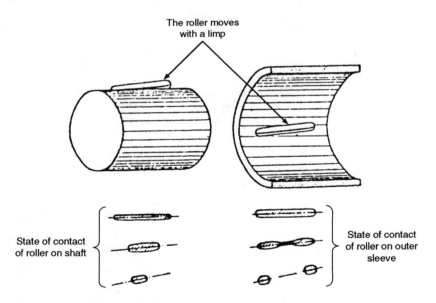

Fig. 38-2 Skewing of roller bearing (Courtesy of Mr. Yamada).

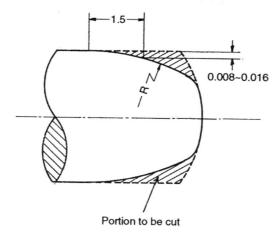

Portion to be cut

Fig. 38-3 Shape of roller ends: Excessive wear of shaft could be prevented by cutting both ends as shown here.

selection of this shape is rather empirical, the optimum shape cannot be determined quickly. Thus, it appears that efforts for determining the optimum roller shape were inadequate.

As a possible third cause, I wonder if the crankshaft itself was machined with an adequate accuracy of the outer diameter. The shaft is originally round. Even though any finished shaft looks exquisite with the naked eye, it may have a triangular or polygonal shape when examined closely, as illustrated in Fig. 38-4. This perfect roundness is very important, even for today's automobiles. Unless the surface unevenness is kept within 0.003 mm, durability will become poor.[38-3] For a precise finish, both excellent machine tool and machining technique are necessary. However, it is possible that both the tools and the techniques were inadequate during this early period.

In addition, the accuracies of the roller itself and the cage, which is a structure to support the roller, may have constituted a problem. Mr. Uozumi indicated that all the rollers were used only after a careful screening (i.e., only rollers with a circularity deviation within 0.002 to 0.003 mm were selected), so it can be thought that inadequate production engineering was covered by manpower. Yet, I have a strong doubt as to how properly the rollers were selected when I remember the skill of student workers mobilized for labor during the war and the one-digit lower accuracy of the actual rollers.

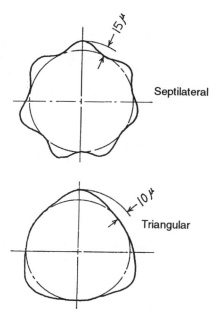

Fig. 38-4 Example of actual crankshaft journal shape: Though the shaft is apparently round, close measurement may show it to be shaped as shown here.

Could the Trouble Be Overcome?

Could the problems with the DB601 engine have been prevented if these technical shortcomings were overcome? It is my personal belief that the problems revolving around the crankshaft could have been prevented. However, I read that this Japanese-built engine often caused problems with the electrical circuit and fuel line as well.[38-4] In particular, the fuel injection pump could not have been of adequate quality. Even in today's diesel engine, the fuel injection pump is the point that requires the most labor and time during development.

A gasoline direct-injection system refers to a method in which the fuel is injected directly into the cylinder as in a diesel engine. The structure of the injection pump itself is basically the same as that of a diesel engine. In the case of a diesel engine, its fuel, which is a light oil, also has a self-lubricating property. However, gasoline does not have this degree of lubricity. Therefore, the lubricating method for the gasoline injection pump is far more difficult than for a diesel engine.

It was as late as 1942 when Japan began to manufacture the fuel injection pump for the diesel engine through a technical agreement with the Robert

Bosch Company. However, machine tools and other production equipment could not be obtained from Germany due to the war. Hence, it was difficult to machine the injection nozzle and other components to the required accuracy. In fact, the Japanese manufacturers had such miserable conditions and equipment that only 5% of the total production could meet the specifications.[38-5] The introduction of the gasoline direct-injection engine in Japan under these conditions was not possible.

Another problem reported with the engine was contamination of the spark plugs, which would be inherent in an inverted engine. The control of lubricating oil and the restriction of oil consumption are basic problems of any engine, so much so that these problems can be considered eternal subjects. In a radial engine, some cylinders are inverted; in an inverted V-type engine, however, all the cylinders are inverted. Therefore, the difficulty of controlling the lubricating oil in an inverted V-type engine can easily be imagined. Controlling the oil is not a project that just anyone can undertake.

Is the Use of Roller Bearings Appropriate?

The use of roller bearings may have been appropriate by the German heavy industry: The German industrial machine had already accumulated sufficient production engineering and empirical knowledge to manufacture and support the incorporation of the roller bearings in its machines. However, roller bearings should not be used unless the infrastructure can support the stringent requirements. The trouble with the ABC engine, as pointed out by Professor Kiyoshi Tomizuka, occurred before roller bearings became widely used. I wonder if the problems with the ABC engine can be attributed to inadequate supporting conditions.

In 1964 and 1967, Honda produced 1.5L and 3L Grand Prix engines, respectively. Both engines incorporated roller bearings in their design. Using these engines, the Honda entry fared well in several races, stirring the blood of Japanese race car enthusiasts. I later heard that the engines had no problems with their crankshafts. When the design is exact and conditions for accurate machining are met, the results will meet our expectations. In conclusion, it can be said that the introduction of the DB600 series engines into Japan during World War II was too much of a technical burden for Japan's engineering level at that time.

When introducing new technology or challenging others for superiority, we should determine the difference of the new technology from that which already exists. Is the new technology merely an extension of existing technology, or is it truly innovative? Does the new technology consist of an advancement of existing technology as well as a completely new idea? If so, to what degree? What field appears to be unknown? The answers to all these questions must be well categorized. Then for each category, those areas requiring preliminary research and study or those that are to be developed in parallel should be examined. Afterward, a development plan should be prepared.

If the proposed project has extensive missing knowledge, then the project should be either modified to use more of the known data or else courageously postponed until the boundaries of existing knowledge are expanded.

A person need not give in to an innovation thoughtlessly. He must determine if the bar in his high jump is within or beyond his ability to jump. After the challenge is accepted, then the distance and speed of the approach run should be carefully planned. This need for careful evaluation in a high jump is the same as that required for a technological jump.

Appendix A38-1 Alfa Romeo P2 Engine

The Alfa Romeo P2 engine had a 61-mm bore and an 85-mm stroke. A sheet metal water jacket is welded to a steel cylinder. The engine is equipped with 16-valve twin overhead cams and a Roots blower driven by the crankshaft. The crankshaft uses only roller bearings. Most Grand Prix race engines at that time used the roller bearing system. The P2 engine was victorious in its first race, which was a 200-mile race held in Cremona in 1924. After its debut race, this car had a brilliant record of consecutive victories, including the French and Italian Grand Prix races[38-1] (Fig. A38-1).

Appendix A38-2 DB601 Engine

Stimulated by the Rolls-Royce aeroengine, Germany secretly began the development of the DB601 engine in 1931. To improve the pilot's visibility, an inverted V engine was chosen (Fig. A38-2, Photo A38-1).

In 1935, a 950-hp engine with a carburetor was completed. In 1937, the gasoline direct-injection system was adopted so as to configure a system in which the proper quantity of fuel could be delivered to the cylinders without respect to the flight altitude or change of gravity of a fighter.

The bore/stroke and swept volume of the engine were initially 150×160 mm and 33.9 liters, respectively. Later, the bore and swept volume were

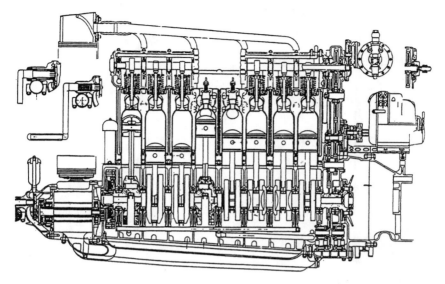

Fig. A38-1 Alfa Romeo P2 engine: 134 PS/5500 rpm, 61 mm bore, 85 mm stroke, 19.9 L displacement. Later, the power was enhanced to 154 PS (1924).

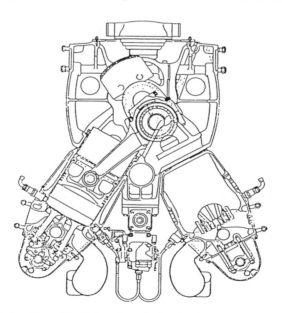

Fig. A38-2 Daimler-Benz DB601 engine: 33.9L displacement, weight 714 kg (1937).

Photo A38-1 Robust and exquisite DB601 engine: [Top] It fascinates not only the old Japanese Imperial Army but also today's people. [Bottom] The connecting rod bearing section, roller bearing, and its cage can be seen (Deutches Museum, München).

expanded to 154 mm and 35.8 liters. Finally, the swept volume was increased to 44.7 liters. In 1945, 2850 hp was achieved by using methanol/water injection (Fig. A38-3, Table A38-1). The most innovative modifications among the many new techniques boldly incorporated into the plan were the governor system, which adjusts the quantity of fuel injection in response to supercharging (boost) pressure, flight altitude, and intake air temperature; and the mechanism that obtains the optimum boost by adjusting the oil volume of fluid coupling according to flight altitude and thereby controlling the rotational speed of the supercharger. Fig. A38-4 shows the principle of the boost control. The oil volume of the fluid coupling was automatically controlled with an aneroid barometer so that rotational speed matches flight altitude or air density.

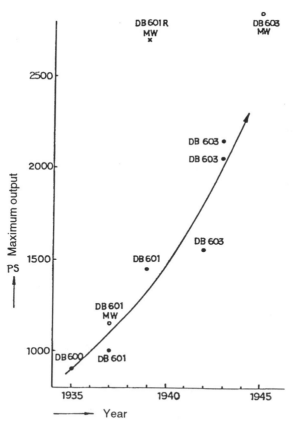

Fig. A38-3 The development process of a DB600 series engine.

Table A38-1. List of DB600 Series Engines

Year Production Began	Name	Swept Volume (L)	Compression Ratio	Supercharging Pressure Ratio	Maximum Output (PS)	Production Quantity
1935	DB 600G Carburetor	33.9	6.5	1.38	950	About 2280 (as Type 600)
1937	601A	33.9	6.5	1.40	1200	About 19,000
	601E	33.9	7.2	1.42	1400	About 19,000
	*601RMW[1]	33.9	8.6	2.43	2700	
1941	605A	35.7	7.5	1.42	1550	About 42,000 (as Type 605)
(1944)	605D	35.7	8.5	1.42	2000	About 42,000 (as Type 605)
1942	603A	44.7	7.5	1.40	1850	About 9000 (as Type 603)
(1944)	603E	44.7	7.5	1.45	2050	About 9000 (as Type 603)
(1944)	603L	44.7	8.5	1.40	2150	About 9000 (as Type 603)
1945	*603N	44.7	8.5	1.75	2850	About 9000 (as Type 603)
1942	610 A[2]	67.8			2980	
1942	604[3]	46.5			2500	
1942	607[4]	44.7			1750	

* Methanol/water injection
(1) For world record-setting Messerschmitt fighter
(2) Twin inverted V24 cylinder
(3) X 24 cylinder
(4) Diesel

Appendix A38-3 Supplement to Failure Analysis of Crankshaft Bearing of DB601 Engine

Insufficient Heat Treatment of Crankshaft

I heard that in Japan the crankshafts were initially subjected to induction hardening. In the case of the DB601 engine, it is obvious that the surface hardness was inadequate, resulting in excessive wear within 100 running hours (Photo 38-3). Later, the induction hardening process was changed to carburizing. At the surface of the crankshaft, the hardness was close to that of the Benz engine, but it decreased from about 1 mm below the surface, as shown in Fig. A38-5. The method of hardening the surface is called *surface*

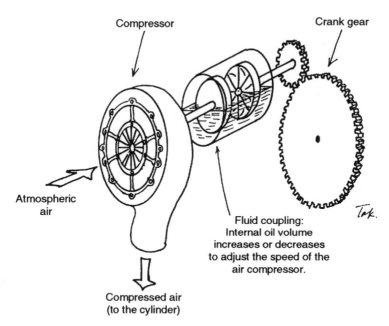

Fig. A38-4 Oil volume of fluid coupling is automatically controlled in response to flight altitude, thereby controlling the boost pressure from the supercharger.

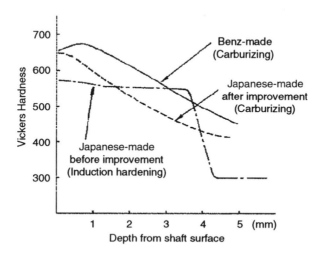

Fig. A38-5 Crankshaft hardness of the Ha-40 engine (Daimler-Benz engine made in Japan).

treatment. This method is intended to leave the inside in a "soft" state for keeping it tough and enhancing the strength and wear resistance of the surface. However, in the case of a roller bearing, a large load is locally applied by the roller, so local deformation must be tolerated. Therefore, it can be guessed that the hardened layer must be about 1.5 mm or more thick.

On the other hand, when observing the structure of the carburized area, the German Benz crankshaft has a neat martensite structure (indicating satisfactory quenching). The Japanese engine crankshaft shows precipitation of troostite, which indicates inadequate quenching (Photo A38-2). The structure of the steel before quenching, particularly the homogeneity of structural components in austenite, is an important factor. It was reported that the use of the Krupp steel made in Germany at that time was satisfactory. The material itself, that is, the steel quality, must have been one cause of that trouble.

It is said that nickel was not used because of the undependable supply at that time. However, the trouble was based on the I 221 material (wartime standard) using the nickel, that is, the highest-class nickel-chrome-molybdenum steel. It can be guessed that the steel manufacturing process also was a part of the problem as mentioned later in this book.

Historical Process of Change to Shell Bearing

I could not understand why the design was changed from a roller bearing to a plain (shell) bearing during the war. I had suspected that the bearing factory had been bombed, as discussed earlier. However, to determine the real reason, I asked my friend at Benz, Dr. G. Fränkle, to investigate this matter. Then, in August 1983, I received a letter from Mr. Heinz Hoffmann, who had been involved in the design of the DB601 engine. Mr. Hoffmann revealed a number of interesting facts. The letter said that, first, the relevant design change followed the historical process shown in Table A38-2. It was true that the roller bearing was replaced with the plain (shell) bearing. However, the replacement was not due to a mechanical problem, but because the Benz in-house production facility could not produce enough of the light alloy cages for roller bearings to meet the wartime demand.

To understand Table A38-2, it is necessary to know the detailed structure. In the initial design, the main journal bearing was a plain (shell) bearing; the connecting rod bearings and the master rod bearing were of a roller type; and the subrod bearing was a plain (shell) type, as shown in Photo A38-3 and Fig. A38-6. The fork-shaped connecting rod is connected to the crank-

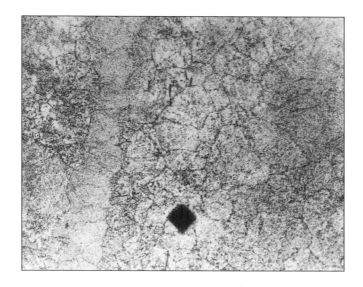

Photo A38-2 [Top] Troostite precipitated on Ha-40 crankshaft, [Bottom] but the Benz-made shaft had a neat martensite structure.

pin via three-row roller bearings, as shown in the figure. On the outer race, the subrod is connected via a plain (shell) bearing. The roller bearing of the master rod was changed to a plain (shell) bearing in the DB605 model

Table A38-2. History of Changes on Crankshaft Bearing of the DB600 Series Engines

Engine	Crankshaft Main Bearing	Connecting Rod Bearing	
		Master Rod	Sub Rod
DB600	Plain	Roller	Plain
DB601	↑	↑	↑
DB605	↑	Plain	↑
DB603A Series 1	Roller	Roller	↑
DB603A Series 2	↑	Plain	↑

Photo A38-3 Initial connecting rod bearings: Roller bearing for master rod and plain (shell) bearing for subrod (Deutches Museum, München).

(Fig. A38-7). Note that this bearing was made, not of thin shell metal as is currently used, but rather of a thick shell metal.

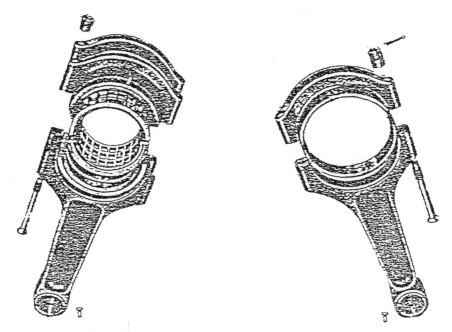

Fig. A38-6 Initial design of connecting rod bearing.

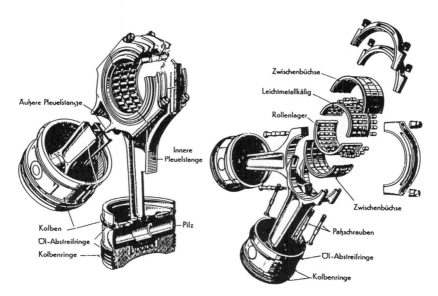

Fig. A38-7 The DB605 plain (shell) bearing.

The new design (plain bearing) was then reverted to the old one (roller bearing) in the next model, DB603. At the same time, the crankshaft main journal bearing was changed to a roller type. However, in the final DB603, the master rod bearing was changed to a plain (shell) type again (Table A38-2). With regard to the repeated changes, Hoffmann said that it was necessary that a roller bearing capable of enduring the bubbling lubricant condition at high altitudes be used. The design of the final model is shown in Fig. A38-8.

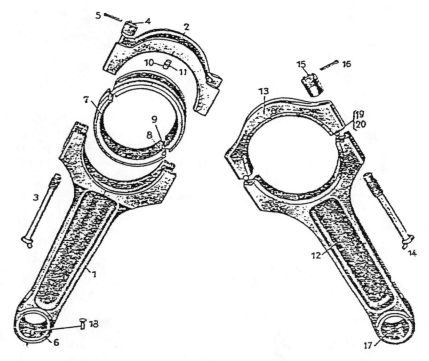

Fig. A38-8 The design of plain (shell) bearing (final model).

Evaluation of Bearing Design

It cannot be denied that the design of the DB600 series crankshaft bearings was unique. However, why was a roller bearing applied? Why was a plain (shell) bearing used for the main bearing? These questions were of some technical interest to me.

As previously mentioned, Vittorio Jano had adopted a roller bearing because he was disappointed with the poor maximum loading of white metal at that time. Subsequently, Kelmet was discovered, and the maximum load capacity of the plain (shell) bearing was substantially enhanced. However, a full-fledged heavy-load bearing was not realized before the advent of thin shell metal.

The old plain (shell) bearing consisted of 5-mm thick bronze (called "back metal"), to the inside of which bearing material was welded. The back metal later became steel, and its thickness was reduced to about 1.5 to 2 mm, which improved the maximum load capacity remarkably.[38-6]

As a result, the plain (shell) bearing is far superior to the roller bearing under satisfactory lubricating conditions. However, the technique of the thin shell metal started from around 1930. In 1931 when the design of DB600 was initiated, it is possible that the technique had not yet been introduced into Benz. This supposition is confirmed from Fig. A38-7, which shows the plain bearing to be made of thick shell metal. Fig. A38-9 sketches the history of the bearings' growth. The time point of the DB600 design corresponds to a transition from the thick shell metal to a thin shell metal. Hence, it can easily be imagined that the Benz engineering staff adopted the roller bearings naturally.

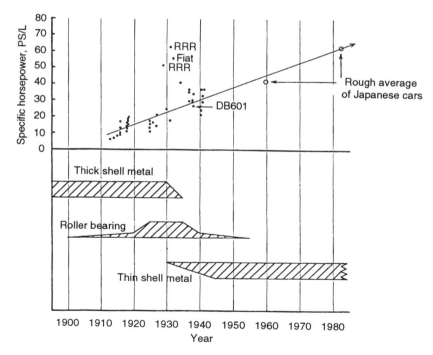

Fig. A38-9 Transition in crankshaft bearing of reciprocating engine.

Then why did they adopt a plain (shell) bearing for the crankshaft main bearing? With respect to the load capacity, the plain (shell) bearing ensures a lighter weight and a more compact design. Besides, the main journal bearing is easier to provide lubricating oil. In contrast, in the connecting rod bearings, lubricating oil must be supplied through an oil hole bored in the crankshaft. Unless this oil hole is properly positioned, the oil supply is apt to become unreliable. The lubricating oil can be influenced by centrifugal force, the oil film thickness, and oil pressure inside the journal bearing at the point at which the oil enters. This point is an important one to be considered during the design phase, even at present.

In our times, computational techniques have advanced sufficiently so that the oil film thickness and/or eccentricity of crankshaft center can be examined with satisfactory precision. These computational techniques were unavailable when the DB600 engine was being designed. Further, since the lubricating oil boils (bubbles) at a high altitude, it can be supposed that the design staff adopted a roller bearing for the master rod because this bearing can rotate even if the lubricating oil runs out. I can understand why a roller bearing was used again after changing to the plain bearing on the master rod. The connecting rod for the final model used plain bearings as shown in Table A38-2 because a proper material could be selected for simplifying the design, in accordance with Mr. Hoffmann's comments. What about an adaptation of roller bearing for the main journal bearing? Is it for increasing the load capacity or for reducing the frictional power loss to balance the friction increase due to the use of the connecting rod plain bearing? Some questions still remain.

As Mr. Uozumi and others have pointed out, one advantage of a roller bearing is that it has a low breakaway torque, which is very helpful at engine startup. This advantage is one of the main justifications for using the roller bearings in the engines of fighters so as to aid in its rapid takeoff.

Leap of Technology

Although I said previously that the introduction of DB601 technology was too much for Japanese technology to undertake at that time, the major items of the technical leap are listed in Table A38-3. For instance, Kawasaki Aircraft had an experience with the Kawasaki- BMW9 on a liquid-cooled V12 aeroengine. This engine later contributed to setting a world record in the *KOKENKI* (KOKEN long-range research aircraft made by Tokyo Gasuden, now Hino Motors). However, the DB601 had a power output per liter of more than twice that of the Kawasaki engine. This experience is the first

Table A38-3. Failures, Causes, Probable Reasons, and Reflection for the Problem on the Ha-40 Engine (Japanese-Built DB601)

Failures	Causes	Reason	Technological Reflection
Excess crankshaft wear	Radical increase of bearing load	Radical increase of power from 17 PS/L (experienced by BMW 17) to 35 PS/L (1150 PS) and to 43 PS/L (1450 PS)	Inadequate technique for production engineering of both accuracy and material
Fuel line trouble	Gasoline direct cylinder injection	Technological leap without experience (including lack of experience with manifold injection)	Inadequate preparation for technical leap Inadequate technique for production control of accuracy for fuel injection equipment (pump, nozzle, etc.)
Electrical circuit trouble	Inverted V engine	Excessive oil up to combustion chamber	Inadequate technique for lubricating oil consumption control and lubricating oil properties Lack of study on ignition system?

leap. As mentioned earlier, several simultaneous technological leaps would have been required before the Japanese could have manufactured the gasoline direct-injection and inverted engine.

Accuracy of Roller Bearing

The accuracy (sphericity) of the Japanese ball-bearing during World War II was as low as 15 μm (0.015 mm), while an SKF-manufactured ball had an accuracy of about 2 μm. Today, even a steel ball of the pachinko (Japanese pinball) machine in a town shop has a sphericity of 5 μm. The bearing for precision ball-bearings has usually been manufactured with a sphericity of about 0.08 μm. I heard that the roller bearing has a circularity of 1 μm or less. Thus, since World War II the precision of the bearing has advanced at a pace that would have been unimaginable during the war, but the basic manufacturing process has remained unchanged. However, the stock material can be improved rapidly because of the vacuum degassing process introduced in the mid-1960s, and the accuracy of roller has been improved sharply by the super finishing. Yet, the accuracy has been enhanced mostly by the steady step-by-step efforts of the bearing manufacturers, that is, improvements made in each step of the manufacturing process and the accumulation of technical knowledge. Engineering is always significantly affected by the underlying knowledge or know-how. In evaluating any engineering product, the engineer should keep an eye out for the scale know-how supporting the product.

For this appendix, information was provided by Mr. Kazuo Kakuda of the Nihon Seiko Company, Mr. Teiji Nagashima of the Teikoku Piston Ring Company, and others. I gratefully acknowledge their help.

Chapter 39

Looking Into the Future: I. What About Stirling Engine?

The dream blooms 150 years after the Scottish clergyman first dreamed it. But when does spring come?

Revival of Stirling Engine

What future does an engine have? Some alternative engines have often been touted as the next-generation engines. The concept of a next-generation engine is based on the premise that such future engines will surpass the present-generation gasoline engine and even the diesel engine in exhaust gas and fuel consumption. Among the future engines, let us trace the trends of the more promising ones.

In December 1972, I was on a ship destined for Malmö, Sweden. The ship cleaved the surface of the dark and calm Baltic Sea, while the sound of the ship's wake was muffled by the night fog. I was standing alone on a dim deck with my feet absorbing the heavy vibrations transmitted from the MAN engine in the engine compartment below deck (Photo 39-1). This was my voyage to a future engine.

After arriving at Malmö, I was promptly taken to the engine laboratory of United Stirling (Sweden) AB. There, I saw an engine connected to a dynamometer. Although the hum of this engine was no louder than the motor of a refrigerator air compressor, it was under full-power operation. Mr. S. Carlqvist, who guided me on the tour, stood a coin edgewise on the engine. The coin trembled slightly, but it did not fall. Furthermore, the exhaust gas was emitted inside the laboratory room without using a muffler.

Photo 39-1 Voyage to a future engine (author): On my ship during the night-crossing of the Baltic Sea in search of the Stirling engine, the heavy sound of the MAN diesel engine was audible on the deck.

The exhaust gas came out through a duct like the one used for a gas ring in a kitchen. In an engine cell in which a conventional diesel engine is under full-power operation, conversation is barely possible because of the loud noise. Besides, the exhaust gas must be vented outside the room via a large muffler. By contrast, this Stirling engine permitted normal conversations while standing beside it, even under full-power operation.

I was greatly surprised. So favorable was my first impression of the Stirling engine that I wondered if diesel engines, which are handicapped by exhaust gas and noise, would be replaced by this Stirling engine. I even thought that not only diesel engines, but also reciprocating engines for automobiles (internal-combustion engines), might be replaced by a sudden revival of the Stirling engine.

Why has interest in the Stirling engine resurfaced 150 years after its invention by clergyman Robert Stirling? Because the engine, which was being studied by Philips of the Netherlands, happened to attract attention as being an engine capable of solving the exhaust gas problem. Then the question arises as to why was an electric appliance company such as Philips would be studying such an old engine.

Before World War II, the Netherlands was eagerly surveying the resources in Borneo (Kalimantan), then a Netherlands colony. The explorers wanted a small portable generator to be used at campsites in the interior of the jungle. Their requirements were: "The engine for the power generator should be able to burn any fuel without emitting a noise, unlike a gasoline engine. Besides, if no sound is emitted, then people can sleep soundly and listen to the radio free from distractions. If such an engine can be made, it would be useful not only for resource surveying, but also for military service."

A combination of the Stirling engine and a generator fit their need. Thus, since 1937, Philips' development project for a portable generator had been continued secretly despite the German Army occupation. Then, the project was forced to change its direction due to the flow of history, that is, the end of colonialism, and Philips' engineering was also inherited by the newly established United Stirling AB.

Faded Charm

When I returned to Japan, I studied this engine even further. The greatest problem with the engine was its output control, that is, how to attach an accelerator. The Stirling engine is a kind of external-combustion engine that uses helium or hydrogen as its working gas. Its principle of operation can be explained as follows. The gas sealed in an engine is heated or cooled externally to change its volume, thereby actuating the piston, which is known as the closing working cycle. This operation is comparable to a pressure cooker put on a gas stove heating element. Therefore, neither a combustion noise nor an exhaust noise is emitted (Fig. 39-1).

In an internal-combustion engine, for example, the pressure of the working gas falls immediately, and the output becomes smaller when decreasing the fuel quantity or throttling the mixture gas quantity. In the Stirling engine, however, it is not easy to decrease the output immediately because the working gas is sealed in the reservoir. Unless the gas is shifted to and returned from a different reservoir, output cannot be controlled. It is technically very difficult to control the output of a Stirling engine in the same way as the accelerator of a normal automobile. In addition, the fuel consumption of this Stirling engine was not good (refer to Appendix A39-1).

The charm of the Stirling engine faded considerably when I realized that its low-noise characteristic could be duplicated even in conventional engines

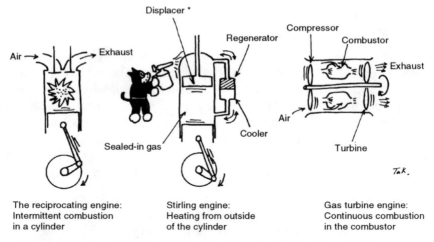

The reciprocating engine:
Intermittent combustion
in a cylinder

Stirling engine:
Heating from outside
of the cylinder

Gas turbine engine:
Continuous combustion
in the combustor

*Displacer serves to control gas transport for expansion and contraction of the sealed-in gas
and transmit an expanding force to the piston (reference is made to a cartoon character
"Norakuro" of Suiho Tagawa).

*Fig. 39-1 Operating principles of reciprocating engine, Stirling engine,
and gas turbine engine.*

due to advances in sound-deadening technology. Moreover, I also realized
that the engine does not generate all the noise heard in an automobile. Noise
is also emitted from the transmission gear and other components of a vehicle as well. To reduce the noise generated by the entire automobile,
noise-reducing measures must be taken steadily and gradually on not only
the engine, but the other components as well (refer to Appendix A39-2).

In addition, the bulk or size of the Stirling engine appears to be larger than
that of a conventional diesel engine, and its radiator requires a capacity 2.5
times larger than that of a diesel engine (Fig. 39-2). Further, the regenerator
and cooler seem to have a much higher cost and lower productivity than do
those of present engines. As a result, a car with an external-combustion
engine cannot leave the garage just by turning the starter once. The engine
requires a long lead time to heat the working fluid. If someone feels that he
cannot wait even for a short warm-up time, then this engine is not for him.

The U.S. Department of Energy (DOE) had researched several kinds of
engines since 1970 to answer the question: "Which engine can save 30% or
more of fuel?" In 1978, the DOE narrowed the candidate engines down to
the Stirling engine and gas turbine. It was planned that one of these two
engines would be singled out in 1983, and its mass production would be

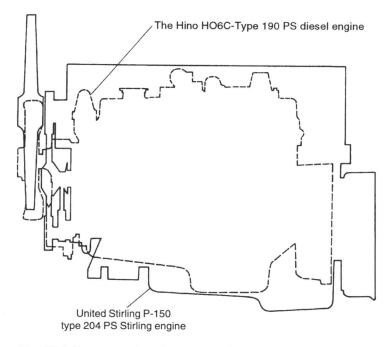

The Hino HO6C-Type 190 PS diesel engine

United Stirling P-150
type 204 PS Stirling engine

*Fig. 39-2 Size comparison between Stirling engine and diesel engine:
Radiator excluded.*

attempted in 1990 (Photo 39-2). The greatest reason for the above is a multifuel feature, that is, the ability to use various kinds of fuel. In particular, the Stirling engine can use any combustible material. It was thought that petroleum-derived fuels would be exhausted in the near future (refer to Chapter 41). Therefore, the multifuel feature had a great advantage.

The DOE project was completed in 1989 as scheduled. The conclusions were that fuel consumption could be decreased by 10-15% when compared with a car equipped with the same class of gasoline engine. Ironically, the noise produced by this supposedly quiet engine was reportedly louder than a comparable diesel engine because of the required cooling system and auxiliary equipment such as the fuel-atomizing air compressor.

In Japan, a similar tack was taken as a part of the 1982 Moonlight project. Various types of engines were studied in both governmental and private research institutions for six years. As a result, the superiority of the Stirling engine to a gasoline engine in fuel consumption was clarified. The Stirling engine is no longer a prime candidate for application to automobiles.

Photo 39-2 The Stirling engine is still under research and development (at SAE Annual Congress in 1980).

However, its value has been established, and research and development have continued as the powerplant for locations other than automobiles. For instance, United Stirling is examining a possible application to deep sea submarines, and Mechanical Technology Inc. NY is devising a hybrid engine with an electric motor (engine consisting of a motor and Stirling engine) to function as a solar-energy-based free piston engine for spacecraft, etc. Thus, the dream of using a Stirling engine is expanding away from its use in automobiles.

Appendix A39-1 Fuel Consumption of Stirling Engine

The Stirling engine was invented by Robert Stirling in 1816. Its cycle is ideally a combination of two constant temperature/volume-processes called the "Stirling cycle" as shown in Fig. A39-1(a). It is an excellent cycle.

Yet, the actual Stirling engine requires heating and cooling at a rather high rotational speed (2500 rpm in the case of the 200 PS engine shown in Fig. 39-2). Therefore, the actual cycle diagram becomes as shown in Fig. A39-1(b). Fig. A39-2 compares fuel consumption of the 204 PS Stirling engine with a similar-sized diesel engine (direct fuel injection) as of 1978. The fuel consumption of the Stirling engine is not always good.

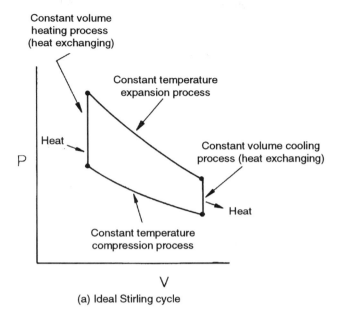

(a) Ideal Stirling cycle

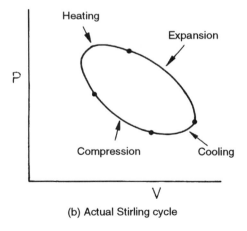

(b) Actual Stirling cycle

Fig. A39-1 Stirling cycle: (a) Ideal Stirling cycle; (b) Actual Stirling cycle.

Besides, the Stirling cycle is sensitive to changes in the ambient temperature. Since the fuel consumption of diesel engines has continually been improved year after year, it is difficult for the Stirling engine to have a better fuel consumption.

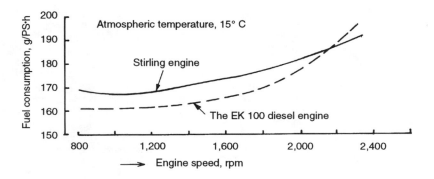

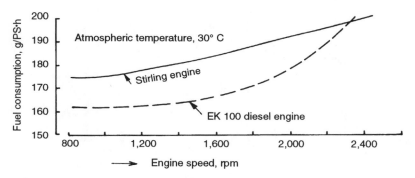

Fig. A39-2 Comparison of fuel-consumption rate between the Stirling engine and the diesel engine (1978): The rate of fuel consumption in the Stirling engine is not always better than the diesel engine. Further, the fuel consumption of the Stirling engine rapidly increases as atmospheric temperature rises.

Appendix A39-2 Noise Emission From a Truck

Fig. A39-3 illustrates the contribution of each sound source to the noise emission from a truck. It is understandable that a truck meeting the 1985 Japanese regulation has a lower noise level at each source. I will estimate the effect of a noiseless engine, if any, mounted on a truck meeting the 1985 regulation.

Human hearing is logarithmically sensitive to noise. So, a certain noise level A can be expressed as follows when the concurrent sound intensity is replaced with I_A.

$$A = 10\log_{10}\frac{I_A}{I_0} \quad \text{(dBA)}$$

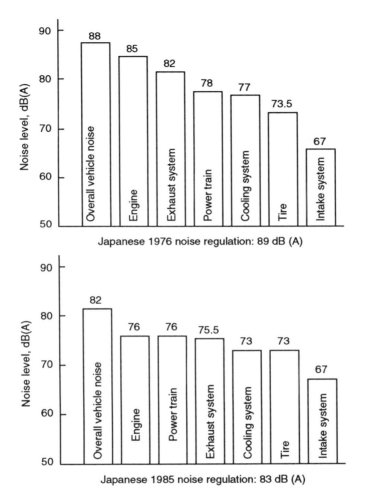

Fig. A39-3 Truck noise has multiple sources. After 1985, the contribution of the engine to the noise level is no worse than that from other sources.

where I_0 represents the minimum audible sound of the human ear.

$$I_0 = 10^{-12} \quad W/m^2$$

In the case of multiple sound sources, the overall sound intensity I_T can be calculated as follows:

$$I_T = I_A + I_B + I_T + \ldots\ldots \quad W/m^2$$

where

I_T = Overall sound intensity
$I_A, I_B, I_C \ldots$ = Sound intensity of each sound source

The overall noise level T can be given by the equation below:

$$T = 10 \log_{10} \frac{I_T}{I_0}$$

$$= 10 \log_{10} \left(\frac{I_A + I_B + I_C + \ldots}{I_0} \right)$$

$$= 10 \log_{10} \left(\frac{I_0 \times 10^{A/10} + I_0 \times 10^{B/10} + I_0 \times 10^{C/10} + \ldots}{I_0} \right)$$

$$= 10 \log_{10} \left(10^{A/10} + 10^{B/10} + 10^{C/10} + \ldots \right)$$

In the case in which a truck meeting the 1985 regulation obtains and uses a noiseless engine, then:

$$T_0 = 10 \log_{10} \left(10^{0/10} + 10^{76/10} + 10^{75.5/10} + 10^{73/10} + 10^{69/10} \right)$$

$$T_0 = 81 \text{ dBA}$$

Thus, even if noise from the engine is completely eliminated from the overall vehicle noise, the reduction is only 1 dB, that is, from 82 to 81 dB. Therefore, it is understandable that the noise reduction of the engine is ineffective for overall vehicle noise when the vehicle already has a low level of noise as a result of treatment of other sources.

Chapter 40

Looking Into the Future:
II. What About the Gas Turbine?

Its character is quite promising, but can it surpass the diesel engine in its fuel consumption performance?

❧

The Hope for Gas Turbine

The gas turbine engine, promoted as a future engine by the U.S. Department of Energy, is an internal-combustion engine. However, the gas turbine engine does not require that fuel burn in a closed space as in a reciprocating engine. As a result, the gas turbine does not have a propensity to knock as does a gasoline engine, and it is not so restricted by frictional loss when compared to a diesel engine. If one wanted to enhance the efficiency of a diesel engine, its compression ratio is restricted by combustion conditions in addition to the frictional loss. For example, an increase in the compression ratio decreases the ignition delay, which induces a higher level of exhaust smoke. The gas turbine also has fewer restrictions on fuel, as well as other advantages. Thus, its continued growth can be expected.

The principle of the jet engine used in all the large airplanes today is the same as the engine for automobiles.

In 1945, after the Japanese defeat in World War II, many Grumman and P51 aircraft were flying freely in the skies of Japan. Near the end of that year, the Lockheed *Shooting Star* appeared in the sky. The *Star* thrust into the sky with a sound of distant thunder. This encounter was my first with the power of a gas turbine. I was extremely impressed. I believed that the general piston engine would eventually be replaced with this new generation gas turbine (Fig. 40-1). The gas turbine for automobiles came soon after. In 1950, England's Rover Company released its prototype car.

Fig. 40-1 Jet plane appearing over the sky in Japan in 1945. The roar of the engine seemed to foretell the end of the reciprocating engine.

Gas Turbine Sleeping in Museum

In 1951 I asked my teacher, Professor Yasusi Tanasawa, to allow me to design a gas turbine as my graduation project. Professor Tanasawa, who had solved the unstable combustion problem of the first Japanese jet engine Ne-20 in Japan and still continued his research, answered me unexpectedly: "It is not for you yet," he said. "You should not select such a subject." Instead, my design project was a rather ordinary 30-hp gasoline engine. I suppose that my instructor responded to my request as he did because of his assessments of the business world and of my capability at the time.

In the spring of 1984, I had occasion to call Professor Tanasawa. When our talk touched on the gas turbine, I heard that he had found the design drawings of the Ne-20 engine among his vast storehouse of documents. I had the good fortune of examining the drawings. As I looked at the drawings, it occurred to me that some desperate spirit that performed round-the-clock labors without food (due to the shortage caused by the War) was even now appealing from each bolt drawn thereon. I read each sheet reverently with a deep impression (Photo 40-1).

Photo 40-1 Even individual bolts in Ne-20 design drawings impressed me with the engineers' desperate spirit: Professor Tanasawa, his wife, and the author (from the right). The design drawings are held in my hand. This was the last time I saw Professor Tanasawa in good health.

The researchers led by Professor Tanasawa had resolved the unstable combustion problem of the Ne-20 engine. On the other hand, Professor Fukusaburo Numachi, of the Tohoku University, and others had resolved the initial poor performance problem of the multistage compressor. I heard that the poor performance had been considerably improved by Mr. Osamu Nagano, who was in charge of design and who manually bent the vane. However, the final design was completed by Dr. Hitoshi Murai (later appointed as president of the Institute of High Speed Mechanics, Tohoku University) and others in the group of Professor Numachi. The success of the engine resulted from the design of the axial compressor blade, that is, a blade row (cascade) was adopted instead of a single aerofoil. After World War II, the Ne-20 was carried away by the U.S. Armed Forces. Later, the Ne-20 was returned to Japan. It is now preserved in Ishikawajima-Harima Heavy Industries Co., Ltd. (Photo 40-2). The first Japanese jet plane, designated the *Kikka*[40-1] and powered by the Ne-20 engine, flew the sky above Japan for only 15 minutes before the war ended. The *Kikka* has been restored and preserved in the Smithsonian Museum (Photo 40-3).

As an item of interest, at a corner of a museum adjacent to the famous Le Mans speedway in France, a somewhat old-style car equipped with a grille resembling the one at a jet engine's nose is attracting visitors' attention. This vehicle, the Socema Grégoire, made a spectacular debut as a turbocar

Photo 40-2 Before the real "Ne-20" engine: Professor Murai, who designed the axial compressor blade of this engine [left], and the author.

Photo 40-3 Restored Kikka: *The nacelle shape, which differed from the original one somewhat, worried me (Smithsonian Museum).*

(gas turbine car) after the 1950 introduction of the Rover vehicle. Yet, this profligate son, or luxurious car, bankrupted its maker, or parent, because of the tremendous development expenses. In the corner of the museum, the son appears to be in meditation, lamenting the fate of the turbocar yet to make a debut (Photo 40-4).

Photo 40-4 Meditating alone surrounded by reciprocating engine cars: the Socema Grégoire 100 hp (Le Mans Museum).

However, a number of companies in the world have continued research and development efforts despite the enormous expenses, and the relevant technology has been steadily advancing. Hino Motors also initiated its research jointly with Toyota Motor Corporation in 1969. They targeted a scaled-down version of a turbine engine for future application to large-size trucks. This joint research was generally directed by Mr. Kenya Nakamura of Toyota Motor Corporation. A car equipped with this engine was successfully driven in a test drive with the one-shaft gas turbine and generator hybrid, which had been simultaneously developed by Toyota. The development of this engine was announced at the international gas turbine conferences in 1971 and 1977.[40-2, 40-3] Toyota Motor Corporation has continued the development of that engine, together with the one-shaft type. The actual car test is now in the advanced stage of development (Photo 40-5).

Photo 40-5 Gas turbine test cars: [Top] Hino bus with a Toyota gas turbine engine; [Bottom] Toyota gas turbine test car.

Why Did Ford Discontinue Its Project?

Since 1953, Ford Motor Company had performed continuing research on gas turbines. In 1966, I visited the Ford Motor Company and had the good fortune of riding in a truck that had the gas turbine as its powerplant (Photo 40-6). I felt that this truck had an advanced style, luxurious interior, and riding comfort that were far superior to trucks made in Japan at that time. However, I did not understand the use of some of the interior furnishings. I asked the purpose of a small door behind the driver's seat. Although I understood the answer to be a toilet, I could not understand how it was used. I repeated my question several times until I realized it was actually a container that kept things warm.

Photo 40-6 This beautiful gas-turbine truck greatly impressed me in March 1966.

Ford originally considered the application of gas turbines to both cars and trucks. In 1960, the company narrowed the field of its gas turbine research to trucks, targeted the beginning of mass production in April 1974, and manufactured 200 gas turbine trucks as a preparatory step in 1973. In June 1973, however, the project was suddenly suspended. Mr. Ivan M. Swatman, who had poured all his energy into gas turbine research since he had joined Ford, left the company. He continued his research on gas turbine as a consultant in San Diego, California. In 1983 I visited him. In his office, which displayed an illustration of the Ford GT707 gas turbine, Mr. Swatman enthusiastically told me about the application of the gas turbine to cogeneration (a power unit that integrates power generation and cooling/heating) (Photo 40-7).

According to Mr. Masumi Iwai (chief examiner of Toyota Motor Corporation), one of the main concerns of the production process for gas turbine is

Photo 40-7 Mr. Swatman, leader of the Ford 707 gas turbine development effort, talked enthusiastically about gas turbine applications. His office had an illustration of the gas turbine hanging on the wall.

its required manufacturing accuracy. The gas turbine must have a manufacturing accuracy ten times greater than the usual automobile engine. Therefore, it can be imagined that if the Ford gas turbine were finished with the same accuracy as general engines, its output would have a variation as wide as $20 \pm 10\%$. An output variation of 20% would signify that no manufacturer could make an operation schedule. I wonder if Ford forgot the Pratt & Whitney production failure of its aeroengine in the 1940s (refer to Chapter 34).

Expecting a Breakthrough for Practical Application

A bright future for gas turbines has long been anticipated; however, the gas turbine has still not been put into practical use for road vehicles. One reason for this delay is its high fuel consumption. The thermal efficiency of the gas turbine engine is higher at a higher combustion temperature. However, the thermal load and stress of turbine blades constitute a problem with gas turbines because the engine depends on continuous combustion. In diesel engines, the maximum gas temperature in the cylinder rises well above 2000°C, but only periodically. In the gas turbine, on the other hand, the inlet temperature, even when composed of a heat-resistant alloy, is limited to approximately 1000°C due to continuous burning. However, when the turbine is produced from certain ceramic materials, the inlet temperature may reach 1350°C or higher. This increased temperature alone can result in a decreased fuel consumption of 20-30%.

Ford Motor Company, after its GT707 gas turbine project, participated in a U.S. Department of Energy (DOE) project in collaboration with Garrett Corporation. The objective of this DOE program was to produce a ceramic turbine (one-shaft type in which the compressor and turbine share a single shaft as illustrated in Fig. 40-1) with a turbine inlet temperature of 1370°C. In a separate part of this project, General Motors Corporation also took part. The GM objective was to complete a ceramic turbine with two shafts (Fig. A40-1). Fig. 40-2 shows the thermal efficiency of future ceramic turbine engines, as predicted by Ford Motor Company.

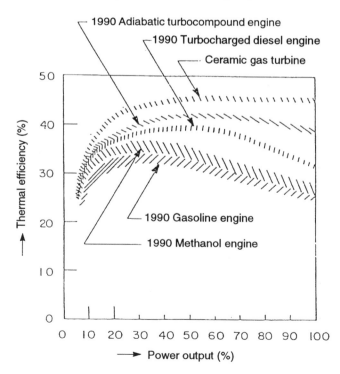

Fig. 40-2 Thermal efficiency of future engine presented by Ford Motor Company (SAE Paper No. 811377).

In accordance with this prediction, the completion of the ceramic turbine seemed realistic. In response to the U.S. initiative, Japan in 1988 decided to establish a national ceramic turbine initiative. In this program, it has been determined that the engine will be of the one-shaft regeneration type (with heat exchanger) and the output goal will be 100 kW. The project is underway with the participation of the major automobile makers and oil companies.

The permissible turbine inlet temperature rose 200°C in the decade of the 1960s, or 20°C a year (according to Mr. Iwai). The efficiency of the diesel engine has been rising year after year. However, if the rise in gas turbine inlet temperature maintains its present rate, the diesel engine will be surpassed by the gas turbine. Can this goal be realized? Technology always has cycles of advancement. A steady rise usually saturates the end of a cycle, requiring a breakthrough to continue further. The gas turbine technology seems to be in this situation. Therefore, the author expects some dramatic breakthrough in gas turbine technology.

Appendix A40 Gas Turbine Jointly Developed by Toyota and Hino

Fig. A40-1 shows the gas turbine engine developed jointly by Hino Motors and Toyota Motor Corporation since 1969. Toyota Motor Corporation has been continually studying and improving this engine.

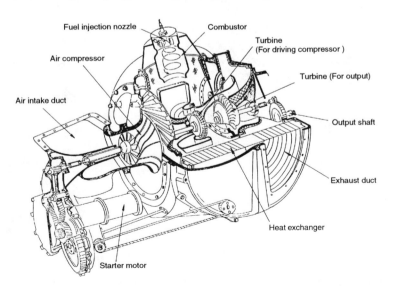

Fig. A40-1 GT-21 engine (1977): 150 PS/50,000 rpm (1977).

Chapter 41

Looking Into the Future: III. What About Hydrogen Engine?

Can this engine become a pioneer of the 21st Century? Toward the Age of Hydrogen Fuel.

In 1986, Hino Motors jointly developed a hydrogen truck with the Musashi Institute of Technology. The truck was equipped with an engine that burned liquid hydrogen, which was injected directly into the combustion chamber toward the end of the compression stroke. Designed by Professor Shoichi Furuhama of the Musashi Institute of Technology, this engine was installed in a truck and entered in the Innovative Vehicle Design Competition held at the August 1986 World Transportation Fair in Vancouver. The vehicle met all the requirements and was one of six finishers from a field of ten. The low-pollution award was presented to this truck, acknowledging its low environmental pollution characteristic.

Mankind consumes a tremendous amount of energy every day. Almost all the energy used for transportation is obtained from petroleum. According to the presently accepted theory, the petroleum and natural gas originates from deposits of organic materials. If so, the quantity of fossil fuel is limited and will be exhausted sooner or later. Yet, Professors Gold and Sorter of Cornell University insist that fossil fuel did not originate from organic material but, instead, was present when the earth was formed from space debris. They point out that methane is contained in the atmosphere of Jupiter, carbon dioxide in the atmosphere of Venus, and carbon in meteorites. From these facts, these professors go on to say that natural gas and petroleum are generated in the earth's crust and by some chemical reaction seep onto the earth.[41-1] Though there are such theories, it is a fact that finding new oil and gas wells has required moving to more remote regions or deeper into the sea. Not only is it difficult to dig out the new wells, but the combination of the carbon and hydrogen could build up toxic exhaust gases. Therefore, some form of alternative energy is needed.

Hydrogen can be generated when water and power are available. Hydrogen may be an unlimited resource because sea water can be decomposed by solar energy. Thus, hydrogen fuel is expected to be widely used in the 21st Century instead of petroleum fuel (Fig. 41-1).

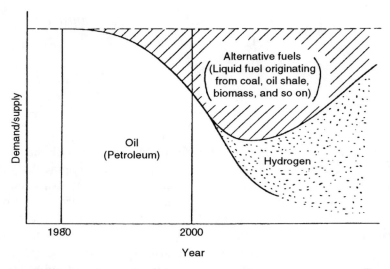

Fig. 41-1 Even though liquid petroleum-derived fuel is currently being used for transportation, the liquid fuel may be replaced with hydrogen in the future (by Ricardo & Company).

Development of Hydrogen Engine

Professor Furuhama has focused his attention on the hydrogen engine as a future engine since 1970, far in advance of other researchers. In 1975, his car was the first hydrogen car to finish a course of more than 2000 km in the Student Economy Engineered Design (SEED) rally held in the United States. His success showcased Japanese technology in this field.[41-2] Hino Motors decided to support Furuhama's far-reaching plan, and he continued to work on the problem. In his first efforts, his hydrogen engine was based on a gasoline engine, but Furuhama eventually designed a hydrogen system based on a diesel engine, which would be called a hydrogen diesel engine. Hino Motors offered a 3.8L (model WO4C) engine as his base engine (Appendix A41). The hydrogen diesel engine was installed on a vehicle, and Hino Motors held a demonstration and test ride on June 2, 1986. The demonstration met with resounding success and greatly impressed the representatives of various organizations, including the mass media. After the final adjustment, the truck left for Vancouver and entered the competition mentioned previously (Photo 41-1). In addition, a presentation of the hydrogen diesel engine was made at the Society of Automotive Engineers Annual Congress in February 1987, and it also made a good impression.[41-3]

At that time, the hydrogen diesel engine was still undergoing academic study, and its sponsors were only Benz and Hino. Afterward, BMW, MAN, Mazda, etc., entered this field, resulting in the work and evaluations being performed on this engine on a worldwide scale. Furuhama has continued to work on his engine, modifying it in several ways, particularly the combustion characteristics. In Japan, the research on hydrogen-utilizing technology was selected as a national project. The hydrogen car is included in this project, which began in the fiscal year 1993.

Appendix A41 Hydrogen Diesel Engine

Fig. A41-1 illustrates the principle of the hydrogen diesel engine. Instead of diesel oil, high-pressure hydrogen is injected through the injection nozzle and ignited with the glowplug (bar-shaped plug made of ceramic) heated to approximately 900°C. The structure of the injection nozzle is illustrated in Fig. A41-2. A diesel fuel injection pump activates the hydrogen injector. To activate the injector, a diesel fuel injection nozzle is mounted upside down on the hydrogen nozzle. When the diesel pump supplies fluid to the diesel nozzle, the hydrogen nozzle operates as is. A conventional fuel injection nozzle is mounted upside down to serve as the delivery valve of the hydrogen injection. This concept is quite a unique one.

Hydrogen is liquefied and stored in the tank at -253°C as shown in Fig. A41-3. The liquid hydrogen is then drawn with the electric pump, and heated and vaporized with the heat exchanger. At 30°C and 80 atm, hydrogen is then injected into the cylinder. The cylindrical fuel tank under the loading platform can be seen in Photo 41-1. The basic specifications of this engine are listed in Table A41-1.

Photo 41-1 The hydrogen truck was first unveiled to the public on June 2, 1986. [Top] Professor Furuhama explaining this truck; [Bottom] Hydrogen-powered freezer van with three different temperature compartments provided by using the latent heat from the vaporization of liquefied hydrogen. This trial method may result in a more comfortable life without polluting the environment.

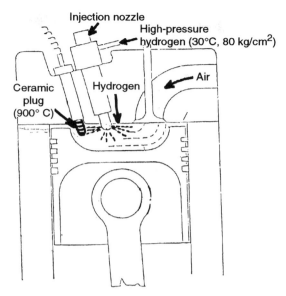

Fig. A41-1 The principle of the hydrogen diesel engine.

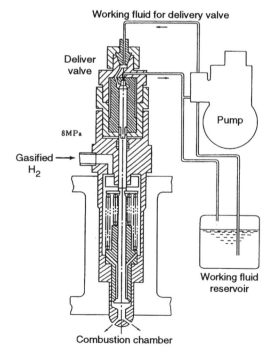

Fig. A41-2 Hydrogen injection nozzle
(from Shoichi Furuhama Hydrogen Car Opens Our Future*).*

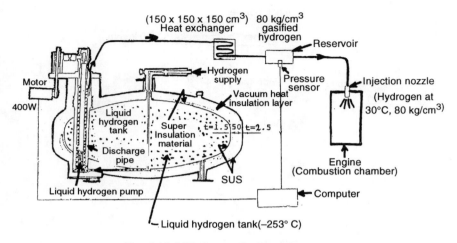

Fig. A41-3 Hydrogen fuel supply system.

Table A41-1. Basic Specifications of Hydrogen Diesel Engine

Basic engine model	W04C (turbocharging)
Bore × stroke	104 mm × 113 mm
Displacement	3839 cm^3
Compression ratio	12
Maximum output	135 PS/3000 rpm

Chapter 42

Looking Into the Future:
IV. What About Hybrid Engine?

Can the hybrid engine system be an ideal motive power, ensuring less environmental pollution and greater convenience?

❁

Is It a Combination Engine or a Miscegenation of Engines?

"Hybrid" indicates a descendant of mixed parentage or a product from origins of different kinds. In general, a hybrid car uses engines of two different kinds. For instance, a submarine cruises with its diesel engine when cruising on the surface of the sea, but its electric motor when below the water's surface. This kind of usage is also called "hybrid" in a broad sense of the term.

In recent years, urban air pollution has been becoming progressively worse in comparison with pollution in the suburbs. Some people have proposed that cars should be powered by electric motors in the urban area and by petroleum-powered engines in the suburbs. This concept can also be used as follows. An electric car has problems such as a shorter driving range, less power, and others. These problems can be alleviated by combining the use of a conventional engine with that of an electric motor. Attempts to form such a hybrid system have been increasing. These attempts include the electric motor, the gasoline engine, the diesel engine, the gas turbine, and the Stirling engine. In addition, several methods of storing the mechanical energy, including compressed air and the flywheel, have been attempted.

Most hybrid engines are dependent on some combination engine that selectively uses two power sources as exemplified by the submarine. For hybrid vehicles, MAN worked out an energy storage and discharge system provided with a motor and a generator, using a permanent magnet on the mechanical flywheel in a vacuum vessel. Although a conventional electric battery was used in the MAN system, Hino Motors succeeded in incorporating a high-performance motor/generator in the flywheel area of a conventional diesel engine. Both the MAN and Hino engines are hybrid in the truest sense of the word, that is, each is a prime mover that utilizes two principles simultaneously. The Hino hybrid engine has been used in hundreds of city buses and several trucks that deliver packages and products in congested urban areas.

HIMR Begins Running

The hybrid system is not a new idea. In 1897, Porsche acquired the patent of a hybrid system consisting of an electric motor and a gasoline engine. The Porsche hybrid system is shown in Photo 42-1. A generator is positioned behind the driver's seat of a normal gasoline engine vehicle. The generator is driven directly by the gasoline engine to generate electric power, which then drives the motor housed in the hub of the front wheel via a controller.

*Photo 42-1 The Lohner-Porsche gasoline-electric hybrid car (1901–1905).
Manufactured by Porsche at Jacob Lohner & Company, the four-cylinder, 16-hp,
Daimler-made gasoline engine was used to directly drive a 10kW generator, whose
power drove a four-pole motor mounted inside the front wheels (Technological
Museum in Vienna).*

It is reported that, during World War II, Porsche attempted to apply this hybrid concept to the Tiger tank in an unsuccessful attempt to counter the Russian T34 tanks. After the war, several attempts to develop the hybrid system were made, but none reached an advanced stage. This failure was because it was difficult to come up with an advantage sufficient to offset such a complicated and expensive design. In recent years, however, numerous similar efforts have been attempted because the exhaust emission regulations are becoming increasingly stringent. In particular, the hybrid system is generating more interest as a deterrent against urban air pollution.

The Hino Motors hybrid system is called the Hybrid Inverter Controlled Motor and Retarder (HIMR). This engine looks similar to a conventional diesel engine as shown in Fig. 42-1. An ultrathin motor/generator is built in the engine. This motor/generator acts as a motor and works together with the diesel engine. Power is delivered from the common output shaft. When the vehicle is driven at slow speeds, less output is needed, and less exhaust is emitted; the HIMR runs using only the diesel engine. This concept is illustrated in Fig. 42-2.

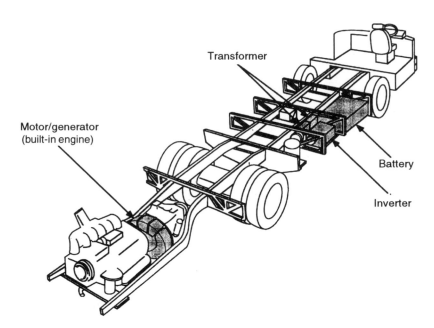

Transformer

Motor/generator
(built-in engine)

Battery

Inverter

Fig. 42-1 Structure of the HIMR bus. The motor/generator is built in the engine, and the inverter size was decreased.

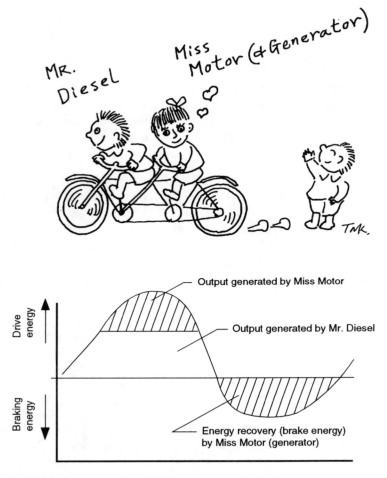

Fig. 42-2 Hybrid system of the HIMR is dependent on the electric motor and the diesel engine working together.

When the vehicle is stopping, the braking energy is collected from the wheels, and the motor/generator is used as a generator. The generated energy is then stored in a battery and used for the next start. When the charge in the battery falls, it is automatically recharged by the diesel engine according to the commands given by a computer. This system, hybrid in the true sense of the term, has realized a substantial reduction of NO_x, smoke, CO_2, fuel consumption, and noise as well as an enhancement of brake performance through recovery of the energy at braking as shown in Fig. 42-3. Unfortunately, the disadvantages of complicated design and high cost remain the same as in previous hybrid systems, even though some features such as controllability have been improved. The problems with the hybrid engine must be solved as mankind becomes more concerned with the need to preserve our environment. A clean and safe environment must exist before higher forms of social improvement can take place.[42-1]

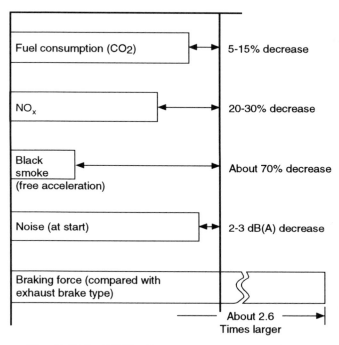

Fig. 42-3 The HIMR effects on environment and safety.

Inverter Most Difficult to Develop

Hino Motors required about 10 years to develop the ultrathin motor/generator (three-phase alternator) and the inverter, which serves to input and output the motor/generator energy via the battery. In the initial development, a special control motor was designed to achieve an ultrathin structure. This motor was initially called the "capacitor switchover resonance type," and Hino Motors began with a scale model. The model rotated very smoothly. We recalled the famous tale of the Columbus egg. In this story, nobody could stand an egg upright on a table; however, Columbus performed this seemingly impossible task by simply hitting the bottom of the egg, flattening it enough to support the egg upright. The moral of this story is that an achievement may seem impossible until it has actually been tried and accomplished. With a sense of relief, we continued with the next stage of development and produced a scaled-up prototype. To our great disappointment, however, the prototype would not rotate (Fig. 42-4).

Fig. 42-4 Although the scale model rotated steadily, the actual machine would not work.

Our research team reviewed the structure of the alternator (in hindsight, the review was insufficient), reconsidered the control system, and applied new materials such as amorphous metal. We were still unable to solve the problem and seemed to hit a brick wall in our developmental efforts. It appeared that the failure in the experiment with the model was attributable to an insufficient understanding of the characteristic number (nondimensional parameter, i.e., π number) at scale change and the law of similarity. The prototype machine was considered to have failed because of immature technology on the alternator and its control.

By this time, Hino Motors had already spent five years on the project. To resolve the current difficulty, our team decided to consult with Toshiba Corporation. However, Toshiba's response after our briefing was discouraging. The company felt that it was impossible to design such an alternator. However, we persuaded a team of Toshiba engineers to examine our prototype. We had them examine all our products including the successfully rotatable scale model, the alternator made of amorphous metal, and the records of our previous efforts. Since the Toshiba engineers were also in manufacturing, they had a great deal of empathy for our attempt. They replied, "We'll try it." The concept, however, was still a difficult one, and time continued to pass mercilessly.

Then, I received a telephone call urging me to come and see the finally completed inverter. I rushed over to the Toshiba site with great expectations. However, I was disappointed when I saw the actual inverter. It was as big as the platform of a four-ton truck (Fig. 42-5). However, the Hino engineers were still optimistic. I left the test site after saying that downsizing would be necessary anyway as the next step. As a result, this monstrous inverter shrunk, as if by magic, thanks to a giant transistor developed by Toshiba.

Fig. 42-5 The completed inverter was as big as the platform of a four-ton truck.

At the end of 1990, the World Environmental Ministers conference was held in Tokyo. The Hino Motors' HIMR attracted the attention of Mr. Akira Fukida, who later became the Japanese Minister of Home Affairs. The HIMR was exhibited in front of the Japanese Diet Building. This exhibition was a tremendous honor given to the young engineering staff, who had dreamed of success and continued to work on the problem until they had solved it (Photo 42-2).

Hybrid System in the Future

The hybrid system appears to be a promising method of complying with the environmental pollution regulations without restricting those transportation methods already enjoyed by many people. The complicated structure and high cost of the system must be improved for it to be widely used. Advances

Photo 42-2 In the presence of many Japanese Diet members, the HIMR bus runs quietly with less polluting emissions.

in the electronic field will ensure a more appropriate control, so the idea of combining an electric motor with another prime mover appears to be promising.

The MAN-designed energy-storage equipment is unique as shown in Fig. 42-6, and future improvement can be expected. On the other hand, improvements in battery technology are expected as well. Internal-combustion engines, such as the gasoline, diesel, and gas turbine engines, will mostly be used as the prime mover for the immediate future. Depending on its application, a fuel cell, and its combination with the catalytic engine described later, may be used. When a combination suitable for each application is eventually selected, I feel that the complicated structure and high cost inherent to a hybrid system will be improved through mass production.

The fuel cell mentioned here can be outlined as follows. When an electric current is passed through water (H_2O), the water is decomposed into hydrogen (H_2) and oxygen (O_2) in a process called *electrolysis*. Conversely, we can conceive of a device that will produce water by reacting hydrogen with oxygen, while removing electric energy. This process is the principle of the fuel cell.

As an application, the fuel cell, which depends on the hydrogen separated by passing water through sponge iron, may be combined with an electric

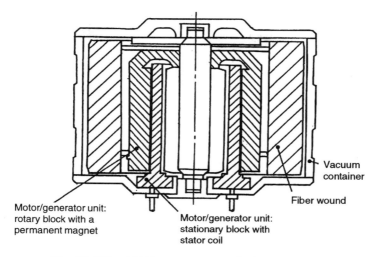

Motor/generator unit:
rotary block with a
permanent magnet

Motor/generator unit:
stationary block with
stator coil

Vacuum
container

Fiber wound

Fig. 42-6 The MAN energy storage/release equipment.

motor to form a hybrid engine. This type of engine is envisaged to be the power of the next generation of engines.

Chapter 43

Onward to the Future

In which direction will the next-generation engines advance?

✄

Comparison of Major Engines at Present and Alternative Engines (Powerplants)

We have already examined three alternative engines, such as the Stirling engine, gas turbine, and hydrogen engine, as well as the hybrid system. Presently in the automobile field, gasoline engines maintain dominance in cars, while diesel engines are first among commercial vehicles. The gasoline engine is dominant in private transport because its energy density (watt/hour per engine weight) and output density (output per engine weight) are about ten times higher than those of the other alternative engines, as illustrated in Fig. 43-1. These density characteristics are very important for application to transport vehicles.[43-1]

The diesel engine is used in commercial vehicles, even though its output density is lower than that of the gasoline engine, because of its excellent fuel consumption performance and durability. As described earlier, the fuel consumption of the diesel engine is about 60% of the gasoline engine (refer to Chapter 33). In addition, its durability (engine life) has been steadily enhanced as discussed in Chapter 8.

It is also important that the ratio of fuel cost to the life cycle cost (total cost from purchase to discard) of the diesel truck has been increasing from year to year, easily clearing the 70% level (in Japanese case) as shown in Fig. 43-2. This higher ratio is because the service lives of both the vehicle and the engine have been increasing and fuel cost has been on the rise. This increased fuel cost is now an accepted part of our transportation economy.

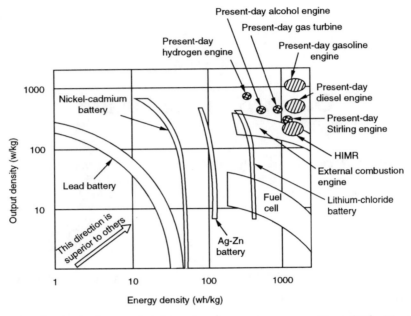

Fig. 43-1 Energy and output densities of various power sources (for vehicles) (actual examples, etc., added based on R&D of Electric Cars, *issued by Japanese Ministry of International Trade and Industry).*

For example, the price of home-delivery service is based on this fuel cost. Considering the widespread acceptance of the characteristics and cost of the leading engine system, it will not be easy for alternative engines to offer advantages striking enough that people will want to change the existing transportation system.

Trade-Off Among Nitrogen Oxide and Other Emissions

Today, the modern internal-combustion engines have been advancing rapidly, and mankind is producing increasingly large amounts of horsepower (Fig. 43-3). Unfortunately, the increase in horsepower signifies that exhaust gas from these engines is also increasing tremendously. For example, Fig. 43-4 illustrates the amount of nitrogen oxide (NO) produced. In an earlier edition of this book, the author predicted that NO would decrease worldwide because of recent gas regulations (the dotted line on the graph). However, because of a host of factors (including the industrial development of Third World countries), these NO levels did not decrease as rapidly as had been expected. The author's expectation of the future exhaust quantity is

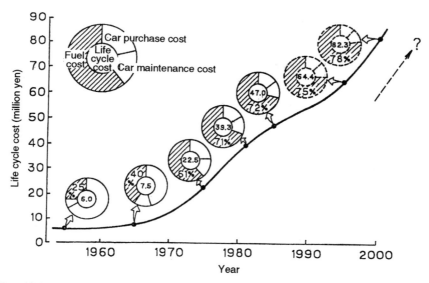

Fig. 43-2 Life cycle cost of diesel truck: Ratio of fuel cost is on a steady rise (based on the Japanese case).

represented by the one-dot chain line. The amount of nitrogen oxides in auto-mobile exhaust appears to be tremendous, but it is far smaller than that of natural generation on the earth as shown in the figure. In the natural world, a great amount of nitrogen oxides has been generated by bacteria.[43-2] It is understandable that the human-produced nitrogen oxides are concentrated mostly in the urban areas and constitute a severe problem. As a result, the emission of nitrogen oxides must be reduced even further. The nitrogen-oxide emission from diesel engines has been reduced to about 35% of its level before Japan regulated it. Even further reduction is expected since the relevant emission from gasoline engines for cars has already been reduced to about 10% of its pre-Japanese regulation level.

Another problem caused by diesel exhaust is particulates. The diesel exhaust contains soot as part of the smoke. Various forms of hydrocarbons attach themselves to this soot, and the agglomerate is called *particulate*. Some people say that these particulates are carcinogenic because cancerous symptoms have been detected in biotests, for example, the Ames Test (a test to measure the effects of a substance on the mutation rate of bacteria). The relationship of these biotests to the actual causing of cancer in humans is still unknown.[43-3] However, this lack of certainty does not mean that we can remain idle. If doubt exists, then we must take preventive measures. This

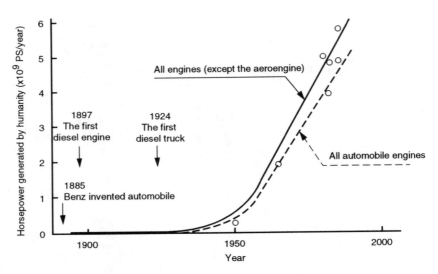

Fig. 43-3 Manmade power on a steep increase.

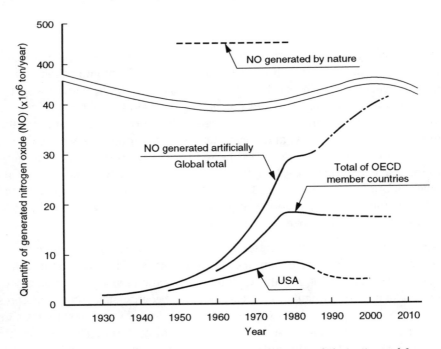

Fig. 43-4 Nitrogen oxides (NO_x) emitted from the automobile (estimated from
Greenhouse Gas Emission OECD 1991)

prevention centers on the improvement of combustion. The key factor in improving combustion is a better mixing of fuel and air (refer to Chapter 15).

By instituting a better mixing, the quantity of particulates decreases; the tendency is, at the same time, for nitrogen oxides to increase. Similarly, strategies to reduce nitrogen oxides tend to increase particulates as well as to reduce power output. Thus, various measures have advantages and disadvantages (Fig. 43-5). Diesel manufacturers in the world have been tackling this difficult problem (Fig. 43-6). The current goal is to satisfy the next set of continuously more severe emission regulations established in each country. In Japan, however, the goal has been generalized even more to search for and find the concept of the next-generation prime mover. This area of research was initiated in 1987 and was assisted by the Japan Key Technology Center. The research has been performed by the Advanced Combustion Engineering Institute Company, Ltd. (ACE), a research company established with capital investment and staff provided by the diesel vehicle manufacturers, parts producers, and other companies interested in the outcome. To date, extremely significant and advanced research results have been obtained on the combustion of diesel engines.

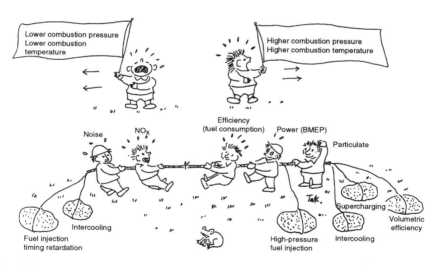

Fig. 43-5 So many contradictions lying in the improvement of diesel combustion. Is that measure friendly or hostile?

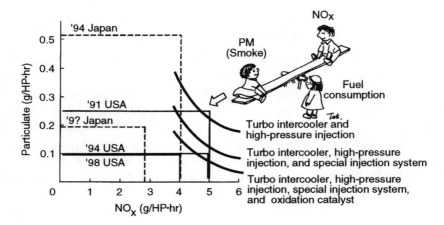

Fig. 43-6 NO_x and particulates have an inverse relationship. Strenuous research in satisfying both conditions has been made so as to meet regulations in each country.

Result of the ACE Research on Combustion; Unique Mode of Combustion

The ACE research[43-4] is based on combustion in the engine by high-pressure fuel injection, thereby examining the long-held view of some engine people that high pressure may be better. The ACE study is outlined below. Photo 43-1 compares the combustion in the conventional diesel engine with that of high-pressure fuel injection carried out at ACE. In 1977 the combustion process was able to be observed in an actual diesel engine while bringing the entire combustion chamber of a practical engine within the field of view. Since then, the following process has been generally accepted by specialists in diesel combustion. The fuel spray injected as shown in the left photo is distributed by the airflow (swirl) into the cylinder, and the fuel is ignited at the point at which the fuel and air are mixed at the stoichiometric mixture level. This point is on the side of the fuel jet. Combustion then spreads sequentially. However, when the fuel injection pressure is increased to a high level (approximately 150 MPa [1500 atm] or higher), ignition occurs not at the side of the fuel jet, but on the leading edge of the fuel jet, or the point at which it collides with the walls of the combustion chamber. As shown on the right photo, the rapid spreading of the combustion process occurs at this point. As a consequence, the high-fuel injection pressure is greatly increased, and combustion proceeds with almost no soot (smoke) or particulates, as can be easily imagined from these photographs. Though this technology could reduce particulates, the NO_x

Conventional engine   High-pressure fuel
injection engine

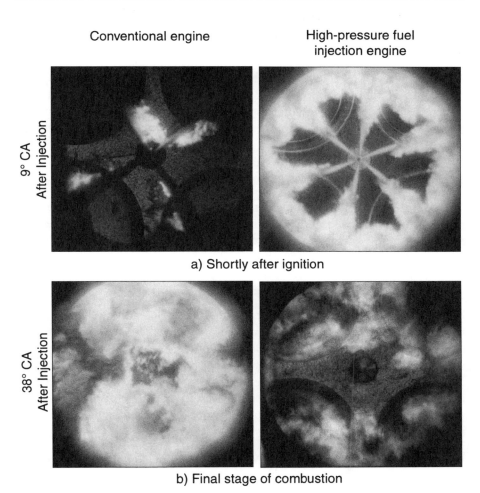

a) Shortly after ignition

b) Final stage of combustion

*Photo 43-1 High-pressure fuel injection results in a unique mode of combustion,
completely free from unburned soot in the final stage of combustion.*

emission still remains. Therefore, the ACE did not stop its study here. Researchers experimented with a technique called *high-pressure pilot injection*. In this method, not only is the fuel injection pressure increased, but a small percentage of the total fuel injection quantity is injected before the main injection. When this procedure is carried out, the amount of NO_x decreases. It first appeared that the research team finally solved both the NO_x and particulate emission problem. However, the technological barrier could not be razed so easily. The particulates, which were minimized by the high-pressure fuel injections, reappeared in even higher density, along with increased fuel consumption, the most important performance parameter.

After six years of research, the ACE had made extensive progress (Appendix A43-1). Since its goal was accomplished, this company was dissolved. To carry on the work of the dissolved ACE, a new ACE was formed with private investment. The new company is now performing vigorous research in its field.

Why Was Diesel Selected as the Basis of Research?

The ACE selected the diesel engine as the basis for the next-generation prime mover because the diesel engine currently has the highest thermal efficiency of any prime mover. It is natural for the diesel engine to be the basis for the next growth. Of course, the diesel engine still has several problems that must be resolved before it can develop into the future engine. These problems have been discussed earlier.

Fig. 43-7 shows the invention year and thermal efficiency of each engine. From this illustration, the efforts of the predecessor in the direction for using resources most efficiently can be imagined. The resources of the earth should not be wasted, and their consumption should be minimized. This rule must not be violated if we are to keep nature unaffected. In thermodynamics, the expression "entropy increase" is used to indicate a disturbance or a waste of energy. In this sense, the minimization of entropy increase must be the basis of engine design.

Exhaust emission is not the only problem with automobiles. In Japan, automobile noise is at its lowest level in the world (Fig. 43-8). Truck noise has been reduced to the level of older cars, and the noise level of cars has also been decreasing. To maintain the level with cars, extensive efforts to reduce truck noise even further have been made.

Progress of Engine-Related Technologies

With all these problems yet to be solved, in what direction will the future engine advance? Fig. 43-9 shows that various requirements for the engine and new technologies related to engine technology both exert influence on what that direction will be. In other words, a number of requirements currently undergoing diversification and change must be met while giving priority to exhaust emission, noise emission, and safety. In engine-related technologies, we all know that electronics and material science have been progressing rapidly.

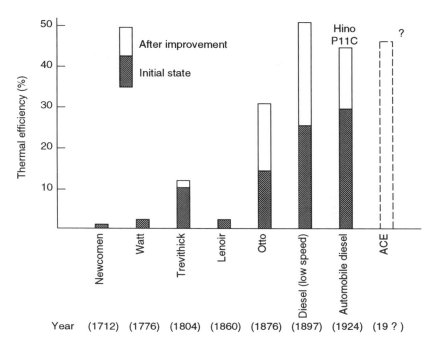

Fig. 43-7 Invention year and thermal efficiency of various engines.

Various electronic controls that have played an important role in development have already been applied to most automobiles. For example, in noise abatement, the vibration of a cylinder head can be simulated in the design stage, so that a lightweight, robust, and noise/vibration-free design comes ever closer to realization (Fig. 43-10).

Progress is also remarkable in the field of material. For example, in 1984, U.S. Polimotor amazed the world by releasing an all-plastic racing engine (2L, 318 hp/9500 rpm). All the components of this engine, including the piston, connecting rod, and valve gear system, were made of Torlon, a thermoplastic composite. The car with this engine actually completed the entire race (Photo 43-2). Besides plastic materials, the rapid growth of other composite materials, such as metallic and ceramic materials, makes the progress of future engines hopeful.

Catalyst and Catalytic Engine

In a conventional engine, fuel and air are introduced into the combustion chamber and there, without external controls, the fuel is burned. As a result,

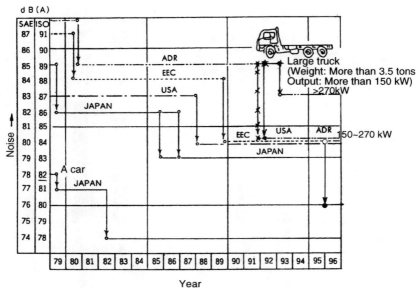

Note:
Values are not for strict comparison because the measuring methods
differ among the countries.

Fig. 43-8 History of vehicle noise reduction (transition of regulation level).

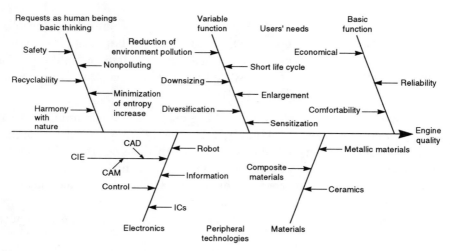

Fig. 43-9 Future direction of engine technology.

toxic substances are emitted. Efforts to suppress the emission of such substances have been made. However, doesn't it seem that a better conversion

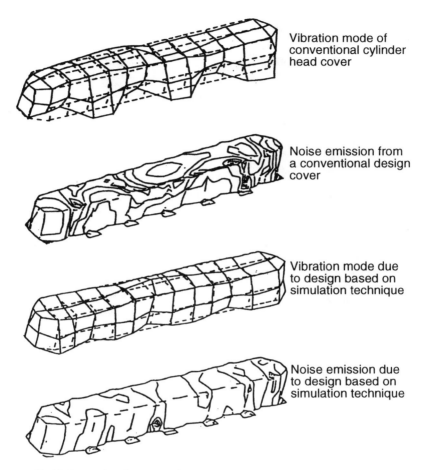

Vibration mode of conventional cylinder head cover

Noise emission from a conventional design cover

Vibration mode due to design based on simulation technique

Noise emission due to design based on simulation technique

Fig. 43-10 Example of noise-reducing measure in design stage through recent simulation analyses (example of cylinder head cover).

method can be thought of to remove energy by converting the matter in the natural world so as to minimize the entropy increase and to prevent the emission of toxic substances?

An idea—if energy is removed by effectively converting matter through some reaction with a catalyst, we might be able to integrate engine exhaust into the environment—is compared with the simple combustion at present in Fig. 43-11. Presently, the use of a catalyst as an aftertreatment is common among gasoline engines. In these catalysts, platinum and palladium or rhodium are supported on a ceramic or metal substrate. When combustion takes

Photo 43-2 A polimotor plastic engine: 2L displacement, 318 PS/9500 rpm.

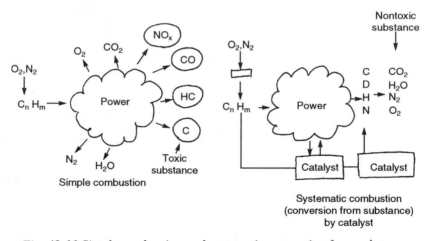

Fig. 43-11 Simple combustion and systematic conversion from substance.

place at the stoichiometric mixture ratio using this catalyst, then these unde-sirable gases (NO_x, HC, and CO) can be scrubbed from the emission. Such a catalyst is called a "three-way catalyst." However, a diesel engine does not allow combustion at the stoichiometric mixture ratio due to high smoke emissions (as explained in Chapter 32), and the diesel is operated with excess air. The catalyst that is effective for gasoline engines is unusable as an aftertreatment for diesel engines. One method of reducing NO_x under this excess air condition is to add a reducing agent to the exhaust. Ammonia is a strong reducing agent and was selected for early development. This method is described later in this chapter. In 1990, however, Mr. Shinji Iwamoto, then professor of Miyazaki University (now Hokkaido University), succeeded in reducing NO under conditions of excess air using zeolites subjected to a specific treatment. Since then, many researchers have made various attempts, but their catalysts have not yet been completed for use in practical engines. Ammonia cannot be used directly in vehicles because it is a strong chemical, and its onboard storage poses difficult problems. Therefore, its use is limited to scrubbing the exhaust of stationary powerplants.

The ACE studied the basics of how to generate energy by conversion of the substance and evaluated different combinations of practical-use catalysts. The ACE researchers came up with the idea that ammonia is produced from the fuel in the vehicle fuel tank, eliminating the need for ammonia storage. Further, the CO generated in the process of ammonia production can be injected into the combustion chamber of the diesel engine. Since CO is a fuel that produces no soot, the black smoke of exhaust can be reduced substantially.

Diesel engines with this system can be run under the conditions of minimum fuel consumption without worrying about NO_x. This concept was identified as the "catalytic engine," and some research on it was carried out. Although the feasibility of the catalytic engine was confirmed, research is continuing on the engine (Appendix A43-2). The vehicle design based on this concept is illustrated in Fig. 43-12.[43-3] The ultimate goal of this research is to create an engine that uses a natural fuel (hydrogen), has a minimal entropy increase (fuel consumption), and produces an exhaust gas that can be assimilated by nature.

Scientific Technology That is Harmonious with Nature

Needless to say, scientific advances have not been restricted to engines. The engine has enabled us to enjoy an almost unlimited convenience and satisfaction. At the same time, the disadvantages of the engine, such as exhaust emission and vehicle safety problems, have become extremely pronounced. Originally, the engine was conceived by Huygens in the 17th Century to

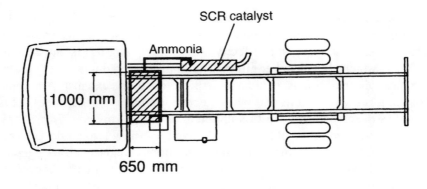

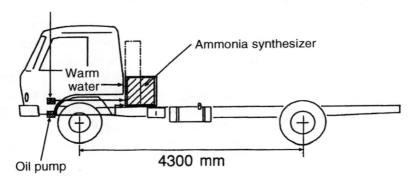

Fig. 43-12 Conceptual diagram of a truck with a catalytic engine.

reduce labor's burden on humanity, that is, the engine originated from humanism (refer to Chapter 1). However, the engine can also result in degrading humanism. The engine and its related scientific technologies have advanced to their present levels based on European rationalism. The earth's environmental conditions have considerably deteriorated. I think it is now time to re-evaluate the engine, returning to its point of origin.

The bases of European rationalism and scientific technologies have consisted of opposing and, therefore, conquering nature. The gardens of Versailles required an enormous amount of water, necessitating some motive power. On the other hand, Korakuen, a representative Japanese garden, is shown in Photo 43-3. The beautiful pond water in the garden was channeled from the Asahi River, flowing through Okayama. No motive power was

*Photo 43-3 A Japanese garden fitted in nature, showing
the Okayama Castle over Korakuen.*

required. The garden is merged into nature by modifying, rather than opposing nature. The early Japanese culture accepted our environment as it was and did not oppose it. In fact, harmony with nature was the very basis of Japanese culture. I feel that future scientific technologies should incorporate the mind of the original Japanese culture, that is, harmony with nature and an embedded presence in nature.[43-5]

However, the logical and mathematical thinking that originated from Descartes is the origin of all scientific technologies. Original thought that supports the advance of scientific technologies cannot grow without this mode of thinking. Therefore, I propose that future scientific efforts merge Japanese thinking with the Descartes system, that is, future technology should be based on the consolidation of these two modes of thinking. Note that the idea of the engine was conceived by Christiaan Huygens as mentioned earlier. His father, Constantine Huygens, was taught personally by Descartes, who had moved to the Netherlands. It may be said that the engine is the technological fruit of the materializations of Descartes' thinking. As mentioned previously, technology has continued along the pathway blazed by his thinking. On this same pathway, the Japanese way of thinking should now be imposed (Fig. 43-13).

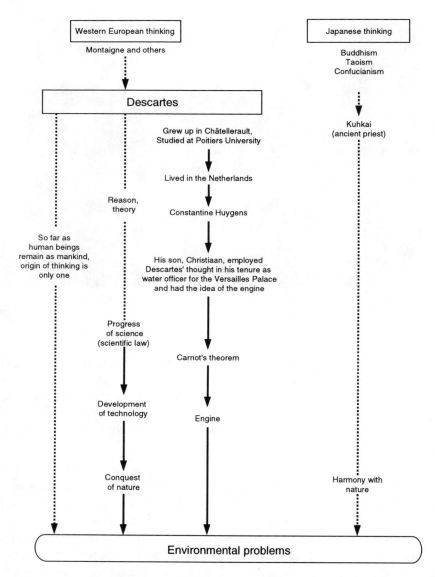

*Fig. 43-13 Scientific technologies must be advanced while keeping a balance between
Descartes' rational thinking and the Japanese objective of being
in harmony with nature.*

In 1967, Arthur Koestler proposed the concept of *holonics*. This concept
means that current individual technologies are to be moved in the direction
that would ensure harmony with the entire environment. This concept is

none other than the superimposition of the Japanese mind on that of Descartes. Our technologies must merge with the concept of holonics.

Presently, the benefits of scientific technologies are concentrated in the northern hemisphere. Many people in other areas of the world also want the benefits produced by this technology. The next-generation scientific technology must correct this imbalance as well as ensure harmony with the earth and with nature. This unmarked trail must first be blazed by the engine, which has been making the greatest contribution to the convenience of mankind today. Both the dream and the work of engineers are unlimited.

Appendix A43-1 Diesel Combustion with High-Pressure Fuel Injection

When setting the fuel injection pressure at a high level (150 to 250 MPa), the state of combustion varies significantly, and the quantity of particulate is reduced widely as shown in Fig. A43-1 (this phenomenon has already been explained). However, the ACE found some other previously unknown phenomena. Direct-injection combustion is roughly classifiable into two types. The first is a system in which the air/fuel mixing is accelerated by the use of an air swirl in the combustion chamber. The second type has been developed primarily in the United States. In this method, fuel and air are mixed by the momentum contained in a spray produced by a comparatively high fuel-injection pressure (90 to 100 MPa), without swirl. The ACE investigated a method in which both air swirl and high pressure were used. Photo A43-1 shows the photographs taken by the high-speed Schlieren photography to examine the effects of the strength of swirl (swirl ratio). According to these photos, combustion appears to be better with the higher swirl ratio since the fuel spray is disturbed and distributed by the airflow. However, as shown in Fig. A43-2, higher swirl has some disadvantages in that fuel consumption, exhaust smoke level, and NO_x emissions are increased. What mechanism causes this combustion procedure to act as it does? First, I rank the results obtained by many researchers, as shown in Fig. A43-3, with regard to fuel injection and combustion. In reference to these formulae, the combustion based on high-pressure direct fuel injection may have the following mechanism.

First, ambient air is entrained into a high-speed jet of fuel forced through a small-diameter orifice to obtain a high pressure. Inside the fuel jet a strong turbulence occurs and fuel droplets evaporate rapidly, mixing with the air. Therefore, ignition does not occur on the side of the jet due to local evaporative cooling and blow-out effects. Instead, ignition occurs downstream of

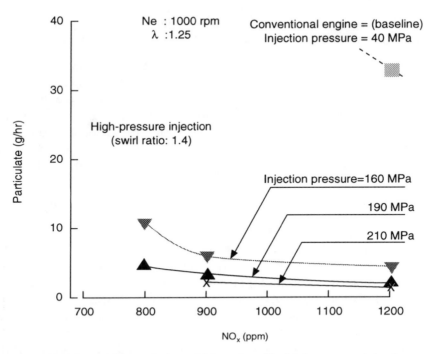

Fig. A43-1 Particulate emission widely reduced by high-pressure injection.

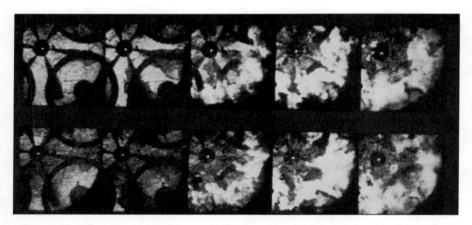

Photo A43-1 Combustion appears to be better with a higher swirl ratio when judged by these photos, but . . .?

the fuel jet or near the wall face of the combustion chamber. Meanwhile, the turbulence energy increases, and the turbulence scale (eddy size) decreases

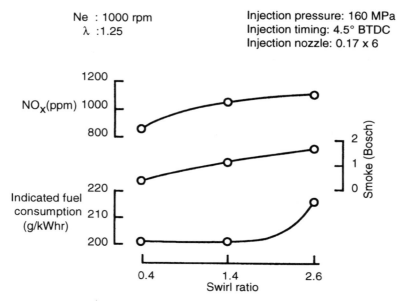

Ne : 1000 rpm
λ :1.25

Injection pressure: 160 MPa
Injection timing: 4.5° BTDC
Injection nozzle: 0.17 x 6

NO$_x$(ppm)

Indicated fuel consumption (g/kWhr)

Smoke (Bosch)

Swirl ratio

Fig. A43-2 Swirl brings about an adverse effect in high-pressure injection.

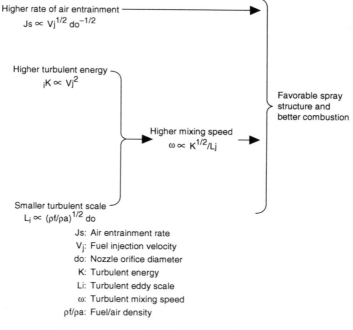

Higher rate of air entrainment
$Js \propto V_j^{1/2} d_o^{-1/2}$

Higher turbulent energy
$_iK \propto V_j^2$

Favorable spray structure and better combustion

Higher mixing speed
$\omega \propto K^{1/2}/L_j$

Smaller turbulent scale
$L_i \propto (\rho f/\rho a)^{1/2} d_o$

Js: Air entrainment rate
Vj: Fuel injection velocity
do: Nozzle orifice diameter
K: Turbulent energy
Li: Turbulent eddy scale
ω: Turbulent mixing speed
ρf/ρa: Fuel/air density

Fig. A43-3 Effect of high-pressure fuel injection.

as noted from the formulae in the figure. Therefore, the mixing of air and fuel is promoted. In consequence, combustion is accelerated and completed in a short time.

On the other hand, if the swirl is higher under these same conditions, then the local air movement probably decreases air entrainment in the fuel jet, and earlier ignition occurs locally. It can be theorized that the rate of combustion in the initial stage is small. Its influence lingers until the final stage of combustion, thus increasing the smoke level and degrading fuel consumption. Meanwhile the NO_x increases due to the increased peak temperature during the combustion (see Fig. A43-4).

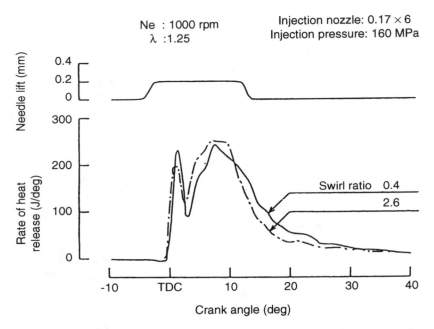

Fig. A43-4 Combustion appears to be better at a higher swirl. However, the first-period combustion is small to make the second-period combustion larger than necessary. The NO_x increases and smoke increases due to inadequate combustion in its final stage.

Fig. A43-5 shows the characteristic change due to pilot injection. As mentioned before, NO_x decreases but other characteristics degrade rapidly. A slight change in specifications brings about a delicate variation of combustion characteristics. Hence, I suppose that this variation should be controlled to defeat the tough enemy.

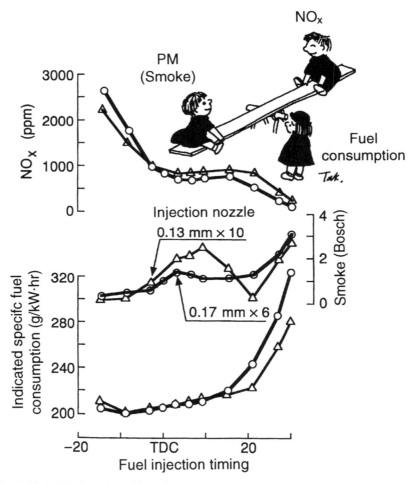

Fig. A43-5 NO_x is reduced by pilot injection. However, the enemy (smoke), who retreated once, has reappeared with a new companion (fuel consumption).

Appendix A43-2 Catalytic Engine

Fig. A43-6 illustrates one of many ideas for a catalytic engine. Today, the most efficient form of engine combustion is diesel combustion. However, diesel combustion always produces NO_x as well as other emissions. One method of minimizing the NO_x is to mix it with ammonia, which can be prepared from a portion of the fuel and then used to decompose the NO_x.

In Fig. A43-6, a minimal amount of fuel is decomposed into hydrogen and carbon monoxide in the catalyst bed A. Then the hydrogen is separated

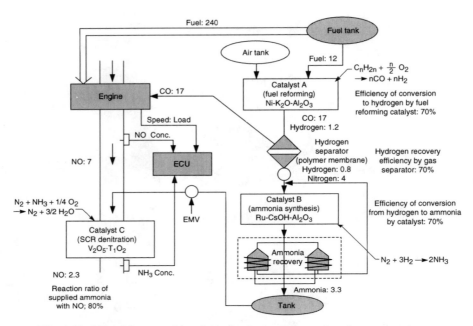

Fig. A43-6 Total image of catalytic engine and flow of each gas constituent
(unit: g/kW-h in ratio).

using the hydrogen separator (polymer membrane). The remaining carbon monoxide is injected into the engine. The hydrogen is then emitted to the catalyst bed B, at which ammonia is formed. The ammonia then reacts with the exhaust in the catalyst bed C, thereby decomposing the NO_x in the exhaust stream. The resulting nitrogen and water are discharged into the atmosphere. To control NO_x in the conventional diesel engine, the fuel injection timing (the time at which the fuel injection is initiated, detailed in Appendix A11-2) must be delayed to lower the combustion temperature. However, this delayed injection timing reduces the engine efficiency. In contrast, the catalytic engine can operate at optimum injection timing while still controlling NO_x, thus resulting in a higher efficiency than the conventional engine.

Epilogue

When we know of a person's success or failure and his enthusiasm for his work, especially when we can see the results of his work, it is unfortunate if we cannot always feel his thoughts and doubts and respect him for his work. Yet, we recall the sorrow and emotions that we felt upon first viewing the person's work weaken and fade with the passage of time. During my research and travels, I often took notes with the intention of retaining these precious impressions and using them as the material for a book reflecting these feelings. However, partially because of my tight business schedule, it was not easy to research and compile a book in an orderly and efficient manner.

I would like to have had more time to polish my words and descriptions. Unfortunately, some of the contents of this volume may be unclear, and some may even have factual errors. Also, I am somewhat embarrassed by my poor sentence structure in English. So, I ask for the reader's understanding as he or she reads this book.

Some products, such as engines or automobiles, are judged to be failures by this book. It is often difficult to answer the question, "What do you mean by a failure?" A product that does not look or perform well may still sell well and be deemed a success by the marketplace. Similarly, a product that has been critically acclaimed by the automobile reviewers may have a limited commercial life. The reasons behind these different reactions may be extremely diversified and only dimly understood.

Sometimes the only way to arrive at some conclusion on these historical cases is simply to guess about the reason because the true causes of the failures of the products discussed in this book cannot be determined without knowing all the facts and conditions surrounding the product. However, I think that a serious analysis and evaluation of these historical happenings and technologies can still be of benefit to serious thought and reflection, even if some of the facts are unknown.

The author now returns his pen to his desk with many thanks for those people who came before him and devoted their lives to the technology in which he himself has such great interest.

Finally, the author expresses his deepest gratitude for the many people who helped in the publication of this book.

Takashi Suzuki
August 1988

References

(1-1) Lelievre, J.M., and J.R. Dulier, *Conquete De Ca Vitesse*, Fd P. Couty (1969).

(1-2) Sass, F., *Geschchite Des Deutschen Verbrennungsmotoren Bau*, Springer Verlag, Berlin (1962).

(1-3) Hardenberg, H.O., *The Antiquity of the Internal Combustion Engine, 1509-1688*, Society of Automotive Engineers, SP-977 (1993).

(1-4) Hirata, H., *A Nation of Lost Power*, (Japanese) Iwanami Books (1976).

(1-5) Payen, J., *Les Moteurs a Combustrien Interne*, Gauthier Editeur, Paris (1964).

(2-1) Frankel, T., *Steam Engines and Turbines*, Smithsonian Institution Press (1977).

(2-2) Sanford, J.F., *Combustion Engines*, Miyajima, Takano Translations (Japanese), Kawade Books, Kawade Shobo new (1974).

(3-1) Sanuki, Matao, *Record of Human Aviation*, (Japanese) Chuko Books (1974).

(3-2) Terada, T., *Ten Volume Collected Works of Trahiko Terada*, (Japanese) Iwanami Books (1961).

(3-3) Toshio, A., *Record of the Technology of the Gear*, (Japanese) Kaihatsu Company (1970).

(4-1) Tanasawa, Y., *The Essence of Industry and Technology*, (Japanese) Yoken-Do (1978).

(4-2) Cummins, Jr., L.C., *Internal Fire*, Carnot Press (1976).

(7-1) Tomizuka, K., *Record of the Internal Combustion Engine*, (Japanese) Sanei Shobo (1969).

(7-2) Devillers, R., *Le Moteur a Explosions*, (1934).

(7-3) Hesling, D.M., "A Study of Typical Bore Finishes and Their Effects on Engine Performance," Sealed Power Company, presented at the 1963 Annual Meeting of the American Society of Lubrication Engineers (1963-5).

(7-4) Basiletti, J.C. *et al.*, "The International Harvester New 300/400 Diesel Engines," Society of Automotive Engineers Paper No. 710555 (1971-6).

(7-5) Wilson, J.V.D., and F.R.B. Calow, "Cylinder Bore Polishing in Automotive Diesel Engine—A Progress Report on a European Study," Society of Automotive Engineers Paper No.760722 (1976-10).

(8-1) Bird A., and I. Hallows, *The Rolls-Royce Motor Car*, B.T. Batsford Ltd. (1975).

(8-2) Tomizuka, K., *Aviation Developments*, (Japanese) Kyoritsu Publications (1944).

(8-3)   Torii, K., "Tribology on Automobile," *J. of JSME*, Vol. 81, No.719 (Japanese)(1978-10).

(8-4)   Shima, S., "Resolving the Lubrication Problem in Automobile Engines (I)," *Heat Engines* (Japanese) Vol. 1, No. 6 (1955-6).

(8-5)   Takao, T., "Cylinder Liners, Piston Rings, and Their Effect on High-Speed Internal Combustion Engines," *The Internal Combustion Engine* (Japanese) Vol. 2, No. 13 (1963-7).

(8-6)   Munro, R. *et al.*, "Cylinder Component Design Reliability and Cost," Institute of Mechanical Engineers, p. 171/172 (1972).

(9-1)   Hiroshige, T., *Translation and Explanation of Carnot and Research into the Combustion Engine*, (Japanese) Misuzu Books (1973).

(9-2)   Suzuki, T., A free translation of T. Hiroshige (Ref. 9-1) into modern Japanese.

(9-3)   Okada, I., *A Book of Thermodynamics*, (Japanese) Omu Company (1969).

(9-4)   Hishinuma, S., "Fairy Tales and Lifespans," *J. of Gakushikai*, No. 743 (Japanese)(1979).

(9-5)   Nishikawa, K., "Effective and Ineffective Energy," *J. of JSME*, Vol. 79, No. 697 (Japanese)(1976-12).

(9-6)   Alkidas, A., "The Application of Availability and Energy Balance to a Diesel Engine," ASME Paper No. 100262 (1988).

(10-1) Kamo, R., and W. Bruzik, "Adiabatic Turbo Compound Engine Performance Prediction," Society of Automotive Engineers Paper No. 780068 (1978).

(10-2) Tagawa, Suiho, *Second Lieutenant Norakuro*.

(10-3) Wallechinky, D. *et al.*, *The Book of Lists*, Bantam Books Inc. (1978).

(11-1) Suzuki, T. *et al.*, "An Observation of Combustion Phenomenon on Heat-Insulated Turbo-Charged and Intercooled D.I. Diesel Engine," Society of Automotive Engineers Paper No. 861187 (1986).

(11-2) Kawamura, H., "The Condition and Future of Ceramic Engine Parts," *J. of JSAE*, Vol. 40, No. 8 (1986).

(11-3) Tsujita, M. *et al.*, "Advanced Fuel Economy in Hino New PII C Turbocharged and Charge-Cooled Heavy Duty Diesel Engine," Society of Automotive Engineers Paper No. 930272 (1993).

(12-1) Sandfort, J.F., *Heat Engines*, (1969); Translation by T. Miyajima, (Japanese) Kawade Publications (1974).

(12-2) Ishii, Y., *The Steam Engine Locomotive*, (Japanese) Chuko Books (1971).

(14-1) Kent, Jack, *Hop, Skip, and Jump*.

(15-1) Suzuki, T., "Resolving the Exhaust Problems in Diesel Engines," *J. of JSME*, Vol. 76, No. 663 (1973).

(15-2) Shiozaki, T., T. Suzuki, and M. Shimoda, "Observation of Combustion Process in D.I. Diesel Engine via High Speed Direct and Schlieren Photography," Society of Automotive Engineers Paper No. 800025 (1980-2).

(15-3) Tennekes, H., and J.L. Lumley, *A First in Turbulence*, The MIT Press (1972).

(15-4) Suzuki, T. *et al.*, "Development of a Higher Boost Turbocharged Diesel Engine for Better Full Economy in Heavy Vehicles," Society of Automotive Engineers Paper No. 830379 (1983).

(15-5) Suzuki, T., "Research into Dealing With Exhaust Emission From High-Speed Diesel Engines," Ph.D. dissertation, Kyoto University (1977).

(16-1) Steinwedel, L.W., *The Mercedes Benz Story*, Chilton Books (1969), Translated by E. Ikeda, (Japanese) Sankei Newspaper Company (1973).

(16-2) Hillman, I., *Auto Car* (22 May 1964).

(16-3) Takahashi, M., "The High Speed Fighter Plane Ki-83," *Machines of the World*, No.94, (Japanese) Bunrin-do (1978-2).

(17-1) Pearson, C.T., *The Indomitable Tin Goose*, Motor Book International (1960).

(17-2) Howley, T., "Tucker Looking Back at the Future," *Collectible Automobile*, July 1985.

(18-1) Sanuki, M., *Heart of the Aeroplane*, (Japanese) Kodansha (1975).

(18-2) Naito, Y., "Thoughts About C6N1," *J. of Visualization Society of Japan*, Vol. 13, Supp. L, No. 1 (Japanese)(1993).

(19-1) Green, W., *Famous Bombers of the Second World War*, MacDonald (1959).

(21-1) Barker, R., and A. Harding, *Automobile Design, Great Designers and Their Work, First Edition*, Robert Bentley Inc. (1970).

(22-1) Bentley, W.O., *The Cars in My Life*, Hutchinson & Co. (1961).

(22-2) Setright, L., "Rolls Royce," *World Car Books*, Translated by I. Taka, San Key Publications (1972).

(22-3) Helk, P., *The Glory of Car Races*, (Japanese) Asahi Newspaper Company (1978).

(23-1) Rassweiler, G.M., and L. Withrow, "Motion Pictures of Engine Flames Correlated With Pressure Cards," Society of Automotive Engineers Paper No. 800131.

(23-2) Wheeler, R.W., *Gasoline Combustion—Past, Present and Future*, Ricardo Consulting Engineers, DP 78/212 (1978-3).

(23-3) Boyd, T.A., "Charles F. Kettering—Pioneer of the Nation's Second Century," *Automobile Engineering*, Vol.84, No.12 (1976-12).

(23-4) von Elbe, L., *Combustion, Flames and Explosion of Gases*, Academic Press (1961).

(23-5) Taki, M., "Analysis of the Knock in High-Speed Compression Machine," *J. of SAE Symposium*, Report 841 (Japanese)(1948).

(23-6) Lichty, L., *Internal Combustion Engines*, McGraw-Hill Book Company (1939 & 1951).

(24-1) Porter, F.C., "Design of Fuel Economy: The New GM Frontal Drive Car," Society of Automotive Engineers Paper No. 790721 (1979).

(24-2) Norbye, J.P., *The Complete Handbook of Front Wheel Drive Cars*, TAB Books (1979).

(25-1) O' Jil, D., *No Enemies! The T34 Tank*, (Japanese) Sankei Publishing (1973).

(25-2) Kadogawa, K., *Tanks*, (Japanese) Keibun Company (1977).

(26-1) Kikuchi, A., *Tanks of the World*, (Japanese) Heibon Company, New Color Books 46 (1976).

(26-2) Mishima, Y., *WW II and Mitsubishi Trust*, (Japanese) Nihon Keizai Shimbun, Inc. (1987).

(26-3) Hofmann, G.F., "The Troubled History of the Christie Tank," *Army* (May 1986).

(26-4) Christie, J.E., *Steel Steeds Christie*, Sunflower University Press (1985).

(26-5) Hara, T., "The Diesel Engine and Me," *Internal Combustion Engine*, Vol. 16, No. 204 (Japanese)(1977).

(27-1) Nozawa, T., "Reciprocating Engine 100 Years," *Aviation Records (Part 2)*, (Japanese) Asahi Newspaper Company (1975).

(27-2) Igaya, Z., *A History of the Hino Motors, Ltd*, Hino Motors, Ltd. (Japanese)(1985).

(27-3) Nakagawa, R., and S. Mizutani, *History of the Nakajima Airplane Engine*, (Japanese) Kanto Company (1985).

(28-1) Clymer, F., *Treasure of Early American Automobiles*, Bonanza Books.

(28-2) Tailer, C.F., *Aircraft Propulsion—A Review of the Evolution of Aircraft Piston Engines*, Smithsonian Institution Press (1971).

(28-3) Setright, L.J.K., *Some Unusual Engines*, Mechanical Engineering Publications Ltd. (1975).

(28-4) Garber, P.E., *The National Aeronautical Collections*, The Smithsonian Institution (1965).

(28-5) Smith, H., *Aircraft Piston Engines*, McGraw-Hill Book Company (1981).

(28-6) Ogston, A.R., "A Short History of Aviation Gasoline Development, 1903-1980," Society of Automotive Engineers Paper No. 810848 (1981).

(28-7) Hempson, J.G., *The Aero Engine up to 1914*, I Mech E, The Newcomen Society (1981).

(29-1) Courau, G., *Les Automobiles a Hälice*, Editions Automobiles, Paul Couty (1969).

(30-1) Draper, C., *The Salmson Story*, David & Charles (1974).

(30-2) Sekiya H. *et al.*, "Lateral Deformation of Cylinder Block," 16th FISITA International Congress 7-5 (1976-5).

(30-3) Tomizuka, K., *Aero Engines*, (Japanese) Kyoritsu Publishing Company (1943).

(31-1) Brouwers, A.P., "150- and 300-kW Lighweight Diesel Aircraft Engine Design Study," Contractors Report No. 756, NAS 3-20830 (1980).

(32-1) Meyer, R.B., "The First Airplane Diesel Engine, Packard Model DR-980 of 1928," *Smithsonian Annals of Flight*, Vol. 1, No. 2 (1964).

(33-1) Lindbergh, C.A., *The Spirit of St. Louis*, Charles Scribner & Sons (1955).

(34-1) Shiga, H., *Two Men of Torpedo Boat Kojin Co*, (1978).

(34-2) Joyner, J.A., "Reduction of Cavitation in Pitting of Diesel-Engine Cylinder Liners," *SAE Transactions*, Vol. 65 (1957).

(34-3) C.H. Mead, *Wing over the World*, The Swannet Press (1971).

(34-4) Risaburo Oba, "On Mechanism of Cavitation Erosion Perspective," *Turbomachinery*, Vol. 10, No.6 (Japanese)(1978).

(34-5) Suzuki, T. *et al.*, "A Modification of Combustion Systems for Low Exhaust Emission and Its Effects on Durability of Prechamber Diesel Engines," Society of Automotive Engineers Paper No. 760213 (1976).

(35-1) Tomizuka, K., *Record of an Eighty Year Lifespan* (Japanese) (1975).

(35-2) Ellis, J., "Voyager: Never Have So Few Tried So Much With So Little," *Air and Space* (October/November 1986).

(35-3) Goldstein, G., "Voyager's Cooler Heads Prevail," *Mechanical Engineering*, Vol. 109, No. 2 (Feb 1987).

(36-1) Tomizuka, K., *A History of the Internal Combustion Engine*, (Japanese) Sankai-do Company (1969) (Japanese).

(36-2) "The Panhard Dyna 55 Engine," *Overseas Engineering Anthology*, Vol. 7, No. 7 (1958).

(37-1) Naruse, M., *In The Womb of Scientific Technology*, (Japanese) (1942).

(37-2) Sanuki, M., "Air Said to Schweinfurt," *Machine Research*, Vol. 11, No. 6. (Japanese)(1959).

(38-1) Nakamura, Y., *The Past, Present, and Future of Racing Engines*, (Japanese) Sankai-do Company (1981).

(38-2) Yamada, K., "Two or Three Problems With the Skewing of Roller Bearings," *Machine Research*, Vol. 11, No. 1 (Japanese) (1959).

(38-3) DeHart, A.O., and D.H. Harwick, "Engine Bearing Design, 1969," Society of Automotive Engineers Paper No. 690008 (1969).

(38-4) Omi, I., "Carrier Bomber Suisei," *Koku Fan*, Vol. 81, No. 1 (Japanese) (1971).

(38-5) *Forty Year Record of Diesel-kiki Company*, (Japanese) Diesel-kiki Company (1981).

(38-6) Sparrow, S.W., "Recent Developments in Main and Connecting-Rod Bearings," *SAE Transactions* (July 1934).

(40-1) *All about WW II Japanese Aviation Technology*, (Japanese) Hara shobo (1976).

(40-2) Kitano, M. *et al.*, "The Development of a Regenerator Seal for Vehicular Use," Paper No. 10, Joint Gas Turbine Congress (1977).

(40-3) Morishita, T. *et al.*, "A Study on a Premixed Combustor for a Vehicular Gas Turbine," Joint Gas Turbine Congress (1977).

(41-1) Soakage, N., "Could Japan Become a Natural Resources Country?" (Japanese) *Sankei Newspaper*, Vol. 1, No. 24 (1987).

(41-2) Furuhama, S., *Reappearance of the Engine*, (Japanese) Kodansha (1982).

(41-3) Takiguchi, M. *et al.*, "Combustion Improvement of Liquid Hydrogen-Fueled Engine for Medium-Duty Trucks," Society of Automotive Engineers Paper No. 870535 (1987).

(42-1) Suzuki, T., "Hybrid System," *J. of JSME*, Vol. 95, No. 882 (Japanese)(1992).

(43-1) Suzuki, T., "Non-emission Engine," *Resources Technology,* No. 224 (Japanese)(1986).

(43-2) *Influence of the Pollutant Materials—To Human Nitrogen Oxide Particulates,* (Japanese) National Research Council (1977).

(43-3) Lewtas, J., and K. Williams, "A Retrospective View of the Value of Short-Term Genetic Bioassays in Predicting the Chronic Effects of Diesel Soot," Fourth Satellite Symposium of the International Toxic Science Academy (July 1986).

(43-4) ACE's Technical Review-No. 1, No. 2, Advanced Combustion Engineering Institute Company, Ltd. (1992).

(43-5) Suzuki, T., "Future Diesel Engines—Problems, Technologies, and Challenges," Calvin W. Rice Lecture, ETCE Conference, ASME (1988).

Index

Oil consumption *(continued)*
  transition in, 46*f*
  in typical truck, 32-35, 36*f,* 37*f*
  see also Lubricating oil consumption
Oil cooler, efficiency enhancement of, 105-107, 106*f*
Oil shock, enforcement of Clean Air Act and, 61-62
Okayama Castle, 420-421, 421*p*
Orgill, Douglas
  comment on Russian T34 tank, 195
  comment on T34 tank, 197
Otto, Nicolaus August, 5
  internal combustion engine invented by, 19
    completion of, 27-29
  stratified charge combustion and, 23-24, 24*f*
    air vigorously whirling in cylinder, 26*p*
    Honda CVCC, 25*f*
    in present measures on exhaust gas, 24-26
Otto cycle
  exhaust loss on, 70*f*
  explanation of, 21-22, 22*f*
Otto four-stroke-cycle compound engine, 89
Otto's double expansion engine, 93, 94*f*
Overhead cam, for Mercedes race car, 172*f*

P36. *See* Curtiss P36
P51. *See* North American P51
P75 airplane, 149-150, 151*f*
P75A Eagle, 151-152, 152*p*
Packard Motor Company, 275-276
  045 dual-windshield Phaeton Dietrich body, 298*p*
  automobiles
    Clipper automobile, 276*f*
    Panther-Daytona automobile, 312*p*
  diesel engine, 277
    advantages of, 287-289
    challenge for lightweight diesel engine, 292-293, 293*p,* 294*p*
    combustion in, 299-301, 301*f*
    cylinder fastened to, 302*f,* 302-304, 303*f*
    DR-980, 302*f*
    shortcomings of, 286-287
    Stinson plane mounting, 295*p*
    Stinson-Detroiter airplane with, 279*p*